Tradition and Modernity
in Spanish American Literature

Tradition and Modernity in Spanish American Literature: From Darío to Carpentier

by
Adam Sharman

CABRINI COLLEGE LIBRARY
610 KING OF PRUSSIA ROAD
RADNOR, PA 19087

TRADITION AND MODERNITY IN SPANISH AMERICAN LITERATURE
© Adam Sharman, 2006.

All rights reserved. No part of this book may be used or reproduced in any manner whatsoever without written permission except in the case of brief quotations embodied in critical articles or reviews.

First published in 2006 by
PALGRAVE MACMILLAN™
175 Fifth Avenue, New York, N.Y. 10010 and
Houndmills, Basingstoke, Hampshire, England RG21 6XS
Companies and representatives throughout the world.

PALGRAVE MACMILLAN is the global academic imprint of the Palgrave Macmillan division of St. Martin's Press, LLC and of Palgrave Macmillan Ltd. Macmillan® is a registered trademark in the United States, United Kingdom and other countries. Palgrave is a registered trademark in the European Union and other countries.

ISBN-13: 978–1–4039–7487–7
ISBN-10: 1–4039–7487–X

Library of Congress Cataloging-in-Publication Data

Sharman, Adam, 1963–
    Tradition and modernity in Spanish American literature : from Darío to Carpentier / by Adam Sharman.
      p. cm.
    Includes bibliographical references and index.
    ISBN 1–4039–7487–X (alk. paper)
    1. Spanish American literature—History and criticism. 2. Modernism (Literature)—Latin America. I. Title.

PQ7081.S525 2006
860.9′112—dc22
                                                              2006045409

A catalogue record for this book is available from the British Library.

Design by Newgen Imaging Systems (P) Ltd., Chennai, India.

First edition: October 2006
10 9 8 7 6 5 4 3 2 1

Printed in the United States of America.

Contents

Acknowledgments	viii
Introduction: Tradition and Modernity, Literature and Cultural Studies	ix

1 The Things that Travel: On Tradition and Modernity in Latin America — 1

- Introduction — 1
- Modernity as Material Reality and as a Philosophico-Aesthetic Concept — 3
- Latin American *modernidad* — 11
- Hybrid Cultures and One Postmodern Critique of Modernity — 15
- A Note on Names: Postmodernism, Postmodernity, or Late Capitalism — 17
- Modernity under Erasure, or, the Limits of Postmodern Relativism — 19

2 Culture Is (Not) Ordinary: The Secrets of the Slow in the Public Sphere — 27

- La ideología de lo culto moderno — 29
- Note on the Word *Culture* — 33
- A Paradigmatic History of Latin American Cultural Studies — 34
- Modernism and Hegemony — 38
- Globalization and the Fast and Slow Economies of Art — 42

3 Fieldwork: Cultural Studies and the Problem of Tradition — 49

- To Create Is to Resist — 50
- The Immanence of Cultural Studies and Hermeneutics — 52

	The Question of Context	55
	The Politics of the Question of Context, or, Avant-Garde Subalternism and the Problem of Tradition	58
	Articulation versus Homology	63
4	***Modernismo*, Positivism, and (Dis)inheritance in the Discourse of Literary History**	**67**
	History and Modernity	67
	Autonomy Domine	70
	El cuchillo divisor	74
	LEMA: Arte y progreso	76
	History and the Proper Name	79
	Rituals	80
5	**Vallejo, Semicolonialism, and Poetemporality**	**85**
	Postcolonial Theory on Semicolonial Times	86
	The Ghost of Lenin	91
	Symbolist Imperial Nostalgias	93
	The (Peruvian) Western Discourse of Modernity	96
	Poetemporality	99
	Two Alternatives for *Trilce* VI	101
	The Peruvian (Western) Discourse of Modernity	106
6	**Borges and a Differently Colored History**	**109**
	The History of Eternity	111
	The Question of Modernity (and Tradition)	113
	A Personal (Platonic) Theory of Eternity	118
	The Eternal Return: '44, '46, '43, '44, '46 . . .	122
	The Context of Nationalism	126
	Otra historia	131
7	**Rulfo and the Mexican Roman Trinity**	**135**
	Transculturation	135
	Pedro Páramo and the Mexican Roman Trinity	138
	"Luvina" and the Time of Tradition	147
	The Origins of Technique	151
	Demo(cra)tic Design	154
	Conclusion	157

8	**This Is Not a Revolution:**	
	Carpentier on the Age of Enlightenment	**159**
	Of Ripe Immaturity: Enlightenment and Popular Culture	161
	The Two Functions of Religion: Birthright and Grand Narrative	163
	The Grand Narrative of Nature	167
	Narrative Art and Magic	175

Conclusion	179
Notes	187
Bibliography	221
Index	231

Acknowledgments

I am grateful to the Arts and Humanities Research Board for the Research Leave Scheme award that enabled me to complete this project. My thanks also go to William Rowe and Phil Swanson for helping me obtain the above, and to my colleagues in the Department of Hispanic and Latin American Studies at the University of Nottingham, who covered for me during that extended absence. I am indebted to Alejandro Riberi and Trevor Stack for their constructive comments on certain chapters, and above all to Guillermo Olivera for generously sharing with me his profound knowledge of Latin American cultural studies. I am grateful, too, to those individuals who have extended me the opportunity to try out some of the material in this book. Prototypes of different chapters were delivered at the Institute of Romance Studies, London; the Borges Centenary Conference, Kings' College, London; the Hispanic Research Seminar at the University of Cambridge; the Department of Hispanic Studies at the University of Aberdeen; the Research Seminar in my own department in Nottingham; and three conferences (Braga, Glasgow, and Valencia) of the Association of Hispanists of Great Britain and Ireland.

A substantially different version of chapter 4 has appeared as "Modernismo, positivismo y (des)herencia en el discurso de la historia literaria," in *¿Qué es el modernismo? Nueva encuesta, nuevas lecturas*, ed. Richard A. Cardwell and Bernard McGuirk (Boulder: Society of Spanish and Spanish-American Studies, 1993), pp. 319–337. The first half of chapter 5, and the odd phrase from chapter 1, was published as "Semicolonial Times: Vallejo and the Discourse of Modernity," *Romance Quarterly*, 49:3 (Heldref Publications, Summer 2002), 192–205. A few paragraphs or sentences from chapter 6 found their way into "Borges y el tiempo de la ceguera," in *Jorge Luis Borges, Intervenciones sobre pensamiento y literatura*, ed. William Rowe, Claudio Canaparo, and Annick Louis (Buenos Aires, Barcelona, Mexico: Paidós, 2000), pp. 249–262. I am grateful to the editors of all of the above for permission to reprint material.

Introduction: Tradition and Modernity, Literature and Cultural Studies

This book has two main strands. On the one hand, it explores the concepts of tradition and modernity in the context of Spanish America. To do this, it draws on the general bibliography on tradition and modernity, but gives special attention to the ways in which these concepts—and the Spanish American historical formations they purportedly designate—have recently been understood by academic work categorized as Latin American cultural studies. On the other hand, the book examines the different understandings of tradition and modernity that underpin the work of an earlier generation (if we can call them that) of selected Spanish American literary writers. The point of this dual focus (theory from the end of the twentieth century versus writing from the first sixty years of the century) is that these literary writers "belong" to the period that the later cultural theorists have taken to constitute the region's true *modernidad*.

This historical appurtenance to the period known as modernity, and to characteristically modern habits of thought, has often sufficed for the earlier (pre-"boom") generation of literary writers to come under fire from the later (postmodern) cultural studies. Although, as its own internal polemics make clear, Latin American cultural studies is neither a single nor a singular thing,[1] we may still be permitted the generalization that, in its view, the canonical literary figures of the first half of the century are simply too bound to the hegemonic modernist moment of literary experimentalism and too wedded to the European tradition of high culture.[2] Although this book is in part a defence of the earlier writers, it does not go down the path of asking forgiveness for them. Its principal labor consists, rather, in excavating the logic that structures the debate and makes such denunciations possible. Its principal contention is that the "modernist" literature of these writers offers up acute interventions in the messy relationship between Spanish American tradition and modernity, and between both of the latter and Western modernity. These interventions can be dismissed out of hand only by a slash-and-burn approach, which conforms closely to the dominant spirit (there is more than one spirit) of modernity.

The book begins with general theoretical and definitional work (chapters 1–3), before moving on to analyses of specific literary grapplings with aspects of tradition or modernity. There is a movement in the early chapters from general questions concerning the philosophical and socioeconomic relationship between tradition and modernity (chapter 1), to the part played by culture in modernity (chapter 2), and, finally, on to the role of literature and the function of literary analysis in cultural studies.

Chapter 1 lays the groundwork for everything that follows. Its starting point is the fact that, according to cultural studies, Spanish American modernity is a phenomenon of the end of the nineteenth and first half of the twentieth centuries. *Modernidad* belongs neither to the period of independence and Enlightenment, nor to the sixteenth and seventeenth centuries, but is a product of the Second Industrial Revolution. This definition is driven largely by a socioeconomic interpretation of modernity, though in the work of someone such as Beatriz Sarlo it is interwoven with the other main interpretation of modernity, the philosophico-aesthetic conception (modernity as novelty, evanescence, change). Focusing on the critique of modernity adumbrated by Néstor García Canclini in the epoch-defining *Culturas híbridas*, the chapter has two working assumptions and develops two main contentions. The working assumptions are, first, that modernity in Spanish America is a differential condition extrapolated largely from the West but necessarily reworked by local materials in the new context; and, second, that modernity is a qualitative and chronological, rather than merely chronological, category (to use Peter Osborne's terms). Spanish American modernity is modern not simply by virtue of the fact that it comes after a "premodern" period, but because the later time is considered qualitatively superior (more technologically advanced, more democratic, etc.) to the earlier epoch.

The two contentions are, first, that it is essential to keep sight of the fact that not everything in the modern age is modern, and thus that the historical phase called modernity is inadequate with respect to its own self-image as destroyer of tradition and the past. This is easily said; it is less easy to maintain this position rigorously in the heat of historical analysis. The more one strives to identify a period as modern, that is, to distinguish it from a preceding period thought to be not-modern, the more one is drawn into treating the contents of the period called modernity as *essentially* or *absolutely* modern. The second contention is that every time variants of the words *modern* or *modernity* are used, even in the most anti-Eurocentric declaration, the European tradition is necessarily invoked. Stuart Hall maintains that modernity is a plural, differential, and relative phenomenon.[3] Loosening up and pluralizing the historical origins of modernity, he shows that it emerges neither from one moment nor from one place. But if modernity had complex beginnings, developed out of interaction with other parts of the globe and took different paths even in the so-called central countries, the idea that a country such as Japan "took a radically different path to modernity" needs qualifying. The radicality of Japan's difference ("a fiercely modern, high-tech economy with a strikingly traditional culture") is circumscribed by the fact that many of the conceptual and technological roots of this radicality are to an important degree profoundly Western. Even when one says that Latin American modernity is decisively not the same as its European counterpart, and even when one says, as García Canclini does, that European modernity itself is not the same as European modernity, one falls back on an idea of modernity that is indissociable from the socioeconomic reality and conceptual tradition of, first, Europe and, later, North America. It is not that the non-West is condemned to imitating a single European concept of modernity (there were many European concepts and lived versions of modernity); it is that the general idea of modernity has deep roots in a Europe that was the first organizing center of a vast colonial enterprise. The centrality of, first, Europe and, then, North America drives the antiethnocentric reaction against modernity; but that same centrality explains why, let us say, a certain European conceptual tradition (which was never exclusively European) is always already inscribed in the attempts to do away with Western modernity. To overlook this entanglement, which it would be facile to consider wholly negative, is to inhabit a simplified intellectual, political, and moral universe, which is at best unsustainable and at worst dishonest.

Chapter 2 deals with Weber's classic stance on culture as a would-be autonomous sphere in modernity. Returning to García Canclini's Weberian argument on modern Latin American culture in *Culturas híbridas*, and sketching in the book's place in the history of Latin American communication and cultural studies, it notes the residual Leninism (or, at least, the 1960s version of Leninism) of a work taken to be exemplary of the postmodern break with Marxism. From his work in the 1960s on the Argentine avant-garde through to this later text, García Canclini has remained steadfastly critical of the elitism of Latin American *vanguardismo* and modernism, insisting on the importance of the public sphere and the values of openness, transparency, and accessibility. *Culturas híbridas* stands as an obituary to a modernity and a modern culture whose rigid stratification has been eroded by postmodernity. Ten years on, *La globalización imaginada* is more conciliatory toward modernist-type cultural production. Where the earlier text gave weight to the demotic impulse behind postmodernity, the later book is more circumspect about the production—and consumption—of fast culture in contemporary life. The chapter argues that the key concept in García Canclini is that of the public sphere, but that this concept is used uncritically. Here I adapt Jacques Derrida's work on responsibility. What García Canclini's (Enlightenment) appeal to the public sphere lacks is any acknowledgment that the idea of an accessible and democratically responsible art might have to confront the possibility that the concept of responsibility necessarily has the structure of secrecy; in other words, the possibility that irresponsibility (not always following the publicly sanctioned rules, and not always allowing one's work to be consumed instantly and by all) might be an integral part of being truly responsible. Without this possibility, critical thought and "slow" art—from any era—have no place in democracy.

Chapter 3 focuses on the difficulty of thinking about tradition from the vantage point of a contemporary cultural studies whose unconscious habits are still recognizably modern. In its embrace of avant-garde aesthetics, William Rowe's work appears to represent a limit-case of Latin American cultural studies. In fact, it makes some of the latter's exemplary moves. Rowe follows García Canclini's critique of the autonomy of modern culture, calling for a new critical practice dedicated to the illumination, not of the literary artifact in its illusory autonomy, but of the entirety of a cultural field. Rowe's immanentist concept of the field erases the boundaries between cultural production and such things as economics, power, and the social imaginary, paving the way to see literature as a means of access to larger formations. This is the defining manoeuver of a modern cultural studies given over to tracking down and intervening in the relationship—the articulation—between cultural production and power. But the synchronic concept of the field brings with it a certain baggage. The methodological (homological) presupposition of the field bestows a privilege on the iconoclastic avant-garde work, which exceeds the field in the direction of the new and cannot account for the historical traces of the past that find their way even into new cultural production. This archetypal modern logic of the field conflicts absolutely with the avowed respect for tradition shown by a García Canclini (in the case of indigenous traditions) or a Jesús Martín-Barbero (in the case of traditional popular and mass culture).

The remaining chapters zoom in on and out of a series of literary engagements with tradition and/or modernity in Spanish America. Chapter 4 deals with the paradigmatic discourse of literary-philosophical modernity. Dominating the early years of the twentieth century, the literary history of Spanish American *modernismo* displays all the rhetorical tropes of the moderns: cut, discontinuity, generational division, the incandescent impulse, the ceaseless desire for the new. However, in their formal and informal attempts at writing themselves into the subcontinent's cultural pantheon, the *modernistas* exemplify not only the discursive tics of modern thought, but also the unavoidable entanglement in the discourse of the preceding generation. Intoxicated by the idea of disinheriting themselves from positivism, they end up submitting to the most traditional, not to say positivist, of modern presuppositions—the idea of historical progress. We are not to conclude from this that the *modernistas* were just as traditional as the positivists and in fact introduced no major changes into Spanish American cultural life. The point is to take seriously the distinct linguistico-conceptual codifications of different discursive rituals, without bestowing on ritual a purely negative value or believing (positivistically) that cultural producers belong to a given ritual without remainder.

Chapter 5 turns to the question of literary modernity and indigenous traditions. It highlights the conflation of two different understandings of Latin American colonialism that have been pressed into service so that César Vallejo can be spoken about in the language of *post*colonialism. The first understanding derives from the period of independence, where the region is supposed to emerge from the yoke of colonialism into a postcolonial situation. In reality, a colonial condition is replaced by a colonial postcolonial condition in which, as Bolívar was keenly aware, Creoles took over from *peninsulares*, and there was never any question of allowing the indigenous population to think they had rid themselves of the European invader. The second understanding, which Vallejo himself makes use of, comes from Lenin's theory of imperialism and posits the entire region as a victim of "semicolonialism." Only by considering the continental antagonism posited in the second case (Latin America versus the West) and the brute fact of the end of Spanish and Portuguese colonialism in the first does it become possible to produce a reading of Latin America en masse as a postcolonial place.

Not only am I deeply skeptical about the intellectual and moral propriety of such a conflation, it may also be the case that the subversion of Western temporality at work in certain of Vallejo's poems is attributable not to any indigenous tradition at odds with the modern view of linear time, but to the time of the lyric poem itself. This theme recurs in the book: to discount the specificity of literary form, that is, the technical repertoire and work of writing, is to discount literature.

Chapter 6 deals with the classical, Platonic conception of the time of eternity as the time of tradition. It is frequently asserted that Jorge Luis Borges's embrace of the time of eternity and related deterministic themes represents a flight from a rapidly modernizing Argentina. Borges himself said as much. To remain content with that explanation, however, is to overlook the way in which Borges musters the time of eternity not just against the abstract notion of modern linear time, but against the deep-rooted, dominant matrix of modern thought, that is, nominalism. We will lead ourselves up a hopeless blind alley if we conclude that Borges is a "traditionalist." On the contrary, Borges's work rewrites as much as it recuperates the cultural archive, and uses tradition as a means to tease, bait, and criticize a modern, aggressive nationalism whose philosophical underpinnings lie in nominalism. Borges's argument with a strident, narrow form of cultural nationalism is writ large into the fabric of a collection such as *El Aleph*, written during a period of intense global nationalist fervor that culminated in the Second World War.

Chapter 7 addresses the configuration of authority, religion, and tradition that makes up the Mexican Roman trinity. There has been a tendency in criticism, especially in work on transculturation, to highlight the traditional-rural or, more problematically, the pre-Colombian dimensions of Juan Rulfo's work, that is, those elements that do not proceed from metropolitan high Western culture. Without discounting the transculturative qualities of Rulfo's writing, there is in the view of religion and the popular classes that lets itself be read in *Pedro Páramo* a pronounced affinity with the modern tradition of Enlightenment. Critical of the Church and peasantry alike, Rulfo's work shows how ill-equipped the crumbling Mexican Roman trinity is to deal with the brute power of *caciquismo*. The paralysis of the trinity finds its figurative equivalent in the representation of a dead village (in the novel) or of a village where time has stood still (in "Luvina"). Both depictions of the time of tradition are to be read as products of writing, rather than simple transcriptions of reality. In these depictions, arch-traditional topoi and stereotypes creep into the text, whereas other elements (such as children and the female labor of childrearing) fall below the threshold of significance. Rulfo's technique may well stand as the literary corollary of the generalized rejection of the Roman trinity, but it does not follow that modern art's aesthetic of fragmentation is necessarily on the side of pluralist democracy.

The final chapter explores the French Revolution as the political incarnation of modernity's apocalypticism. Detailing the ripple effects of the French Revolution in the Caribbean, Alejo Carpentier's *El siglo de las luces* is a counter-Enlightenment text of demystification. The novel does not give up on Enlightenment, but does introduce more Romantic emphases, together with decidedly anti-Enlightenment materials. Alongside non-Western medicine, magic, the body, and popular and black culture, Carpentier gives a special place to religion and nature, which function as themes to reinscribe a certain popular antirationalism and as grand narratives to make modernity look like a rather small chapter in the history of the world. By highlighting the novel's important emphasis on characters' force, action, and freewill (which takes it close to Sartre but also to eighteenth-century thought), critics have neglected to see that the novel's discourse on nature, even and especially its discourse on evolutionism, falls back on traditional predestinationism. To privilege human will at the expense of the book's strand of premodern deterministic fatalism is to miss the point that Carpentier is tilting at all (modern) expressions of *tabula rasa* rationality, voluntarism included. This finds support in something that has also gone unnoticed, namely, that superstition or magic does not appear just at the novel's propositional level, but is embedded in the novel's narrative art. *El siglo de las luces*, no less than the Century of Lights itself, contains premodern fabric.

The book criticizes cultural studies at many junctures, but cannot get away with claiming that it owes nothing to cultural studies. It is often the case, for instance, that a chapter focuses on broad social, cultural, or theoretical questions at the expense of textual analysis. Although I attempt to redress the balance at various moments, this focus is unavoidable if one is to engage seriously with the problematics posed by cultural studies. From start to finish, the book is marked by a type of thought, and above all by a particular idiom, which it shares with that "discipline." This shared conceptual and linguistic apparatus can best be understood as belonging not to cultural studies (Latin American or otherwise), but to that thing called "Theory." Cultural studies, literary theory, and critical theory would be the hyponyms of the superordinate theory, that body of thought and work which begins, in the

Anglo-Saxon academy, with the modernizing tools of structuralism and semiotics. What perhaps distinguishes cultural studies is its tendency to turn its back on the high-cultural tradition, incarnated precisely in literature. In its most strident guise, and despite its postmodern idiom, cultural studies represent another modernizing force convinced of the obsolescence of outmoded cultural forms and the no less archaic-conservative disciplinary habits that accompany them.[4] A cursory glance at contemporary power formations suggests just how overdetermined the rejection of high culture is and how problematic it becomes to maintain that the abandonment of the high is per se politically progressive.

More nuanced cultural studies expand the horizons of what can pass as worthy of study and cast light on the subtle articulations between culture and power. But even they frequently overstate such articulations, to the extent that cultural politics suddenly becomes as urgent and as significant as politics itself. This urgency assumes its most urgent form, by definition, in the desire to intervene in the present. The result is not just that an outmoded form of literary study is willingly left behind (a form that is now insignificant, since it belongs to a long-gone era in which high-cultural forms, together with the high-cultural study of those forms, were hegemonic), but that the literature of that same, nonurgent period is sacrificed, too.[5] The risk run by such presentism, as it instrumentalizes cultural production of the past, really is the exhaustion of difference.

CHAPTER 1

The Things that Travel: On Tradition and Modernity in Latin America

Introduction

According to conventional understanding, modernity is the name given to an epoch of European history that marks the passage from the age of revelation, where to produce means to discover or reveal the already given, to the age of production, understood as the technoscientific invention of something hitherto unknown, an age bound up with the new value placed on *humanitas*. Leaving aside for a moment the question of whether such a definition is or is not Eurocentric, recent work on Latin American modernity done under the aegis of cultural studies defines modernity differently.[1] This definition has not been sufficiently discussed. In contrast to the idea of European modernity as an epoch beginning sometime around the year 1500, Latin American cultural studies holds that modernity arrives in the region not before the end of the nineteenth century and possibly as late as the 1920s and 1930s (Sarlo, Martín-Barbero) or even the 1950s (García Canclini, Brunner).[2] In short, Latin American modernity is a child of the Second Industrial Revolution.

If this new work on Latin American modernity diverges in respect of chronology, it shares with the older understanding the conviction that modernity is a historical phase.[3] Latin American modernity may arrive at a different time but, notwithstanding a "certain flexibility," it remains an epochal phenomenon. Two clarifications are called for. The first is that, when applied to non-Western parts of the globe, the word *modernity* cannot mean "a historical phase of Western civilization," but must mean something like "a general condition extrapolated from a phase of Western civilization." Reworking what Hardt and Negri say of the concept of modern sovereignty, one can say that modernity emanates largely from Europe but was born and developed in the midst of Europe's relationship with its colonial outside.[4] The second clarification is that even if modernity in the new republics is an extrapolation rather than a simple graft from the West, it is still not a purely temporal affair. Modernity is a qualitative as much as temporal concept. Modernity may designate a historical period or condition, and modern may describe certain contents of that period, but even when used thus as descriptors of chronology, both noun and adjective have a qualitative value. Modernity, one hears in the pathos of descriptions of it, is "better" than the age or condition that preceded it.[5] This qualitative dimension is apparent whenever the term modernity is used in a second sense. Modernity has come to mean the general quality of being modern, where modern means whatever is deemed qualitatively superior or "up with the times." Modernity in this sense is less a historical phase than a spirit or quality. Paradoxically it then becomes possible to say of the early period of modernity that it was not very "modern" (they had no computers and it took an age to get anywhere). But even when the word appears divorced from the classical period of modernity, it is still tied to the philosophical debates of the eighteenth century, which engendered the idea of the modern age. This convergence of chronology and quality suggests that rival socioeconomic and philosophico-aesthetic concepts of modernity are closely intertwined. These two clarifications (apropos of the abstraction that is a traveling modernity and the qualitative as much as chronological character of the category modernity) are guiding assumptions throughout this chapter and throughout the book as a whole.

In addition to these two guiding assumptions, as it outlines the recent debates in Latin American studies the chapter develops two contentions. First, the historical-cum-sociological bent of much of the work on Latin American modernity has laid emphasis on pinpointing the moment modernity arrives in the region. Even when such attempts are theoretically aware that modernity (or any historical period, for that matter) is a mixed configuration, the desire to define and delimit the area's modernity leads to a treatment of things and people that forgets this insight. The proper name modernity works its magic, bewitching us into believing that the modern is one and undivided, that is, into totalizing the contents of the modern on the basis of the fact that they are present in the same historical juncture. The first contention, then, is that not everything in modernity is modern. The banality of the contention is equaled only by the hastiness with which it is forgotten in the so-called historical analysis of culture.

Second, one of cultural studies' central concerns has been to supersede the historical phase and conceptual apparatus of modernity, that is, leave behind the universalizing philosophical discourse of modernity and the neocolonial development models of socioeconomic modernization that swept the region after the Second World War. The subtitle of the seminal text of Latin American cultural studies, García Canclini's *Culturas híbridas*, is *Estrategias para entrar y salir de la modernidad*. To leave modernity, it goes without saying, is at the same time to step out of the political and philosophical shadow of the West. The interest of García Canclini's manifesto-text is that, for all its championing of postmodern relativism, there is a troubled consciousness in its pages sensitive to the problems of entering or taking one's leave of modernity. The second contention, then, is that there are historico-theoretical reasons why leaving (Western) modernity is neither possible nor desirable. If *modernity is the name of a differential generalized condition primarily of European origin but necessarily reworked in a new context*, then in the process of abstraction by which modernity takes (uneven) shape in Latin America the historical traces of the West are not lost. Before exploring these two contentions further, however, an indispensable first step must be to rehearse in detail the two primary ways of defining modernity.

Modernity as Material Reality and as a Philosophico-Aesthetic Concept

There is a long-standing conflict between the socioeconomic and the aesthetic (romantic antibourgeois) concepts of modernity:

> It is impossible to say precisely when one can begin to speak of the existence of two distinct and bitterly conflicting modernities. What is certain is that at some point during the first half of the nineteenth century an irreversible split occurred between modernity as stage in the history of Western civilization—a product of scientific and technological progress, of the industrial revolution, of the sweeping economic and social changes brought about by capitalism—and modernity as an aesthetic concept. Since then, the relations between the two modernities have been irreducibly

hostile, but not without allowing and even stimulating a variety of mutual influences in their rage for each other's destruction.[6]

Although the two distinct modernities may be mutually antagonistic, this antagonism does not prevent their close association. If they did not touch in profound ways, they could not conflict. Distinguishing between the two modernities cannot hide the fact that the socioeconomic concept already contains a philosophy and, despite what Baudelaire says, the philosophico-aesthetic concept is already marked by the social. It remains to trace the nature of this inscription.

The standard socioeconomic paradigm deploys a periodizing conception of modernity, viewing it as either a single phase or a series of subphases of Western society. Viewed in the singular and on the grand scale, modernity has traditionally been taken to refer to a historical phase in the development of Western civilization that displaces the Middle Ages. The origins of this single and singular modernity lie in its leave-taking of an earlier age built on the premises of a "divinely ordained system of aristocracy, monarchy, land-ownership, and ecclesiastical authority."[7] It is difficult to say exactly when this leave-taking begins. Convention has it that the beginnings of modernity are to be found in the seventeenth-century scientific revolution, but there are important dissenting voices. Ernst Cassirer pushes the origins of modern *thought* back in time by considering Nicholas Cusanus to be the first modern thinker.[8] Matei Calinescu reminds us that the idea of modernity was born in the Christian Middle Ages.[9] Jürgen Habermas follows Hegel by locating the beginnings of the modern age around 1500, a beginning marked by the three "monumental" events that are the Renaissance, the Reformation, and the discovery of the New World.[10]

Stuart Hall's levelheaded approach to modernity highlights the porosity not only of the temporal but also the geographical borders of modernity.[11] Mindful of attributing any single starting point to modernity, on the grounds that the processes that formed modern societies began at different times and "operated across several centuries and in a slow, uneven way" (p. 8), *Formations of Modernity* takes the history of the modern state back to Ancient Greece and Rome; the account of the economy becomes "mainly an eighteenth-century story"; the analysis of the industrial social structure focuses on the nineteenth century; the chapter on cultural formations begins with the Reformation; and the chapter on the West's relations with the rest of the world starts with Portuguese maritime exploration of the fifteenth century. In sum, modernity is an uneven affair, differential in temporal terms but in spatial terms, too, since not all its conceptual and technical resources originate in the West, and since this historical phase of the West is born precisely out of the colonial clash with other, non-Western historical times.

C.A. Bayly has taken this logic to an extreme by arguing that modernity should not be called Western at all but may more faithfully be termed a "common" modernity.[12] Among other things, Japanese industrialization, together with Jan de Vries's idea of demand-side "industrious revolutions," is mustered as evidence that non-Western peoples were at the same time actively engaged in making the modern world. However, Bayly's book speaks with a forked tongue. The dominant argumentative form of *The Birth of the Modern World* is the adversative: bold antiethnocentric proposition, qualified by "however" or "That said" or "and yet," and duly followed by a list of the multiple, and ultimately decisive, factors which ensured that, from the mid-nineteenth century, "the flow of events was now more firmly from Europe and North America outward." These factors include: usable land, agriculture, food availability, coal, inventions, stable legal and financial institutions, the commercial middle classes, the public sphere, military capability, the idea of progress, liberalism, socialism, and science (see pp. 60–64, 72–74, and 114). Although some of these factors are found in other parts of the globe, things seen separately elsewhere come together in Europe, and it is Europe that initially articulates most the flow of things and people. What Bayly says somewhat despite himself, Enrique Dussel says explicitly: modernity is not exclusively European, but it is a world-system that for centuries had Europe at its center. Europe organizes and controls modernity. "Modernity was the fruit of the 'management' of the centrality of the first world-system."[13] The word *common* masks the Western and, ultimately, imperial-colonial dimension of modernity. It is the West that most occupies the common ground, not to say the common land—both of which cease to be common. The West does not always have things its own way. But even when Bayly cites the powerful modernizing impetus of Japan's Meiji regime (1868–1912) as evidence of "uniformity," such evidence can easily be recoded as evidence of "Westernization." The first illustration in Bayly's book is a nineteenth-century Japanese print depicting a Japanese woman in Western dress seated at a Singer sewing machine.

Although they name the phases differently, Bayly and Dussel share the consensus view that this modernity, which is dominated but not made exclusively by the West, has received renewed impetus at certain decisive moments, such that it may usefully be subdivided into smaller phases. Marshall Berman divides modernity into three periods: the first beginning with the sixteenth century and running through to the French Revolution; the second beginning with the Enlightenment and comprising the early nineteenth century; the third stretching out from the latter part of the nineteenth century.[14] Hardt and Negri's *Empire* likewise isolates three "moments" in the constitution of European modernity. The first is the revolutionary plane of immanence, that is, the shift away from a thought of transcendence toward the idea of a world made by the creative powers of humanity. The second moment is the counterrevolution that attempts to keep those creative forces in check. The third and final moment is the formation of the nation-state as the locus of sovereignty, which gathers up some of the old forces of transcendence to keep humanity's powers in check by intercalating the state as the proper form of mediation. Dussel, in contrast, divides modernity into just two phases. The first, beginning in 1492, he calls the "Hispanic, humanist, Renaissance modernity." This first modernity is managed by Spain along political, economic, and intellectual lines, which are still clearly linked to the older "interregional" system formed by the Ottoman-Muslim world, India, China, and Europe. The second phase, which is formulated in the first half of the seventeenth century, is the "Anglo-Germanic" modernity, which truly comes to constitute the first "world-system." This second modernity begins with Amsterdam and "frequently passes as the *only* modernity." For Dussel, modernity must be understood as something stretching back as far as the fifteenth century, and the New World, or what he calls "Amerinidia," considered part of this modernity, for only then can the extent of the deformation of the subcontinent by the second (rationalizing) modernity be grasped.

These alternative ways of dividing up modernity prepare the ground for different judgments on modernity (which I shall return to later). But whether one takes modernity to be a single long phase, a series of subphases, or a temporally uneven phenomenon, the description of the socioeconomic reality of modernity throws up a number of common themes. These include: developments in science and technology that allow for the wholesale manipulation of nature and bring forth the demystification of world and cosmos; the dominance of secular forms of political power and authority operating within borders defined (eventually) by the nation-state; economic development conducted through the medium of a monetarized exchange economy and reenergized by the Industrial Revolution; the emergence of a dynamic social order offering greater possibilities of movement between social strata; the decline of a religious worldview and the rise of a rational, secular, materialist culture.[15] If the social and cultural changes in question were propelled by the techno-scientific and politico-economic transformations listed above, they were also moved by factors that belong more properly to the sociocultural sphere itself, factors such as the new academies and learned societies, developments in the printed word, increased literacy, and the establishment of a periodical press. From the second half of the seventeenth century, and in the guise of erudite journals, "universal" libraries, literary clubs, newspapers, tea- and coffeehouses, and Masonic lodges (Israel, p. 59), Western and central Europe witness the formation of a new kind of public sphere for debate outside the usual formal political, judicial, and ecclesiastical bodies and institutions. In the broadest possible brushstrokes, such are the contents of the material reality of the (European or Western) modern age, contents that make up a composite, uneven Ur-modernity, which will not have existed in any one time or place and certainly not in isolation from more traditional contents.

The second interpretation of modernity sees it primarily as a spirit or experience. Calinescu calls it the aesthetic concept of modernity, but in order not to lose sight of the early philosophical underpinnings of this aesthetic concept, which later famously hardens into the aggressive aestheticism of Baudelaire, it is more satisfactory to call it the philosophico-aesthetic concept of modernity. While giving due space to the creation of a new public sphere, Jonathan Israel's account of the "Radical Enlightenment" argues primarily that modernity was in important respects a formal "philosophical" affair. It was philosophy and scholarship that led the challenge to the traditional view of the world:

> During the later Middle Ages and the early modern age down to around 1650, western civilization was based on a largely shared core of faith, tradition, and authority. [. . .] Mid-seventeenth-century Europe was still, not just predominantly but overwhelmingly, a culture in which all debates about man, God, and the World which penetrated into the public sphere revolved around "confessional"—that is Catholic, Lutheran, Reformed (Calvinist), or Anglican issues, and scholars fought above all to establish which confessional bloc possessed a monopoly of truth and God-given title to authority. It was a civilization in which almost no one challenged the essentials of Christianity or the basic premises of

what was taken to be a divinely ordained system of aristocracy, monarchy, land-ownership, and ecclesiastical authority. (Israel, pp. 3–4)

Roughly from 1650 onwards, learned scientific and philosophical treatises were in the vanguard of the assault on theological dogma and paved the way for the new public sphere with its corresponding social change (Israel, p. 82). The philosophical dimension of modernity is not an interesting, if inessential byproduct of socioeconomic change, but lies at the heart of modernity. If tradition is received knowledge and the authority of the ancients, modernity is experience and experiment, challenge and criticism, the production of something formerly unknown, the invention of the new. It stands to reason that not everything in the modern age has this force. Modernity is the name bestowed retrospectively on an era by those anxious to capture the qualities—of critique, change, development, but also rupture—deemed to be new and of greatest value. Modernity is not an idle name invented by philosopher-aesthetes; it is a nomenclature that reminds us at every turn of the criticism of dogma and the opening onto the human.[16]

One of the most significant contents of the philosophico-aesthetic concept of modernity is the modern understanding of time. Neither the advent of a historical consciousness nor what Octavio Paz calls the modern "cult" of perpetual change can be grasped in isolation from the modern understanding of time. If, for the ancients, today repeats yesterday, for the moderns, it denies it.[17]

> In primitive societies the temporal archetype, model for the present and future, is the past—not the recent past, but an immemorial past lying beyond all pasts, at the beginning of the beginning. Like a well spring, this past of pasts flows constantly, runs into and becomes part of the present; it is the only actuality which really counts. Social life is not historic but ritualistic; it is made up not of a succession of changes but of the rhythmic repetition of the timeless past. Always present, this past protects society from change by serving as a model for imitation and by being periodically actualized in ritual. [. . .] Our era breaks abruptly with these ways of thought. Having inherited the unilinear and irreversible time of Christianity, it adopts the Christian opposition to cyclical conceptions but, simultaneously, denies the

Christian archetype and affirms one that negates all the ideas and images of time that man has made for himself. The modern age is the first to exalt change and convert it into a foundation. Difference, separation, otherness, plurality, novelty, evolution, revolution, history—all these words can be condensed into one: future. Not past nor eternity, not time which is but time which is not yet and which will always be to come: this is our archetype. (Paz, *Children,* pp. 9–10, 17)[18]

The historical period known as modernity knows other conceptions of time, but the time of change is its archetype.

However, modern time does not just flow ceaselessly forward; it constantly interrupts itself, habitually rehearses the rupture with time that precisely defines modernity as an epochal new beginning. "Because the new, the modern world is distinguished from the old by the fact that it opens itself to the future, the epochal new beginning is rendered constant with each moment that gives birth to the new. Thus, it is characteristic of the historical consciousness of modernity to set off 'the most recent [*neusten*] period' from the modern [*neu*] age" (Habermas, p. 6). In this schema, the present, which is by definition the most recent moment that gives birth to the new, is always the most prominent. But by virtue of the fact that the present repeats the founding ruptural move of modernity, it "continues" the modern project: "A present that understands itself from the horizon of the modern age as the actuality of the most recent period has to recapitulate the break brought about with the past as a *continuous renewal*" (Habermas, p. 7). Paz says something important in this respect apropos of the relationship between the modern and the new. "The new," he writes, "is not exactly the modern, unless it carries a double explosive charge: the negation of the past and the affirmation of something different."[19] In other words, modernity is a qualitative, not just a chronological, affair. Not every moment in time is hailed as a break with the past; only certain preferred moments are adjudged to be qualitatively superior to the past and thus count as truly modern. It is the *quality* of the temporality that opens up a new period, not the mere fact of chronological succession. This qualitative understanding is closely related to the colonial moment.[20] And it was this same understanding that was generalized in the latter half of the nineteenth century into the ideas of *Neuzeit* and *modernité*, "thereby coming to be understood as constitutive of the temporality of modernity as such" (Osborne, p. 71). That the qualitative understanding of time should be constitutive of the temporality of modernity is just what sustains the late-nineteenth-century aesthetic concept of modernity,

> the historical force of whose fundamental objects "lies *solely* in the fact that they are new" [. . .]. The logic of the new, fashion, and aesthetic modernism as a "rebellion against the modernity of the philistine" which nonetheless works within the same temporal structure, may all be understood as the result of an aestheticization of "modernity" as a form of historical consciousness and its transformation into a general model of social experience. (Osborne, p. 71, citing Benjamin and Calinescu)

The qualitative understanding of the modern age does not, however, point solely in the direction of the aesthetic concept of modernity. Although the aesthetic and socioeconomic definitions of modernity conflict, the aesthetic concept not only has its origins in the historical conjuncture of modernity but articulates the fundamental premise of social reform.[21] Namely, criticize and change, dissent and create. When Baudelaire speaks of modernity as a spirit or attitude, he rules out the idea that modernity is a determinate historical phase. For Baudelaire, modernity is just what transcends a historical phase, being modern is a heroic choice. But what this voluntaristic aesthetic concept of modernity overlooks is that aestheticism is already an epochal phenomenon, or is at least in some way tied to the historical times (if aestheticism, or the cult of novelty, reaches new heights in modernity, it is not an absolutely modern phenomenon). Following Paz on time, it is an archetype of modernity, which does not mean that it owes everything to the modern era. The upshot of this partial historicization of Baudelaire's conception of the modern is that there is a profound convergence between Calinescu's two conflicting modernities. Baudelaire's search for the ephemeral is connected to Hegel's lightning bolt (which, however, must strike not once but repeatedly), and both of the latter to the spirit of change.[22] The aestheticization of the concept of modernity, which is transformed into a general model of social experience, sees in modernity not just the emergence of new political structures and economic practices, but a radically different "mode of vital experience" (to use Berman's phrase), something like a new spirit, or a spirit of the new. We miss the essential if we fail to see that the drive for continuous aesthetic renewal finds its corollary in the cluster of dynamic *social* concepts (revolution, progress, emancipation, development, crisis, *Zeitgeist*) that, together with the expression modern age, either emerged or acquired their new meaning in the eighteenth century.[23]

Latin American *modernidad*

Beatriz Sarlo's work on Buenos Aires takes the city's *modernidad* to be a socioeconomic reality *and* an aesthetic experience marked by lightning strikes of the new, which Sarlo evokes in rhapsodic prose.[24] The modernity in question has little to do with the classical definition of modernity as that phase which displaces the Middle Ages—which is not to say that important aspects of the older sense do not find their way into these debates. However, in common with recent accounts of European and North American modernity, the debate surrounding Latin American *modernidad* has generally homed in on Berman's third phase of modernity, that is, on the years stretching out from the end of the nineteenth century.[25] While the period of Sarmiento clearly exhibits some of the signs of modernity consistent with Berman's second period—signs such as the advent of modern technology and changing social patterns propelled by economic growth, for critics such as Sarlo modernity only arrives in Argentina in any significant way in the second two decades of the twentieth century. *Modernidad* is neither the general passage from the epoch of *traditio* to the epoch of production as invention, nor is it synonymous with the project of Enlightenment.[26] *Modernidad*, for Sarlo, refers to the closing years of the nineteenth century and, more especially, the inaugural ones of the twentieth. Nuances apart, all the work on Latin American modernity by Sarlo, García Canclini, Jesús Martín-Barbero, Carlos Monsiváis, Brunner, and Julio Ramos binds the region's modernity to the Second Industrial Revolution. Framed in Latin America by the formation of nation-states and the formally free incorporation of the latter into the capitalist world economy, it is an era characterized by the expansion of the railway network, the advent of the telegraph and automobile travel, the growth of steam shipping, the arrival of cinema, radio, and the airplane, and the beginnings of mass democracy.

The interesting thing about Sarlo's work, as we have said, is that she complements the socioeconomic view of Buenos Aires modernity with a philosophico-aesthetic understanding of it. Here then, at the entry to a new century, Sarlo can find material socioeconomic and technological changes in the fabric of the city, which seem themselves to be the stone, steel, and electric incarnations of that perpetual change identified by Paz as the spirit of the modern age. Under the geometric modern streets run sewers, drains, and the tunnels of the first underground system; and, above ground, the tram tracks, electricity lines, telephone cables, water pipes, and lighting.[27] Here, in Buenos Aires in the 1920s and 1930s, the ferment and change of modernity is found not in the prose of philosophers or the free verse of poets, but in (and under) the streets themselves.[28]

Whereas Martín-Barbero concurs with Sarlo that the 1920s and 1930s form the key years, García Canclini and Brunner emphasize later decades, above all the 1950s.[29] It is important to register different handlings of these respective modernities. If in Martín-Barbero there is a historian's desire to isolate a key period (the 1930s), there is also recognition that Latin American modernity does not begin at that moment. He thus invokes Bolívar, Martí, Mariátegui, and the region's nineteenth-century national bourgeoisies as vital modern forerunners. In contrast, Brunner writes of the need to identify a genuine "constelación de cultura propiamente moderna como tal." For him, Sarmiento, the *modernistas*, those championed by Martín-Barbero, and even early-twentieth-century university reform are all isolated "new" (not "modern") moments that do not amount to modernity:

> Digamos así: la reforma universitaria de Córdoba (1918), igual que determinados elementos de la Revolución mexicana, o las ideas de Mariátegui y Martí, representan momentos—siempre ambiguos desde el punto de vista cultural—de irrupción de elementos nuevos en las culturas tradicionales, pero por sí solos no fundan la modernidad. Su advenimiento tendrá que esperar hasta encontrar un piso (social, tecnológico y profesional) favorable sobre el cual sostenerse.[30]

One can sympathize with Brunner's one-Martí-doesn't-make-a-modernity approach, but to reserve the word modernity for a time when the region finally achieves a critical modern mass is to flirt with one of the founding habits of modern thought, which cuts off the present moment irremediably from tradition and the past. A compromise solution is to look for a critical mass that might merit the name modern, while avoiding the expectation that such a mass could be *absolutely* modern.

However, it is the work of another Argentine writer, who shares the focus on Berman's third phase of modernity, that has most influentially addressed the modernity of Latin America as a whole. Néstor García Canclini's approach to modernity conforms more closely than Sarlo's to a socioeconomic view, and is accordingly critical of the philosophico-aesthetic discourse of the moderns. He identifies four constitutive

The Things that Travel 13

movements of modernity: the emancipating project, the expansive project, the democratizing project, and the project of renewal:

> Por proyecto *emancipador* entendemos la secularización de los campos culturales, la producción autoexpresiva y autorregulada de las prácticas simbólicas, su desenvolvimiento en mercados autónomos. Forman parte de este movimiento emancipador la racionalización de la vida social y el individualismo creciente, sobre todo en las grandes ciudades.
>
> Denominamos proyecto *expansivo* a la tendencia de la modernidad que busca extender el conocimiento y la posesión de la naturaleza, la producción, la circulación y el consumo de los bienes. En el capitalismo, la expansión está motivada preferentemente por el incremento del lucro; pero en un sentido más amplio se manifiesta en la promoción de los descubrimientos científicos y el desarrollo industrial.
>
> El proyecto *renovador* abarca dos aspectos, con frecuencia complementarios: por una parte, la persecución de un mejoramiento e innovación incesantes propios de una relación con la naturaleza y la sociedad liberada de toda prescripción sagrada sobre cómo debe ser el mundo; por la otra, la necesidad de reformular una y otra vez los signos de distinción que el consumo masificado desgasta.
>
> Llamamos proyecto *democratizador* al movimiento de la modernidad que confía en la educación, la difusión del arte y los saberes especializados, para lograr una evolución racional y moral. Se extiende desde la ilustración hasta la UNESCO, desde el positivismo hasta los programas educativos o de popularización de la ciencia y la cultura emprendidos por gobiernos liberales, socialistas y agrupaciones alternativas e independientes. (*Culturas híbridas*, p. 51)

The notable thing about this account is that the contents of modernity are variously positive and negative. The expansive project, for instance, both extends knowledge of nature and begets the industrialization that will threaten the natural world. Such a plural view of the projects of modernity does not diminish the fact that the projects define part (the most modern part), rather than the totality, of the historical phase called modernity.

More Bermanesque than Berman, García Canclini asserts that, at least from the point of view of culture, modernity only really takes hold in the subcontinent in the 1950s, propelled by economic growth, urbanization, the growth of the market for cultural goods, the introduction of new communications technologies, and the emergence of radical political movements.[31] Although *Culturas híbridas* adopts a solidly socioeconomic conception of Latin American modernity, it is at the same time a critique of traditional sociology. This critique is two-pronged: it criticizes sociologists, first, for peddling a melancholic negative comparativism (Latin American modernity is always late and defective in relation to the original European model), and, second, for positing an exclusively positive understanding of modernity. On the first issue, García Canclini maintains that there is no simple correlation *anywhere* (either in Europe or in Latin America) between socioeconomic modernization and cultural modernism. The most advanced economic modernization does not necessarily produce cultural modernism and it therefore serves little purpose to compare the fortunes of Latin America with an idealized, though quite erroneous, image of how that process supposedly happened in the metropolitan centers. Whenever Sarmiento traveled to one of the world centers in search of modernity, he invariably returned disappointed.[32] On the second question, García Canclini follows the line most associated with Adorno and Horkheimer's "dialectic of Enlightenment," according to which the unpalatable aspects of modernity are not unfortunate accidents of, but are integral to, the modern project.[33]

Culturas híbridas argues that, on the basis of the constitutive tension between a liberating progressive rationality and the oppressive forces of instrumental reason, the four projects of modernity in Latin America maintain a necessarily awkward relationship with indigenous traditions. By virtue of a process of reasoning that yokes together "indians"/tradition/rural life/preservation of the past, while construing all of these things as separate from, and antithetical to, urban life/modernity/movement toward the future, the dual harbingers of progress that are the philosophical discourse of modernity and the socioeconomic processes of modernization can find no place for the indigenous-traditional in the modern age.[34] García Canclini's essential point is that in the last quarter of the twentieth century in Latin America indigenous-traditional and modern cultures have come to intersect much more, and that as a result the bipolar analytical categories of modern thought are inadequate to the new "hybrid" object. By the late 1980s, modernity, which only took hold in the 1950s, had run its course, displaced by a postmodern world to which only the categories of postmodernism are adequate.³⁵ It is worth following closely García Canclini's critique of the antagonistic habits of modern thought, for even if it is anchored in a later period, at every juncture it is critical of the cultural configuration and analytical categories of the first half of the twentieth century, which is the concern of this book.

Hybrid Cultures and One Postmodern Critique of Modernity

The reality of contemporary Latin America is, in García Canclini's famous phrase, that of a "multitemporal heterogeneity"—a conjuncture formed by the meeting of three broad "temporalities" that belong respectively to indigenous traditions, Catholic, colonial hispanism, and capitalist modernity. The word *temporality* derives from Perry Anderson (who takes it from Althusser), who writes variously of "historical times," "historical temporalities," and a "differential temporality."³⁶ These near-redundant terms are intended to designate significant strands of a culture (i.e., institutions, manmade objects, social customs, works of art), which have a common historical origin but persist, in some shape or form, in a later historical formation. Above all, more than one such temporality goes to make up a given historical conjuncture, and insofar as modernity is the negation of plural temporalities, this plurality is essential to the critique of the modern understanding of time and, by extension, history.

In the modern view of time as irreversible flow, entities move together in synchronized step; one false move and they are rapidly replaced by other things more able to keep up. (The indigenous are welcome to join modernity, on the condition that they cease being indians.) As Bruno Latour puts it: "The moderns have a peculiar propensity for understanding time that passes as if it were really abolishing the past behind it. They all take themselves for Attila, in whose footsteps no grass grows back."³⁷ This is not simply an idea. It corresponds, for Walter Benjamin, to the inexorable forward drive of the material reality of modern capitalism itself, to what he calls the storm of progress that blows from Paradise.³⁸ Without this storm, without this "harsh disciplining" (Latour) at the hands of the moderns, peoples and entities would be seen in their true light, as pertaining to "all sorts of times" and possessing "all sorts of ontological statuses" (Latour, p. 72).

García Canclini concurs with Latour in his critique of the modern spirit of Attila. But what distinguishes him from Latour, who is otherwise right to say that there is no country which has not reached the point of mixing up times, is that García Canclini endows the term "temporality" with a broader, more anthropological—more decisively ethnographic—meaning than that intended by Anderson. He has in mind not different times of the same tradition, but those that belong to radically different cultural traditions. For García Canclini, these broad historical temporalities—each of which is a generalization—do not coexist in isolation; they contaminate, intersect, and cross-fertilize one another. For this reason, one cannot sensibly choose between modernization and local "traditionality." The storm of modern development may blow hard but it does not suppress traditional popular cultures.[39] Correspondingly, if modernization does not eradicate popular culture, nor does traditional popular culture remain unchanged. Urbanization in Latin America, by which cities now account for 70 percent of the total population, means that peasant and traditional culture of the rural areas no longer represents the majority of popular culture in the region, which is now to be found in the cities, the putative seats of modern life. And even when traditional, rural culture remains in the countryside, it seldom goes untouched by the technical and economic resources of modernity. We recall García Canclini's account of his epiphanic meeting with the Oaxacan artisan who moved effortlessly "del zapoteco al español y al inglés, del arte a la artesanía, de su etnia a la información y los entretenimientos de la cultura masiva, pasando por la crítica de arte de una metrópoli" (*Culturas*, p. 225), and who as a result shared none of the melancholy García Canclini assumed must accompany the (to him) obvious subordination of tradition to modernity.[40]

Leaving aside the question of the balance of power in such commerce, at the descriptive level García Canclini's point about the intersection of the modern and the traditional is well made. As he argued in *Las culturas populares en el capitalismo*, artisanal products may occupy a structural place in modern capitalism *and* be historical manifestations of pre-Colombian times.[41] His construction of an armory of theoretical concepts appropriate for the analysis of hybrid cultures responds to the changed and changing landscape of contemporary Latin America. From the vantage point of 1989, the so-called postmodern phase of history has witnessed a significant deepening of the intersection of traditional and modern temporalities, and, by virtue of its readily accessible telecommunications, decentralized networks of power and expanded markets, made possible the creative cross-fertilization of cultural forms. Having thus departed from the historical phase that was modernity, it is necessary to part company with the bipolar habits of modern thought.

A Note on Names: Postmodernism, Postmodernity, or Late Capitalism

> "We have to name the system": this high point of the sixties finds an unexpected revival in the postmodernism debate.
>
> —Fredric Jameson

The notion of postmodernity used (equivocally) by García Canclini is not a universally agreed one.[42] Closely tied to a relativist, antiethnocentric tradition of progressive Left critique both within and beyond Latin America, it nonetheless differs significantly, for example, from Fredric Jameson's North American model. Postmodernity for Jameson designates the moment—of late capitalism—when society has modernized to such an extent that the residual and the archaic have been expelled from the present. If the new in modernity is experienced as new by virtue of the fact that the old and the traditional sit alongside it (Apollinaire's Paris included grimy medieval monuments and the latest airplanes), in contrast postmodernity has done away with history:

> The postmodern must be characterized as a situation in which the survival, the residue, the holdover, the archaic, has finally been swept away without a trace. [. . .] Everything is now organized and planned; nature has been triumphantly blotted out, along with peasants, petit-bourgeois commerce, handicraft, feudal aristocracies and imperial bureaucracies. Ours is a more homogeneously modernized condition; we no longer are encumbered with the embarrassment of non-simultaneities and non-synchronicities. Everything has reached the same hour on the great clock of development or rationalization (at least from the perspective of the "West"). This is the sense in which we can affirm, either that modernism is characterized by a situation of incomplete *modernization*, or that postmodernism is *more* modern than modernism itself. (pp. 309–310)

This sense of postmodernity clashes head on with García Canclini's understanding. The latter's insistence on the historical traces left by pre–Colombian culture in contemporary artefacts, and indeed the very notion of plural temporalities, responds to Jameson's injunction to think the present historically in an age that has forgotten how to think historically in the first place (p. ix). When García Canclini writes of Latin America as that place "donde las tradiciones aún no se han ido y la modernidad no acaba de llegar" (*Culturas*, p. 35), he is describing the late 1980s, not the beginning of the twentieth century; in other words, he is speaking about the period affirmed by Jameson as the (postmodern) age from which tradition has been eradicated without a trace.

In Jameson's account, postmodernity is another name for late capitalism. What then rears its head is the specter of a narrative of modernization (pronounced dead by García Canclini) in which capitalism brings about the hybridization of cultures in Latin America as a preliminary step on the path toward the gradual elimination of the traditional-archaic-indigenous from the region, a process that, for economic reasons, would occur later in Latin America than elsewhere. According to this logic, it is not that there are two postmodernities (North and Latin American); rather, there is a single logic of modernization (called globalization), which dictates that certain ("advanced") countries enter postmodernity whereas others ("the developing") know aspects of the postmodern but have not yet fully arrived in postmodernity.[43]

Jameson's schema is in part shared by Peter Osborne. For Osborne, who thinks that postmodernity is but another manifestation of the logic of modernity, modernity must be thought of as a differential temporality spatialized at the moment of colonialism.[44] But, equally for Osborne, it is meaningless to construe the different temporalities which make up modernity in isolation from a whole.[45] In this respect, the abstractions "temporality" and "modernity" hinder analysis. Once one descends from such abstractions to the level of material things, bodies, and people, it becomes easier to appreciate the fact that intersection—the knottedness of daily life—is routine. What this means for García Canclini's conception of historical temporalities is that it is a moot point how far capitalism has "synchronized" (the word is his) the different times; and whether, as a consequence, another name for two synchronized temporalities might be one temporality. García Canclini is not oblivious to this (Althusserian) problem. His affirmation of the historical traces deposited by pre-Colombian cultures in the present is not a politically naive celebration of the harmonious coexistence of autonomous cultural times. "Tenemos presente que en este tiempo de diseminación posmoderna y descentralización democratizadora también crecen las formas más concentradas de acumulación de poder y centralización transnacional de la cultura que la humanidad ha conocido" (p. 45). As soon as one inquires into the articulation between relatively autonomous temporalities, one brings them into a comparative analytical and moral framework, and rapidly comes up against the limits of relativism. García Canclini knows this better than most; but knows, too, that because modern and traditional temporalities necessarily intersect, it does not follow that the distinction between the two is "dissolved."[46] He understands, first, the logical difficulty of suddenly deciding to do without one of the terms, and, second, the ethicopolitical necessity of holding onto the term *tradition* not just as an "idea," but as a lived part of social reality, no matter how crisscrossed by the modern it may have become.[47]

What is less clear in *Culturas híbridas* is whether the implications of this unavoidable comparativism have been folded back into the question of modernity itself, that is, into the postmodern critique of the difference between modernity and postmodernity. I should like to offer a thesis as to why, in addition to reasons having to do with the political moment, there are historico-theoretical reasons for the fact that the original project of modernity should haunt García Canclini's work.

Modernity under Erasure, or, the Limits of Postmodern Relativism

In later work, and following the deepening of the debt crisis and the ravages caused by neoliberal privatizations in Latin America, García Canclini is more sanguine about postmodernism, and above all about the contents of postmodernity, and more inclined to hold on to the idea of modernity, or, in effect, fold postmodernity back into (an uncertain) modernity: "Instead of affirming that modernity is an era that has been superseded by post modernity, as was believed in the 1980s, or that modernity is an unfinished project, as argued by Habermas, it should be thought of as an open and uncertain movement."[48] In point of fact, *Culturas híbridas* had already harbored a nagging doubt about the attempt to have done with modernity, a doubt that is expressed as a problem associated with the voluntaristic desire to enter or leave a modernity now viewed as an all-enveloping "condition."

> Las reconversiones culturales que analizamos revelan que la modernidad no es solo un espacio o un estado al que se entre o del

que se emigre. Es una condición que nos envuelve, en las ciudades y en el campo, en las metrópolis y en los países subdesarrollados. Con todas las contradicciones que existen entre modernismo y modernización, y precisamente por ellas, es una situación de tránsito interminable en la que nunca se clausura la incertidumbre de lo que significa ser moderno. Radicalizar el proyecto de la modernidad es agudizar y renovar esta incertidumbre, crear nuevas posibilidades para que la modernidad pueda ser siempre otra cosa y otra más. (*Culturas híbridas*, p. 322)

Why does it prove difficult to have done with modernity and why does postmodern relativism prove inadequate as a means of evading the shadow-criteria of Western modernity?

The first thing to say is that not everything in the modern age is modern. The modern age contains recognizably modern institutions, cultural practices, and social mores, together with modern forms of social and political organization, but it also knows traditional or "antimodern" ones.[49] In addition, it knows examples of all of the aforementioned that combine strains of both the traditional and the modern. The name modern age is a coup executed by the moderns themselves in order to claim the entire epoch as their own. When Hegel spoke of the modern age, he baptized a manifold reality using the name of one of the parts that he saw as the most important and distinctive of the age. In order to give due weight to the profound political, social, and philosophical changes of the time, Hegel bestows the name of the attitude and action responsible for them upon the entire age. Only by believing in the representativity of the name could we believe that the modern age did not know intersections between the traditional and the modern. If in Hegel's time there had been a conventional system for designating world epochs—based, say, on the Greek alphabet—the problem would have been less acute. Hegel could have called the new epoch the "gamma age" and we would then have had to consider the many and varied things that went to make up the gamma age, without ever imagining it was composed of just one homogeneous thing. But Hegel chose to be more partisan. To claim the epoch for his own.

Not everything in the modern age is modern.[50] Bruno Latour's formulation of this postulate is that "modernity" as such did not take place. We have never been modern, he says. Latour does not mean by this that we are locked into tradition, that, really, truth be told, we never quite managed to drag ourselves into the modern age. He means that modernity, as a single definable entity capable of arriving (and departing), never arrived. *Anywhere*. Even at the height of so-called modernity, "we" were more (or less) than modern. We were always already crossed by different temporalities. This is just what Perry Anderson says when he introduces the notion of historical temporalities taken up by García Canclini.[51] And García Canclini echoes Anderson when he writes of Latin America as that place where modernity has not completely arrived and traditions have not yet disappeared. Not everything in the modern age originates in the modern age or conforms to the qualitatively superior ideal of the modern. As a consequence, the modern age cannot be said to constitute a single historical temporality capable of arriving (or departing). Because the historical phase called modernity was never anywhere fully present in its self-identical modernness, one is not prevented from speaking of it or debating its beginnings. But in so doing one is, first, identifying the emergence of certain new forms that come into being in the midst of other older phenomena; second, acknowledging that these new things may well owe a debt to prior traditions (the Ancient Greece, for instance);[52] and, third, recognizing that such temporal slippage is also a geographical one, that is, that the West's path to modernity to a certain extent began elsewhere (for instance in Egypt, i.e., Africa, rather than Greece).[53]

The second proposition concerns the ideological baggage of modernity. If modernity is the name of a historical phase of Western civilization, to speak of the "modernity" of some other place is not to use the word in that initial sense. To say that a historical phase of Western civilization had arrived in Peru would be to incur in the ultimate Eurocentrism—as though Peru had lived out the whole of European history, including the Renaissance, Neo-Kantianism, and the Tolpuddle martyrs, from the year 1500 on. Historical phases do not travel elsewhere; elements or "forces" of a historical phase travel elsewhere.[54] To speak of the "modernity" of Peru is to abstract and generalize the word, such that on the surface it no longer means "a historical phase of Western civilization." "Modernity" comes, rather, to designate a generalizable "condition" endowed with certain elements (capitalist economy, scientific worldview, a new sensorium) capable of traveling. The traveling contents of modernity are reworked, transformed, resisted, and crossed with new materials in the new context.

However, the contents of the new modernity continue to bear the imprint of the West (which is why the abstracted term appears "on the surface" not to refer to the historical phase of Western civilization). To speak of modernity is to invoke the development of a world-system whose center was Europe and whose origins were largely European.[55] This has implications for any relativist analysis (which is really an absolutist analysis) of a local modernity, which henceforth is never exclusively local. The comparative dimension of modernity cannot be volatilized by an unmelancholic relativist "postmodern" critique, without also volatilizing the colonial dimension. It is because modernity is to a large extent European (and, later, North American), and because any local non-Western modernity is still attached to the West, that the full geopolitical, colonial implications of the spread of modernity can be grasped and, indeed, modernity become the object of blame. Dussel's invocation of two modernities allows him to judge the "Hispanic, humanist, Renaissance modernity" negatively and positively (it produced a philosophy, still in touch with the scholastic-Muslim-Christian and Renaissance traditions, of "the highest importance"), whereas the second, "Anglo-Germanic" modernity is valorized in an exclusively negative manner. The second modernity produced a rationalist philosophy that corresponded to the efficacious management of an entire world-system through the rationalization of the life-world, and its economic, political, cultural, and religious subsystems (Dussel, "Beyond Eurocentrism," p. 15). The historical entanglement of Latin America in Europe is clear. Equally clear is Dussel's desire to break with the European political legacy. What is less clear to Dussel is the extent of the entanglement in the conceptual legacy of modernity and the fact that to disavow the second modernity en masse is to be ignorant of one of the main sources of the conceptual reservoir from which one draws and, indeed, deprive oneself of valuable conceptual resources for its critique.

Hardt and Negri's construction of European modernity is better able to account for their own position. Their three "moments" of modernity are also two "modes" of modernity (in this, their concept of modernity is clearly differential). These two modes, the radical revolutionary process of transcendence and the reactionary forces of order, are not sequential but coeval. In other words, whereas Dussel assigns value diachronically (first phase of modernity good, second phase bad), *Empire*'s strategy is to distribute value synchronically, identifying good and bad (the two modes) in each phase. The heuristic advantage of Hardt and Negri's model of modernity over Dussel's is that it leaves itself room to apportion the blame for political and philosophical reactionariness to elements within modernity rather than to modernity (or, at least, Dussel's second modernity) as a whole and is thus able also to recognize that at least some of the resources used to criticize European modernity emanate from European modernity.[56] As Dussel says, Europe was the center of modernity. As such, the conceptual matrix of modernity was largely European. To invoke the European tradition is not to slide back into the clutches of the philosophical discourse of modernity, held to be the analytical corollary of attempts to universalize the social, political, economic, and technological criteria of European modernity during the colonial moment.[57] It is to acknowledge that one cannot not rehearse the legacy of the philosophical discourse of modernity whenever one speaks of modernity. This does not mean one is condemned to a single practical *European* definition of the modern. One is condemned to a general concept of modernity each time one asks the question of what a specific modernity might be. The history of European colonialism and the conceptual apparatus of European modernity are embedded in the name modernity. Not only in the object called Latin America, but in the fabric of the critical language on Latin America. Not everything passes by way of European modernity. Alejo Carpentier is right to have the character Sieger say in *El siglo de las luces* that the black slaves did not have to wait for the French Revolution to proclaim themselves free on innumerable occasions. But, by virtue of colonialism, the cluster of dynamic social concepts (revolution, progress, emancipation, development) that either emerged or acquired their new meaning in the eighteenth century ensure that the discourse on modernity is tied, *though not condemned*, to a European language and conceptual resource bank, which are inseparable from the general idea of what is meant by modernity in the first place.

When García Canclini writes above of creating new possibilities that will allow modernity always to be something other, he plunges headlong into the linguistic waters of a modernity centered on Europe and in the process allows us to see what we had argued earlier: namely, that Calinescu's two bitterly conflicting modernities are joined at the hip. García Canclini's interest is clearly in a socioeconomic concept of modernity, though not in a sclerotic modern socioeconomic reality. Therefore, in his invocation of the project of modernity, which is above all an appeal to a *socioeconomic* modernity (with democratic institutions, educational provision for all, etc.), he draws upon the European philosophico-aesthetic idea of modernity as that impulse for change which "recapitulates the break brought about with the past as a *continuous renewal*" (Habermas). The European conceptual system travels and is transformed, but such transformations do not escape history.

It is like the function of a certain word-processing package that allows one to position the cursor over a footnote number and see a little box with the contents of the footnote pop up onto the screen. The box can be closed and its contents forgotten; but it and they are always there.

However, if the organizing matrix of modernity is European in significant respects, and if in thinking about modernity one is tied to the European tradition, one is neither tied nor condemned to accepting that tradition as an absolute. Exactly which European tradition would one accept? The French? The German? The English? The Scottish? If the European tradition is closely bound up with the possibility of thinking modernity in general, it is not identical with it. The general is never absolutely incarnated in any specific instance of the general. The concept of modernity is at once a general and a specific one; and thinking it entails thinking the tension between the general and the specific. Modernity may believe its general concepts, such as the concept of progress, to be absolutes, but it is clearly possible to advocate progress in certain areas while rejecting it in others, that is, to think the gains of a common law, common schooling, and universal rights against the abuses of universalism and the common ground.[58] To give up on the categories of modernity, in the name of postmodernism, is to run the risk of giving up on the nodal points of power capable of exerting most force on the shape—or misshapenness—of the decentralized whole.[59]

Where, one might ask, does this leave postmodernity? Philosophically speaking, if the name sticks, postmodernity will come to be seen as the continuation of the modern period. Postmodernity will be marked by the modern habit of striving to break with the past, but because such striving occurs at a chronologically later moment than classical modernity, the past it attempts to break with has already experienced multiple renewals and the tradition it attempts to depart from (or even, as in certain strains of postmodernism, embrace) has already been repeatedly fractured and reset.

Jameson's account of postmodernity, or late capitalism, is not a melancholic one. Recalling Marx's judgment on capitalism, he injures us to think postmodernity positively and negatively at the same time, as catastrophe and progress all together. Naming a historical phase should not prevent attempts at labeling smaller shifts that occur within the whole, although one should be constantly vigilant about ruptures or transitions that purport to leave the contents of an earlier phase behind. Although not without a certain acuity and heuristic value, to speak of the "passage" from "enlightened" to "neoliberal" modernity is to speak the language of totalization.[60] A totalization that would deprive Latin America of vital resources to criticize neoliberalism. On the contrary, modernity is differential and porous. The beginnings of Latin American modernity do not lie solely in the Second Industrial Revolution and nor is its current configuration exhausted by "neoliberalism." Both early and late Latin American modernities include traces of "la modernidad ilustrada," as well as the older humanist modernity in which people first "declared themselves masters of their own lives, producers of cities and history, and inventors of heavens" (Hardt and Negri, p. 70). The critique of modernity does not so easily dispense with tradition(s). Especially if Latin America has never been the issue of the Jamesonian postmodern.

CHAPTER 2

Culture Is (Not) Ordinary: The Secrets of the Slow in the Public Sphere

> Queremos proponer aquí una vía antropológica.
>
> —Néstor García Canclini[1]

Néstor García Canclini's *Culturas híbridas* is a violent book. Even if it does not thematize violence, and even if it is written in order to open up a cultural field hitherto considered restricted and undemocratic, *Culturas híbridas* is a violent book. It confronts instances of a "modern" culture deemed violent in its elitism and meets their violence with a violence of its own, refusing to judge them on their own terms, assessing them according to the dictates of a "scientific" sociology of culture, and moving on apace. Much of the book's suasive force, but also its violence, derives from this pace, the sense that a critical eye is ranging rapidly over objects from all walks of life in a ceaseless mapping of the materials that form the hybrid cultures of Latin America in the late 1980s. A decrease in speed, or at least a gesture in the direction of a decrease in speed, together with a less hostile view of high culture, may be observed in *La globalización imaginada*.[2] Suffice it to indicate for the moment that the question of speed in that book is closely related to the question of democracy and the public sphere; to the possibility that what he comes to call the "slow" economy of high-artistic production might better serve the democratic interests of the public sphere than the fast culture that more generally circulates there.

That slow art should be more public-spirited than public art, more indeed than the public sphere itself, is emphatically not the argument of *Culturas híbridas*. The book begins by analyzing modernity's un-public-spirited attempt ("una de las utopías más enérgicas y constantes de la cultura moderna") to construct autonomous fields of knowledge and artistic production (*Culturas híbridas*, p. 51). This is the book's abiding object of critique: the power of the modern organization of the sphere of culture, which works according to a bipolar logic that distinguishes tenaciously between what is deemed to be culture and what is thought to fall below the threshold of culture. The whole book is a critique and denunciation of the oppositional habits of modern thought. García Canclini's argument is twofold. First, that the modern organization of the sphere of culture was an elitist, socially divisive enterprise. Second, that the modern "ideology" (we shall return to this word) of a cultural sphere divided into autonomous fields no longer corresponds to the empirical reality of contemporary society, which knows only cultural crossings, interactions, and hybrids.

My concern in this chapter is with García Canclini's objection to the would-be autonomization of art. Since his early engagements with 1960s' Argentine experimental art, his writings have consistently criticized the antidemocratic credentials of cultural avant-gardism, an obsession that returns in *Culturas híbridas* in the shape of an attack on early-twentieth-century Latin American modernism. In spite of his "postmodern" differences from the tradition of Enlightenment, he shares that tradition's belief in the values of light, transparency, the public, and publicity. What is out in the public sphere, what is expressive of public opinion and available to the people, foments democracy; what hides from public spaces in restricted institutes, or what is expressive of unpopular opinion and barely accessible to the people, is prejudicial to democracy. For all its positive aspects, Latin American modernism is, in the final analysis, judged to be undemocratic. Given the parlous situation of the public sphere in many Latin American countries at the end of the millennium, García Canclini's concern for the values of openness and the common good is understandable. But the question of the relationship between high art and democracy, or between modernism and the public sphere, is not a simple one, and is certainly further complicated by the presence in *Culturas híbridas* of a quasi-Leninist scheme for the valorization of art, which relies heavily on a pragmatic view of art at odds with the unprogrammatic, indeed properly irresponsible, dimension of responsibility that lies at the heart of democracy. What if, as Jacques Derrida suggests, the very concept of responsibility had the structure of a type of secrecy, of mystery even? What would that mean for the judgment of high, or slow, culture?

La ideología de lo culto moderno

The modern organization of the sphere of culture is characterized, in Max Weber's famous analysis, by the creation of specialized, autonomous domains of culture. García Canclini summarizes Weber (in fact, Habermas on Weber):

> Lo moderno se constituye al independizarse la cultura de la razón sustantiva consagrada por la religión y la metafísica, y constituirse en tres esferas autónomas: la ciencia, la moralidad y el arte. Cada una se organiza en un régimen estructurado por cuestiones específicas—el conocimiento, la justicia, el gusto—y regido por instancias propias de valoración, o sea, la verdad, la rectitud normativa, la autenticidad y la belleza. La autonomía de cada dominio va institucionalizándose, genera profesionales especializados que se convierten en autoridades expertas de su área. Esta especialización acentúa la distancia entre la cultura profesional y la del público, entre los campos científicos o artísticos y la vida cotidiana. (p. 52)

García Canclini's concern in the first chapter of *Culturas híbridas* is the specialized field of the modern arts, which begins to take shape in sixteenth- and seventeenth-century European society as artistic production ceases to be dependent for its funding and content on religious and political commissioning and begins to be produced "for its own sake," expressing and responding to concerns considered properly aesthetic. The upshot of this process of autonomization is that high art ceases to work for the people. Whereas in traditional societies art used to be a public practice at the heart of the collective, expressing and reformulating communal concerns, in modern societies art is limited to the aesthetic of the *beaux arts*, the refined taste of the few. Modernity spawns a dualistic discourse of distinction. Arts on one side, crafts on the other. The modern-urban-individual-high is set over and against the traditional-rural-collective-low. Modernity valorizes the former, deprecates the latter. One is "art," the other falls below the threshold of art. If modernity obsessively "collects" all its cultural production, it puts it into carefully segregated places. "Las artesanías iban a ferias y concursos populares, las obras de arte a los museos y las biennales" (p. 38).

Because the modern arts acquire the dimensions of a specialized field, it follows that the study of the arts should itself become a specialized area of expertise. In the process of differentiation characteristic of modernity, the distance between the specialized artist or connoisseur of art and an uninitiated public is exacerbated. As a result, the contradictory predicament of modern art is that it must create an ever-larger audience for its work in order to bring forth an autonomous artistic field, and yet every effort at specialization distances its products from the reach of the multitude. What this ever-greater need for an ever-greater public foregrounds, and this is García Canclini's central point, is the extent to which the idea of modern art as an autonomous field is a chimera. Whereas modern aesthetics—indeed the very notion of the aesthetic as a discrete realm of the human faculties—is premised on the autonomy of art and ineffable uniqueness of the creative process, such autonomy is illusory. No more than any other cultural product can the products of high art avoid the "dependencias inesquivables del mercado y las industrias culturales" (p. 78), the imbrication in the economic network of production, distribution, and consumption. No more than they can high-artistic products escape becoming "goods."[3] The discourse of modernity persists with the hymn to autonomy because it confers distinction upon the producers and consumers of artistic goods, whose tastes are uncontaminated by the baseness of commercial interest and the passions of rural popular or urban mass culture, from which high culture is to be rigorously distinguished.

Although García Canclini's work ostensibly takes place under the aegis of a new paradigm in Latin American (though not only Latin American) cultural studies, which developed as a critique of the Marxist paradigm of the 1960s and 1970s, the imprint of a classical Marxist theory of ideology on *Culturas híbridas* remains visible. For García Canclini, the theory of the autonomy of artistic production is quite simply a falsehood. It passes off as true what is in reality an inverted image of the truth. The manifest socioeconomic determinations of cultural production in modern society are ignored by the ideological discourse of modernity, which avers the precise opposite: namely, that art constitutes an autonomous sphere, indeed that art is produced and consumed in ways directly opposed to the commercialization of modern times. Against this discourse, which seeks to define art according to its intrinsic value, García Canclini sides with what we might call the socio-attributionist theory of art, according to which, in its crudest formulation, art is whatever a particular social group calls art. In point of fact, even if one of his definitions of art seems to us illogical in dismissing "a priori aesthetic values" altogether (the artistic is to be defined not according to "valores estéticos a priori sino identificando grupos de personas que cooperan en la producción de bienes que al menos ellos llaman arte" [p. 58]), the first definition offered in the book is conciliatory: "Que el arte no es sólo una cuestion estética: hay que tomar en cuenta cómo se la va respondiendo en la intersección de lo que hacen los periodistas y críticos, historiadores y museógrafos, *marchands*, coleccionistas y especuladores" (p. 39). What is art is not only an aesthetic question. That is, aesthetic questions do play a part in the definition of art.

García Canclini believes it is postmodernism that has finally laid to rest the theory of the autonomy of art, allowing us to see the interconnectedness of cultural and economic modes of production.[4] But such a vision has only become possible by virtue of the empirical evidence thrown up by the lived reality that is postmodernity.[5] It is important to note that it is not that postmodernity as a historical phase has produced a state of affairs in which art ceases to be autonomous; rather, he says that in postmodernity the diminution of the autonomy of art has become more pronounced.[6] In other words, art's lack of autonomy was also evident in the period known as modernity:

> Si bien la influencia en el juicio estético de demandas ajenas al campo es visible a lo largo de la modernidad, desde mediados de este siglo los agentes encargados de administrar la calificación de lo que es artístico—museos, bienales, revistas, grandes premios internacionales—se reorganizan en relación con las nuevas tecnologías de promoción mercantil y consumo. (p. 71)

Because he takes his examples from the contemporary visual arts, García Canclini can highlight with ease the degree to which art is indissociable from economic circuitry, the extent to which "taste" is influenced by what sells in the international marketplace. And yet, the high visibility of the interaction between artistic production and the market in contemporary society, or "postmodernity," should not prevent us from being able to identify that relationship already at work in the historical phase called modernity. García Canclini writes of the "loss" of symbolic autonomy in postmodernity, where we would say that there was no such autonomy in the modern period either, or at least that there existed only a relative or semiautonomy.[7] There may have been a greater degree of autonomy in late-nineteenth-century Europe than is the case in contemporary times. The European elites had substantially more control over the circuits of production and distribution of high culture, and the opera houses, theatres, and salons all give the impression of constituting an autonomous high-cultural field. This does not obviate the fact, however, that even such a relatively independent sphere was still clearly implicated in the economy of capitalism. The contrast between the "modern" cultural field and the contemporary one that García Canclini calls "postmodern" shows an *exacerbation* of that interaction:

> Lo culto moderno incluye, desde el comienzo de este siglo, buena parte de los productos que circulan por las industrias culturales, así como la difusión masiva y la reelaboración que los nuevos medios hacen de obras literarias, musicales y plásticas que antes eran patrimonio distintivo de las elites. La interacción de lo culto con los gustos populares, con la estructura industrial de la producción y circulación de casi todos los bienes simbólicos, con los patrones empresariales de costos y eficacia, está cambiando velozmente los dispositivos organizadores de lo que ahora se entiende por "ser culto" en la modernidad.[8] (pp. 76–77)

The exacerbation of the interaction between high and popular culture produces the positive result of democratizing cosmopolitanism, even if the democratization in question, at least in Latin America, has been achieved largely by private enterprise and the culture industry. Here, despite differences in the definition of postmodernity (see chapter 1), García Canclini coincides absolutely with Fredric Jameson. Postmodernism bids farewell to the Great Writer.[9] Its fundamental feature is the effacement of "the older (essentially high-modernist) frontier between high culture and so-called mass or commercial culture, and the emergence of new kinds of texts infused with the forms, categories, and contents of that very culture industry so passionately denounced by all the ideologues of the modern, from Leavis and the American New Criticism all the way to Adorno and the Frankfurt School" (Jameson, p. 2). García Canclini's overriding point, however, to which I shall return in due course, is that if the present configuration of culture in society has allowed us to see this cultural hybridity more clearly, it is not the case that the discourse of modernity has been dispensed with. Paradoxically, "la ideología de lo culto moderno—autonomía y desinterés práctico del arte, creatividad singular y atormentada de individuos aislados—subsiste más en las audiencias masivas que en las elites que originaron estas creencias" (p. 77).

Note on the Word *Culture*

García Canclini's critique of the modern conception of culture stands foursquare with the British cultural studies project that began in the late 1950s. For Raymond Williams, the most widespread, modern use of the word *culture* renders it synonymous with "the works and practices of intellectual and especially artistic activity [. . .]: **culture** is music, literature, painting and sculpture, theatre and film."[10] According to this understanding of the word, culture is refinement, good taste, the product of breeding, and a good education. In one of those linguistic shorthands that use the noun to mean a superior aspect of the noun, culture belongs to the "cultured," the "cultivated," the *cultos*. It is not that everyone else is, by comparison, poorly educated or rudimentary in their culture; it is as though everyone else were totally without education, manifestly below the threshold of what could be considered culture. For Williams, this is the Cambridge teashop conception of culture.[11] It is not a matter of comparing types or even degrees of culture, but of distinguishing between culture and its absence. There are echoes in this scheme of all imperialist or colonialist enterprises, and of the early anthropological encounters between the West and the so-called primitive. What is perceived as cultural superiority is expressed hyperbolically as the absolute opposition between culture and nonculture itself.[12]

Cultural studies, and the García Canclini of *Culturas híbridas*, recovers one of the other uses of the word *culture*: culture in the broadest possible sense of "a particular way of life, whether of a people, a period, a group, or humanity in general" (Williams, *Keywords*, p. 90). In this expanded, "anthropological" meaning of the word, the concept of culture is opened immeasurably to recognize the fact, the "first fact," that everyone participates in culture. In Williams's famous saying, "culture is ordinary." To Williams the phrase is self-evident. It simply corresponds to the reality he knew growing up in a working-class family on the Welsh borders and is therefore an almost banal starting-point. "Culture is ordinary: that is where we must start." And yet it is worth remarking on that phrase as it appears and is reworked in the essay that originally appeared in 1958, since Williams goes on to mention something that is wont to fall from view in debates on cultural studies, namely, that there is a second fact, a second aspect of culture. Culture is the known meanings, the traditional, accepted, common coinage of a whole way of life. But culture is also the new meanings forged by individual, creative acts through exposure to the arts and learning. The two aspects, the two senses of culture are inseparable:

> A culture has two aspects: the known meanings and directions, which its members are trained to; the new observations and meanings, which are offered and tested. These are the ordinary processes of human societies and human minds, and we see through them the nature of a culture: that it is always both traditional and creative; that it is both the most ordinary common meanings and the finest individual meanings. We use the word culture in these two senses: to mean a whole way of life—the common meanings; to mean the arts and learning—the special processes of discovery and creative effort. Some writers reserve the word for one or other of these senses; I insist on both, and on the significance of their conjunction. The questions I ask about our culture are questions about our general and common purposes, yet also questions about deep personal meanings. Culture is ordinary, in every society and in every mind. (P. 6)

Why does Williams end the paragraph with a statement that he has gone out of his way, insistently, to contradict? For if culture is ordinary, in every society and in every mind, culture, as Williams says, is also "special," extra-ordinary. Williams means that the presence of new observations and meanings, of the finest individual meanings and special processes of discovery and creative effort, is an everyday phenomenon found in every society. The extra-ordinary is ordinary. The known meanings and the new meanings are "ordinary processes of human societies and human minds." Because Williams wants to emphasize that the tension between traditional and new meanings is constitutive of all cultures, he concludes with the phrase, "Culture is ordinary, in every society and in every mind." From our perspective, however, the phrase is too ordinary. If the extraordinary aspect of culture is common, it is for all that no less special and must be hung on to as such, especially in an era that profiteers from peddling and packaging the mediocre or mundane as extraordinary. In short, culture is and is not ordinary, is and is not extraordinary. Culture is (not) ordinary. This is the first fact, which one is never simply done with.[13]

A Paradigmatic History of
Latin American Cultural Studies

Let us repeat what García Canclini writes apropos of the modern understanding of culture. "La ideología de lo culto moderno—autonomía y desinterés práctico del arte, creatividad singular y atormentada de individuos aislados—subsiste más en las audiencias masivas que en las elites que originaron estas creencias." If the discourse of modernity subsists in contemporary times, so, in García Canclini's own prose, does the discourse of classical Marxism—not least the view that the culture industry is the principal pedlar of the ideology of modern high culture. This should perhaps come as no surprise, given the close kinship between cultural studies and a certain spirit of Marxism. But nor should it go unremarked, especially as García Canclini was one of many Latin American practitioners of cultural studies to interpret the "postmodern" turn of the 1980s and 1990s as a watershed in respect of the dominant paradigm of the preceding decades. The postmodern moment was to recuperate *lo popular* and *lo masivo* from the jaws of a Marxist, Enlightenment-influenced concept of culture that had looked with suspicion on popular and mass culture as the products of ideological mystification.[14] Before proceeding to explore García Canclini's criticism of a Latin American modernism that, it believed, had gone some way toward giving semantic space to popular and mass culture, it will repay us to elaborate on García Canclini's place in the general project of Latin American cultural studies, and specifically on the relationship between *Culturas híbridas* and the older, Marxist–Leninist paradigm.

It has become commonplace in the retelling of the history of Latin American cultural studies to locate its beginnings in a social sciences context.[15] This narrative finds support in contemporary observations which note that what has come to be known as cultural studies in Latin America has its academic power-base in the social science faculties, whereas the North American (and U.K.) variants operate primarily out of literary, or at least humanities, departments.[16] As a crude rule of thumb, the above account is substantially true. It is not without significance, however, that many of the main practitioners of Latin American cultural studies were either formed outside, or indeed would see their work as taking shape at best in the interstices of, the social sciences (García Canclini trained in the history of art, Beatriz Sarlo and Nelly Richard in literature, Jesús Martín-Barbero in philosophy).[17]

The history of Latin American cultural studies dates from the late 1960s and begins, in one important respect, with communication studies, the analysis of the mass media. There had been a prior tradition of media investigation in Latin America but it had followed U.S. sociological functionalism and mass communications research of the 1950s and 1960s. In an era dominated by development models of modernization and by economic, technological, and political plans driven by the United States, such research was administrative and "integrated," that is to say, closely involved with television companies (usually satellite companies of North American corporations) and state projects, and seeing its principal mission as that of providing information about audiences through surveys and *estudios de efectos*. From the late 1960s, communication studies in Latin America acquires a radically different character in line with an altered historical context. This new historical conjuncture was formed by a number of factors that include: the failure of import-substituting industrialization and disquiet at U.S. development models of modernization; political pressure from the United States; the rise of repressive regimes and revolutionary movements in the region; the international context of an emerging *tercermundismo*, including formal international organizations (UNESCO); and, finally, the general rise of what one could loosely call subaltern resistance (movements of decolonization, the Vietnam war, the civil rights movement in the United States). Latin American communication studies set out not merely to study, but also where appropriate to denounce through ideological critique, the workings of the media and related branches of the culture industry. "El estudio de la comunicación en esos años asume el discurso de la denuncia y se articula a él como a su 'forma' de decir la toma de posición: si la comunicación es escenario privilegiado de la dominación, su abordaje como campo de estudio implica plantearse de qué lado se está."[18]

The alliance between Latin American communication studies, or what came to be seen as the overarching discipline of cultural studies, and both Marxism and dependency theory was a close one. Communication or cultural studies insisted upon and demonstrated the political urgency of intellectual work, especially in a context increasingly marked by military dictatorship.[19] In the debate sparked in the mid-1970s by the Argentine journals *Lenguajes* and *Comunicación y cultura*, the question of whether intellectual work should be political is not at issue. In a national and regional context shaped by military dictatorship and structural economic "adjustments," and in an international context marked by the growth of movements of national liberation and a generalized third worldism, both the more formalist, semiotic *Lenguajes* and the more materialist, cultural studies *Comunicación y cultura* shared a generalized intellectual politicization that considered it the duty of the intellectual or academic to be engaged in political work. But whereas Eliseo Verón of *Lenguajes* considers the truth-value of academic work to be a matter of its scientific quality (which may then be placed in the service of ideological critique),

Culture Is (Not) Ordinary 37

Héctor Schmucler of *Comunicación y cultura* follows the Leninist position according to which the ultimate truth of academic work lies in praxis, that is, in its ability to conjoin with a revolutionary practice. "Sólo es 'científico,' elaborador de una verdad, un método que surja de una situación histórico-política determinada y que verifique sus conclusiones en una práctica social acorde con las proposiciones histórico-políticas en las que se pretende inscribirlas."[20]

Under the new influences of semiotics, British cultural studies, French poststructuralism, and Gramsci, 1980s' and 1990s' Latin American cultural studies moves away from the categories of classical Marxism, and dependency theory, toward a less Manichean view and theory of culture.[21] Marxism is characterized by a bipolar division at the economic level between exploiters and exploited; by a naked division at the political level between dominators and dominated; by a model of culture that construes subordinate culture as the product of ideological duping achieved by the dominant culture; and by a model of subjectivity that posits the subordinated as passive subjects of someone else's cultural reality. The new paradigm shifts the accent onto the Gramscian notion of hegemony rather than domination; onto an appreciation of residual and emergent subaltern forms of culture; and onto a model of subjectivity predicated on the capacity of subjects to receive cultural products in a more complex, less passive manner than that suggested by orthodox Marxism. Jesús Martín-Barbero, with whom this last position is perhaps most closely identified, voices the problem with ideology critique thus:

> La ideologización impidió que lo que se indagara en los procesos fuera otra cosa que las *huellas del dominador*. Y para nada las del dominado y menos las del conflicto. Una concepción 'teológica' del poder—puesto que se lo pensaba omnipotente y omnipresente—condujo a la creencia de que con sólo analizar los objetivos económicos e ideológicos de los medios masivos podía saberse qué necesidades generaban y cómo sometían a los consumidores. Entre emisores-dominantes y receptores-dominados ninguna seducción ni resistencia, sólo la pasividad del consumo y la alienación.[22]

Why, then, a decade and a half after the debate between *Lenguajes* and *Comunicación y cultura*, and in the midst of an era characterized by a continued suspicion of the categories furnished by classical Marxism, does García Canclini maintain a Leninist position, supposing that this

"Leninism" is not simply an unguarded use of an outmoded lexicon? The beginnings of an answer appear to lie in the geopolitical, institutional context of García Canclini's work, which marks a significant difference from the context in which cultural studies operates in the Anglo-Saxon world, a difference that, paradoxically, aligns the former's work with the original British cultural studies project. By virtue of their very "success", cultural studies in the United States and, in more uneven fashion, the United Kingdom have been institutionalized in the academy.[23] As a consequence, they find themselves almost necessarily in direct conflict with some of the founding tenets of the early project (especially in what concerns the site and ethos).[24] García Canclini's work, in contrast, and indeed his institutional position at the hub of a network of projects and state-financed plans in Mexico, holds on to the ideal that his variant of cultural studies (which he calls urban anthropology) might be a direct intervention in the *polis* (and beyond).[25] *Culturas híbridas*, of course, subscribes to the Marxist principle that the transformation, not merely the analysis, of society is the ultimate objective of cultural studies; but it also adheres to the Leninist idea that the truth of intellectual and artistic work will only emerge from the latter's embeddedness in a given historico-political situation. One needs to keep this absolutely to the fore when reading the book's account of modernism in Latin America.

Modernism and Hegemony

García Canclini's claim regarding high-cultural modernism in Latin America in the early part of the twentieth century is that, occasionally despite its best efforts, it is used by the elites as a means of elaborating a global project of hegemony. Following Perry Anderson, García Canclini argues that it is not the case, as classical, especially Marxist, reflection theories would have it, that culture simply follows the developmental rhythms of the economic base. Modernism does not "reflect" a state of achieved modernization. In both Europe and Latin America, modernism takes hold in countries that formed a complex intersection of historical temporalities, an intersection, in other words, in which there had been no simple substitution of the ancient and the traditional by the modern.

Although rapid industrial development and urbanization did permit significant modern innovations in the Latin American field of culture—including the creation of an artistic and literary market, and,

Culture Is (Not) Ordinary 39

beginning in Argentina in 1918, a lay and democratically organized university—the formation of autonomous scientific and humanistic fields was confronted with high rates of illiteracy and "premodern" economic structures and political habits (p. 87). In other words, modern*ism* does not betoken the full and complete arrival of modern*ity*. Either in Latin America or elsewhere. The star of modernism nevertheless rises in the new republics because it proves a fertile cultural means for the elites to negotiate the passage of modernization. With its discourse of "distinction" and nineteenth-century European idealist conception of art as the spiritual calling of the select few, modernism is an ideological tool polishing the bipolar discourse of modernity.

García Canclini does not excoriate all Latin American cultural modernism, seeing in Brazilian modernism, Peruvian *indigenismo* and Mexican muralism genuine "reelaboraciones deseosas de contribuir al cambio social" (pp. 90–91). The avant-gardes were neither mere imitators of European trends, nor denationalizers, nor insignificant. Notwithstanding such concessions, the problem that García Canclini sees facing the cultural modernists is that they want to demoticize their production, by incorporating popular culture, the vulgar, the ordinary, the mass-cultural, and the sacrilegious, but, precisely because they are fleeing from the perceived hegemony of traditional cultural forms (such as *modernismo* and the realist novel), they end up becoming more fragmented and antirepresentationalist, that is, more specialized and less accessible.

García Canclini's approach to the avant-gardes is an "anthropological" one, based on the anthropological notion of ritual. Where the avant-garde might see their work as cultural or political acts, he views it as a ritualistic reenactment. Although rituals are usually traditional, conservative repetitions of the status quo, there are rituals that are transgressive. For all their subversive energy, however, these rituals are "impracticable transgressions," that function ultimately as a culture's sanctioned escape-valves, officially permitted violations of the established order through which society defuses the demand for change. The same may be said of the avant-gardes. Though transgressive in their very origins, this transgressiveness soon becomes institutionalized through "la incorporación progresiva de las insolencias a los museos" (p. 62), and as society gradually comes to terms with an accepted space of the unacceptable. Profoundly attached to the modern aesthetic of novelty, the avant-gardes cultivate what Octavio Paz calls "la tradición de la ruptura" and develop what García Canclini himself calls "ritos de egreso" (rites of exit), perpetual attempts to get out from where they currently are. To be in the history of art one has to be constantly leaving it:

> Dado que el máximo valor estético es la renovación incesante, para pertenecer al mundo del arte no se puede repetir lo ya hecho, lo legítimo, lo compartido. [. . .] No hay peor acusación contra un artista moderno que señalar repeticiones en su obra. Según este sentido de fuga permanente, para estar en la historia del arte hay que estar saliendo constantemente de ella. (P. 65)

In this programmatic desire to escape programmaticity there is a deep narcissism, an infantile libertarianism that by definition cannot settle long enough, in any one place or on any one meaning, to build a collective symbolic alternative to the dominant order. Instead, García Canclini sees the avant-gardes as locked into what Pierre Bourdieu calls the logic of sacralizing desacralizations, that is, acts that scandalize no one but the believers.

In the final analysis, and finalism is just what is at stake, García Canclini's thesis concerning cultural modernism, and especially the modern and postmodern avant-gardes (between whom he sees little difference), is not that it is an agent of ideology, even though the modern critical discourse surrounding it frequently is. His point about cultural modernism is that, like the contemporary avant-gardes in general, it is a political irrelevance. In point of fact, we will not have understood the full reach of his argument if we conclude, prematurely, that García Canclini thinks that modernism is a political irrelevance. García Canclini thinks that *all* cultural production is potentially a political irrelevance. It is just that, by virtue of its restricted audience, modernism is even more politically irrelevant (if such a thing is possible) than other, more popular cultural forms. Modernism's irrelevance is exemplary.[26]

This judgment on modernism, which is a judgment on culture in general, derives from a handed-down version of Leninism, according to which, as we have seen, intellectual and artistic work is judged not by its degree of scientific or artistic internal truth but according to praxis, its success in intervening in the polis.[27] Because García Canclini is not a 1960s' Leninist, it is understood that such praxis does not set out to remove the existing order altogether, but rather to reform it.[28] By means of carnival satire, journalistic humor, graffiti, myths, literature, and comic strips (Lenin would never have said this), culture can open up "diagonal" or "oblique" avenues of critique where traditional politics is blocked by its very conventionality. Occasionally, these primarily "metaphorical" gestures of critique lead on to unforeseen "prácticas transformadoras" (p. 317). The problem with such cultural politics, however, is that they have an "eficacia simbólica limitada." This is why García Canclini insists on the importance of the distinction between *action* and *acting*. How do we assess the political value of a symbolic intervention, of a Carnival satire, or of a journalistic parody? Are they real actions, "intervenciones efectivas en las estructuras materiales de la sociedad" that bite deep into the political arena and produce demonstrable change, or are they performances (acting), which simulate social actions but only rarely succeed in operating as an action (p. 317)? Although he moves away from the revolutionary ideal of Marxist–Leninism that informed 1960s' and 1970s' Latin American cultural studies, García Canclini holds on to a residual tenet of Leninism, a principle of meaningful political intervention, which he calls symbolic action. In this respect, and as he says apropos the avant-gardes' sacralizing desacralizations, high literature of the kind that is our concern throughout this book is a performance, not an action. Literature has "limited symbolic effectiveness," in other words, is severely restricted in its political scope. Despite the fact that literature has already worked through some of the concepts that have now found their way into cultural studies, it remains the case that in the building of a counterhegemony literature remains insignificant.[29] To contribute meaningfully toward an alternative hegemony, literature would need to be a traditional action; by virtue of its irremediably modern condition, it cannot be.

García Canclini's logic with respect to high-cultural modernism in *Culturas híbridas* is a politicoteleology. Because the end state of Latin America in the 1920s and 1930s was characterized by the hegemony of a Western-oriented elite, the modernism that the latter used to negotiate the passage of cultural modernization must, in the final analysis, be considered collusive or, where resistant, inconsequential. The final achieved state of the subcontinent is duly read back into each constituent part of the whole. On the surface, this way of evaluating art would seem to belong to the political logic of art propounded by the twentieth-century vanguards themselves. The *raison d'être* of the historical avant-garde was not merely to produce an *aesthetic* shock. The decisive point about the historical avant-garde is that, long before cultural studies, it attempted to problematize the nature of art and disturb the institution of art itself. The vanguards were more interested in producing a shock whose tremors would rock an individual's core social, religious, and political beliefs, and even their comfortable sense of selfhood. In reality, however, the criterion used by *Culturas híbridas* to judge modernism derives from a 1980s' version of a 1960s' version of Leninist praxis. García Canclini views avant-garde production as ritualistic reenactment rather than meaningful symbolic actions that succeed in being truly political. The avant-gardes fail in their bid to be political because, as Schmucler would have it, the truths of their work fail to align themselves with a social practice in tune with the historico-political propositions in which such truths attempt to inscribe themselves. The avant-gardes could not hope to be political in this sense because they foster an aesthetic, perceived by many as alien and inaccessible, which disturbs conventional truths and makes the avant-gardes themselves congenitally out of tune with social practice or the public sphere. In writing of the "failure" of vanguard art, and enumerating the successive frustrations of surrealism, bauhaus, and constructivism, García Canclini applies to art the Leninist criteria by which intellectual work must be judged. It is the logic of all or nothing, enunciated from a necessarily ulterior moment when the end-point of an artistic movement can be identified and its political effects read off. Such are the prejudices of cultural history, of the teleology of *istoria* itself, which operates by identifying and isolating beginnings and endings. If García Canclini can remain resolutely upbeat about contemporary manifestations of hybrid cultural production in Latin America (Mexican public sculpture for instance), in fifty years another cultural historian seeking to assess the political contribution of such work will calmly pronounce its limited symbolic effectiveness.

García Canclini's narrative of cultural history in *Culturas híbridas* both asks too much and too little of literature and the other high arts. Too much, because it charges the arts with the mission of effecting significant direct sociopolitical change. Too little, first because it reduces the arts' temporal scope, restricting them to producing effects only around the time of their initial emergence; and second, because it reduces the nature of the arts' effectivity, condemning them to producing only political effects, squeezing out traditional (in both high-cultural and popular senses of the word) considerations that have to do with the internal value of art, considerations of beauty, awe, astonishment, sensuality, pathos, and pleasure.

Globalization and the Fast and Slow Economies of Art

A decade after *Culturas híbridas*, García Canclini undergoes a change of heart with respect to high, especially literary, culture. This change is introduced into a "project," which otherwise maintains a high degree of consistency. Much in *La globalización imaginada* remains the same as in the earlier work. Methodologically, the benefits of a social scientific perspective are reaffirmed; this reaffirmation constitutes a critique not only of traditional aestheticism, but of cultural studies itself, which in the eyes of "el antropólogo latinoamericano" lacks serious engagement with the hard realities of the economic dimension of culture; the resulting level of analysis is always grand, always schematic. Ideologically, globalization is deemed to have deepened the mercantilization of culture, such that the market has now penetrated into the very logic of cultural production; this process, from which high culture cannot remain exempt, is cast as a narrative of decline. On one level, the very broad level of official cultural policy, a response to this decline must be to ask the question that nobody wants to talk about at the great intergovernmental gatherings: the question of the culture industry. It is the old Marxist question, and it is one reason why García Canclini remains important: it is the question of the conditions of production (of culture) and the ownership of the means of (cultural) production.

But there is something different in *La globalización imaginada*. This difference follows on from two of the basic tenets of the earlier work: first, the idea that culture itself must effect change; and second, the idea that the world of culture is slowly but surely coming under the sway of the market and the culture industry:

> Las novedades tecnológicas y las altas inversiones económicas facilitan hoy megaexposiciones itinerantes de artes visuales, producciones editoriales, musicales y televisivas multinacionales, editar todo con calidad semejante y difundirlo de inmediato en el mundo entero. Pero dejan poco espacio y poco tiempo para el riesgo, la corrección y los experimentos sin ganancias masivas aseguradas. [. . .] lo más inquietante de la globalización ejecutada por las industrias culturales no es la homogeneización de lo diferente sino la institucionalización comercial de las innovaciones, la crítica y la incertidumbre. (Pp. 162–163)

Uniform quality, immediate diffusion, no risk, commercial institutionalization. Let us add "speed" to that diagnosis, since the only surprises left in cultural production are those demanded by a voracious market anxious to "acelerar la obsolescencia de lo conocido" in order to increase sales (p. 183). One understands at once what one solution to this problem of the massification of culture will be (García Canclini has always been pushing at the very definition of "mass culture" to make us understand that even high culture is massified): a slow culture that cannot so readily be consumed, a culture that is not uniform, a culture that is risky and experimental by virtue of the fact that its risks and experiments cannot be accommodated within the paradigm of the shock of the new.

When the values of high culture hold arrogant sway, it becomes necessary to recover other cultural forms and modes of reception. When an era is dominated by the heightened commercialization of all culture, the question of what resists commercialization must pass by way of a meditation on those cultural forms that seem uncannily to call forth the specter of the high, which is now born again as the slow.[30] We may speculate that García Canclini's gesture in the direction of what looks like a progressive understanding of high culture is a reaction to Beatriz Sarlo, who, in her 1994 book *Escenas de la vida posmoderna*, grounded her remarks in the context of the destruction of the Argentine state education system, which was now failing to equip its citizens to be receivers of anything other than someone else's undemanding mass-produced culture.[31] I choose the following passage to illustrate García Canclini's stance on this subject, because it touches on two important issues, though without perhaps being able to elaborate sufficiently on either. The first idea returns insistently toward the end of the book and may be called a slow aesthetics of interruption. By virtue both of the book's own high-speed survey-like quality, and of the essential difficulty involved in any attempt to present or publicize the recondite ways of complex literary texts, this slow culture can only be gestured to, not analyzed as such. The second idea is that culture is not necessarily ordinary:

> "¿Por qué dar tanta importancia a la cuestión estética al debatir políticas culturales?" me preguntaba un funcionario de un organismo internacional. Efectivamente, el énfasis en la búsqueda estética pareciera sólo interesante para grupos minoritarios y por tanto opuesto a la vida pública, que acostumbra asociarse con lo que puede ser compartido por todos. Sin embargo, el arte importa aquí de un modo paradójico. Los escritores y artistas no devorados por el *establishment* cultural, o que aun siendo recibidos por él rechazan la agenda única con que el mercado estructura la esfera pública, cumplen una función contrapública en tanto introducen temas locales o formas de enunciarlos que parecen improductivos para la hegemonía mercantil. Quienes requieren

usar tanto tiempo para una actividad privada de dudosos réditos (¿cuatro años para escribir una novela que van a leer dos mil personas?), y confiesan dedicar semanas o meses a decir en una página de un modo asombroso lo que algunos viven o a discutir lo que muchos prefieren olvidar, son personajes contrapúblicos. Al menos para quienes suponen que la vida pública es la de la racionalidad capitalista, por ejemplo las telenovelas en las cuales producir un capítulo de una hora requiere invertir entre 100 y 120 mil dólares, y filmarlo en tres días para luego venderlo a más de cien países [. . .]. Al trastornar las relaciones habituales entre lo público y lo privado, entre experimentación cultural y rendimiento económico, la economía lenta de la producción artística cumple la función pública de incitar a repensar lo que la economía apremiante de las industrias simbólicas impone como público, fugaz y desmemoriado. (Pp. 199–200)

This is a clever way of reasserting the traditional value of the public sphere. It involves conscripting that most awkward, and seemingly unpublic, thing called art to perform the duties of the public sphere, which the latter is itself incapable of doing. Because the public sphere has been given over to transitoriness, falling prey to an accelerated version of modernity's hunger for the new, it falls to a certain type of art to interrupt this dememorializing flow, to act as reservoir of the traditional memory and values of a genuine public sphere. In short, the counterpublic is more public than the public sphere. This is a bold thing to say for someone who has always opposed unpopular art as at best impotent as a political instrument, and at worst inimical to the values of a democratic public sphere.

Let us develop this insight further. In the Enlightenment order of knowledge, the creation of a democratic public sphere is wedded to the fortunes of publicity. Democracy needs light, transparency, total visibility; no dark corners and no secrets. In principle everyone should be able to see the truth of the workings of the *res publica*. In contrast, slow literature, García Canclini says as much, is not for everyone—that is why it is counterpublic and that is where it derives its critical purchase from. Adapting Derrida's work on the aporia of the concept of responsibility in ethical thought, we can say that a slow work of art cannot be altogether responsible before the public sphere. A slow work of art can only be composed on the basis of knowledge (a decision made without one being minimally informed of the facts of grammar and semantics, without one knowing what one is doing, would be the height of irresponsibility). But if composing a work consists merely in following a body of knowledge given in advance in the public sphere, then the work in question is irresponsible (since it becomes instead the mechanical application of a program). In other words, responsibility involves being responsible (following the guidance offered by knowledge) and irresponsible (not always following that guidance) at the same time. The concept of responsibility is thus tied to the notion of heresy, that is, to a departure from a publicly stated doctrine, or in García Canclini's terms, from the public sphere itself. And insofar as this heresy maintains a certain distance with regard to what is publicly or officially declared, responsibility is not to be thought of as an absolutely public affair that must always take place in the full glare of publicity; rather, from this point of view, responsibility is bound to a type of secrecy:

> The concept of responsibility [. . .] presents itself neither as a theme nor as a thesis, it gives without being seen [*sans se donner à voir*], without presenting itself in person by means of a "fact of being seen" that can be phenomenologically intuited. This paradoxical concept also has the structure of a type of secret—what is called, in the code of certain religious practices, mystery. The exercise of responsibility seems to leave no choice but this one, however uncomfortable it may be, of paradox, heresy, and secrecy. More serious still, it must always run the risk of conversion and apostasy: there is no responsibility without a dissident and inventive rupture with respect to tradition, authority, orthodoxy, rule, or doctrine.[32]

As a consequence, to declare, or publicize, the counterpublic values of slow art (values that are more public than those of the public sphere), that is, to bring them out into the open and submit them to democratic transparency, to the full glare of publicity in the open space of the *res publica*, is to run the risk of presenting their secrets as a thesis, of making them conform to a program—here a programmatic slowness. In other words, one risks depriving them of that element of secrecy, that degree of irresponsibility which originally made them counterpublic and, hence, more public-spirited than the public sphere. This has always been the risk run by discourses on art and more especially by any sociology of art, and any politicoteleological theory of artistic "effectiveness." The moment one broadcasts what works of art do and do not do in a systematic manner that makes them susceptible to being incorporated into a public project, one risks domesticating them, instrumentalizing them, subsuming them within a public project from which all mystery and all heresy have been excluded. This is the danger not only of García Canclini's concept of art; it extends to his concept of the public sphere itself. A public sphere that is transparent, accountable, and always respectful of its own tradition, authority, orthodoxy, rule, or doctrine is in the final analysis an irresponsible public sphere (since it follows knowledge uncritically), which merely reproduces itself in programmatic fashion.

Although *La globalización imaginada* makes an attempt to appreciate the internal value of high art, albeit still deploying an instrumental understanding of art (slow literature is valuable since it will do "x" for us), in point of fact García Canclini had already said something similar in *Culturas híbridas*. We have already seen the early concession: "What is art is not only an aesthetic question . . .". But there is another, more revealing moment in the earlier book. Why, in his commentary on the intertwining of money and taste in the field of modern art, does he lament the fact that "lo mejor, o al menos lo más cotizado del arte latinoamericano, no se verá en nuestros países" (p. 76)? Despite the rider ("or at least the most expensive"), and for all his reservations about the modern project, he holds fast both to the democratizing movement begun in the historical phase known as modernity and to the liberal-humanist ideal that the best of anything worth having (which may well also be the most expensive) should be available for all to enjoy. It is the difference between a degraded populism and an ambitious democratizing project. The difference between a project that exalts the ordinary but is suspicious of paradox, heresy, and secrecy, and a project that believes that the extraordinary should reside among the many as a matter of course—even if the extraordinary does not always, or easily, reveal itself. Culture is (not) ordinary: that is where we must start.

CHAPTER 3

Fieldwork: Cultural Studies and the Problem of Tradition

William Rowe's *Hacia una poética radical: Ensayos de hermenéutica cultural* is a book that, as Rowe is fond of saying about cultural fields, radiates ideas.[1] In an era obsessed with programmatic—that is, assessable—research, it calls for "intellectual adventure," while unable itself, not surprisingly and perhaps by virtue of an essay format that rehearses similar arguments in relation to different case-studies, to escape a certain programmaticity.[2] The book deals with literature produced in Peru, Paraguay, and the Southern Cone of Latin America against a backdrop of undeclared civil wars and other less apparent, more symbolic forms of violence. Announcing itself as a work of cultural studies, it is a cultural studies grafted onto an avant-garde literary-critical project. What is unusual about the book is that it deploys insights derived from a post-quantum theoretical field in the service of a "cultural hermeneutics." In short, the most radical twentieth-century thought is enlisted to renew one of the most traditional theoretical legacies. Rowe's otherwise unique work is paradigmatic of contemporary cultural studies' central mission, which is to understand the power relations that structure a cultural context. These power relations are articulated through a diverse range of cultural materials. "Radical poetics" (*po(i)ēsis* as "creation") designates just one set of cultural materials, an avant-garde writing and reading project, which attempt to forge new conceptual and communicative possibilities. And yet, the synchronic, immanent concept of the field, and the privilege accorded to the iconoclastic object that fractures the field in the direction of the new, are just what become problematic for a Latin Americanism anxious to recover traditional, historical subaltern forms of cultural expression from the clutches of a modernity bent on burying them. The dream of an ordered simultaneity that is the idea of the field may well sacrifice the autonomy of the aesthetic object, but it also sacrifices the possibility that the "radicality" of both field and object may derive from the persistence of other older, "premodern" traditions or modes of sensory perception. It is not just that the articulations between the contents of a field need to be traced more clearly, or the codes of literature better understood; it is that the concept of the field needs radical revision.

To Create Is to Resist

The theoretical first part of *Hacia una poética radical*, which has mini essays on Raymond Williams and the development of British Cultural Studies, the specific characteristics of the Latin American cultural field, war and Cultural Studies, cultural criticism in Peru and Argentina, and Martín Lienhard's work on diglossia, maintains nevertheless a circumspect relationship to theory itself. Rowe is skeptical of the current Anglo-Saxon rage for theory in the humanities, which he believes symptomatic of a diminution in the ability to read and which forms part of a larger shift—at the expense of "intellectual adventure"— whereby the university becomes a producer not of knowledge, but of protocols; not of concepts, but of applications. Rowe is close here to Deleuze and Guattari's dictum, "To create is to resist," faithful to their belief that the value of philosophy lies essentially in the creation of concepts in order to facilitate the becoming of subjected peoples.[3] Rowe does not cast aside theory; his interest is in a circulation between theory and text. In order to achieve a "radical poetics," he proposes a return to precategorial thought, taking up the idea of the frame (*marco*). What any frame does—and one always needs a frame—is selectively to delimit a field or object of analysis. One of Rowe's abiding concerns is the question of the position from which this framing takes place.

On this issue, Rowe singles out and criticizes the practice of deconstruction for aspiring to an "analytical immunity" outside the social space. This seems an ill-judged accusation if directed at the work of Jacques Derrida, the main practitioner of deconstruction, who spent more than forty years showing the mutual contamination that occurs between the apparently most unrelated conceptual practices. The truth is that there are profound similarities between Derrida's work and that of Rowe—not least the shared insistence on the importance of texts, the value accorded to poetry, and the deep mistrust of programmatic, commodifiable knowledge.[4] And then there is Heidegger. Rowe turns to Heideggerian hermeneutics for one of the most rigorous philosophical explorations of the problem of the ground from which interpretation is exercised. Understanding is not defined by a detachment from the material world; it is characterized by a being-there, Heidegger's *Dasein*, a situatedness that is an experience of the world. This place is not easily divined. The terms habitually used to define it "son ellos mismos componentes de una interpretación, y así infinitamente" (p. 22). Or, again: "Se aclara, por decirlo así, desde el mismo piso que se busca aclarar" (p. 24). Such is the difficulty, such is the challenge of discovery. The word is Rowe's: "Descubrir la situación en la que se está—esa es una motivación clave de los estudios culturales" (p. 22). It is a key motivation and a topos of Rowe's own work.[5] However, this discovery is no classical revelation of that which is already there. The hermeneutical circle is "expansive" and "porous"; it never quite returns us to the same point. Put more radically: "Un nuevo mundo requiere nuevos modos de pensar y, a la inversa, pensar de una manera nueva suscita mundos nuevos" (p. 23). The essential here is that thought takes place in the world and is not a possessing of that world; it is an openness to and a dialogue with it. A dialogue which, crucially, is shot through with time.

The place of time, the movement of time, and thus the movement of place are of paramount importance. Rowe writes from within a post-Einstein, post-quantum theoretical context that does not believe in the metaphysical possibility of an absolute, privileged point of entry into a culture which would not itself affect the field of analysis. He borrows a lovely passage from Gertrude Stein on the idea of the composition:

> The composition is the thing seen by every one living in the living they are doing, they are the composing of the composition that at the time they are living is the composition of the time in which they are living. It is that that makes living a thing they are doing. (P. 27)

It would henceforth never be enough for the classical scholar to know the field objectively from outside by (impossibly) exhausting the material. Rowe's clever alternative, in his project of cultural studies, which, by definition, wants to understand a Vallejo poem *and* the cultural space in which it was produced, is to say: why not choose a point of entry (e.g., a poem) that sheds light not on the totality of the composition (which would be impossible), but on some of the *processes* that constitute both it *and* the diverse cultural space-times?

The Immanence of Cultural Studies and Hermeneutics

Having sacrificed an illusory objectivity, and with it a naive empiricism, the model that underpins Rowe's enterprise is a by now familiar relational one. Although he concedes the difficulty involved in investigating a field, he writes nonetheless of the need to "comprend[er] cada elemento en sus múltiples relaciones con los demás elementos" (p. 31).[6] How does it become theoretically possible to dream of comprehending this endless relationality taking avant-garde literature as a starting-point?

In order to dream this dream, Rowe must as a point of principle erase any putative generic difference between literature and other walks of life. Such a manoeuver is accomplished, first, by claiming that, in contrast to the relative autonomy that Pierre Bourdieu ascribes to the Western European literary field, in many Latin American countries no autonomous literary field exists, if indeed it exists in any. Second, he turns to Deleuze and Guattari's seminal musings on the plane of immanence, the effect of which is to buttress the conviction that there can be no transcendence and no hierarchization in the world of cultural production. Since, by definition, the plane of immanence has no supplementary dimension, it becomes impossible to conceive of an event that would take place "outside" or "beyond" it; any event that did occur would merely entail an alteration of the plane of immanence of which it was a constitutive part. "The plane is like a desert that concepts populate without dividing up. The only regions of the plane are concepts themselves, but the plane is all that holds them together. The plane has no other regions than the tribes populating and moving around on it" (Deleuze and Guattari, pp. 36–37). In turn, the act of placing things together in the same plane, "sin jerarquizaciones o dualismos" (Rowe, *Hacia una poética*, p. 34), is what produces the field. In affirming the specificity of the field and the immanent relationship of poetry to the field, Rowe rules out the specificity and autonomy of the aesthetic object, disqualifying the possibility that there might be a specific field called poetry. If Althusser maintains the relative autonomy of literature, Rowe's scheme pushes toward the Foucaultian turn in which all cultural production reveals a field that knows no distinction between base and superstructure, and that thus grants no autonomy to art itself. Even when Rowe is scrupulously attentive to apparently poetic detail (rhythm, rhyme, etc.), the dictates of the theory demand that such detail become constitutive parts of the larger social imaginary rather than remain merely poetic.

This constitutive move of cultural studies finds vital support in Michel Foucault's immanent theory of power, which, stripped down to its bare essentials, makes space for the affirmation of cultural power in a way that does not bring the latter under the sway of politics or economics. Foucault paved the way for this immanentist conception of power in the still unduly deterministic *Surveiller et punir*, but it is not until the first volume of *Histoire de la sexualité* and related essays around the same time that he hits upon a general immanent theory of power that both provides a corrective to Marxist and liberal theories and, in the process, allows the domain of culture to take a properly active role in the configuration of power. If, in the traditional view, power is in the hands of the sovereign, if power is his property to be unleashed, like a thunderbolt, upon those who do not have power, those who are not "in power," then all social action and cultural manifestations fall below the threshold of power and have no bearing on it. If, in contrast, power does not come from above, or from a central source or imposing building, but comes instead from everywhere, from an endless web of *relations* in which nothing is without power, then culture, too, is the carrier of a certain power.[7] In the same way that culture is not outside society, culture is not outside power (which is not to say that everything carries an equal amount of power). What is commonly overlooked in Foucault's "analytics" of power is the fact that he leaves space for a much more traditional-looking type of power. In other words, there are two types of power: there is "power" (*le pouvoir*) and "Power" ("*le*" *pouvoir*) (see *La Volonté de savoir*, pp. 122–123). The first is the new, disciplinary, capillary, relational, molecular kind of power—a force field in which everything has a certain charge. The second is the traditional power of the state, of bourgeois democracy, and of capitalism—which says "no" and "if you do that, we will put you in jail." It is the former understanding of power that provides *cultural* studies with its *raison d'être*.

But why, if all cultural forms exist cheek by jowl on the power-plane of immanence, would we not turn to popular literature or television game shows, rather than experimental literature, to illuminate the field? Why persist with avant-garde literature? The classic modernist answer of the kind ventured by Theodor Adorno, and about which I shall say more in due course, is that the formal laws of high literature mark out a vital distance from social reality, which affords a privileged vantage point from which it may be criticized. Rowe's own response is to say that the choice between popular and high cultural forms is a false one; it is precisely a question of studying *all* cultural forms. One of the book's major strengths is its contention that cultural studies would do well to rethink the confusion—which has led to the rejection of the study of high literature—between artistic works on the one hand and the snobbish reception of the latter on the other. Because such works have been *appropriated* as a form of cultural capital should not lead to the condemnation of the objects themselves.

But, to return to my main theme, the clever methodological alternative that Rowe proposes, which consists in selecting a point of entry "que manifieste y haga visibles algunos de los procesos por los que los varios espacio-tiempos culturales se van construyendo como tales" (p. 28), allows room for objectivist desires. At the theoretical level, Rowe will repeatedly emphasize the importance of time and—precisely because cultural production will always affect, that is, change the composition—the importance of time's disruptive energy. But there are two sets of metaphors in his writing that militate against the quantum insight. First, the spatial metaphors of ground, site, floor, territory. Second, the metaphorics of light, sight, illumination, and the eye. Despite his suggestive invocation of the audible at various junctures in the book, there is a marked, and highly classical accent on vision and visibility. Declaring that the difficult part of the hermeneutic project relates to allowing lived experience to become visible, he speaks tirelessly of "illumination," "revelation," "discovery," "making visible," "pon[iendo] en evidencia," a metaphorics already at work in the seductively commonplace expression "the thing seen by everyone" in the passage quoted from Stein. (Is such a democratic vision possible?) Particularly telling is the metaphor of radiation Rowe borrows from Eric Mottram, which, he says, "combina un sentido de ordenamiento espacial (radio geométrico) con otro de iluminación" (p. 31). In "Force and Signification," a key essay from the early 1960s, Derrida shows with exemplary rigor how the structuralist privileging of space works together with the principle of illumination to dream the thoroughly classical dream of an ordered simultaneity, a dream that desires the revelation, the unveiling, the discovery of a world already to be found in place, not the invention of a new one.[8]

Therein the tension that underpins Rowe's book. On the one hand: the quantum insight, whose own force disqualifies the objectivity of the field it aspires to know, and whose objects might themselves escape a determinate field. On the other hand: a hermeneutics, with its demand for the faithful unveiling of authorized truth, allied to cultural studies, a modern-day hermeneutics with an additional ethico-political desire. Neither hermeneutics nor cultural studies can easily accept the dislocations of time or indeed the law of iterability which dictates that *every* cultural production exceed its epoch. If cultural production did not in its essence exceed the time and place of its composition, there would be no access to it and no cultural studies.

The Question of Context

I am, of course, closely echoing Derrida's understanding of the relationship between meaning and context, which, without denying the structural, contextual dimension of meaning, insists on reinscribing its *productive* aspect. In broad terms, Derrida's reasoning is that to think of meaning as determined by context is to rule out history and the possibility of change, since under such circumstances a given context would only ever produce a text that in turn reproduced the given context, and so on to infinity. On the contrary, for Derrida, the relationship between context and meaning can never be determining, since every sign can be cited, put between quotation marks, and in the process "break with every given context."[9] Moreover, this break with a given context is not just something that befalls a sign as an unfortunate accident (when, for instance, it is cited elsewhere); it is constitutive of signs in general. By their essence, and in their very spacing, a sign is not tied to a context, since for a sign to be a sign at all, it must have the capacity to signify beyond, and quite literally break with, the real context of the moment of its production (a spoken word breaks away from the mouth; a written sign from the pen and contiguous signs). This is not to say that a sign is valid outside of a context. As Derrida puts it in "Limited Inc abc," in a manner that recalls Gertrude Stein, signs at one and the same time engender *and* inscribe themselves, or are inscribed, in new contexts. "For a context never creates itself *ex nihilo*; no mark can create or engender a context on its own, much less dominate it."[10] Contrary to a popular misconception of Derrida's work, none of the above amounts to ruling out historical reconstruction or due attention to a sign's cultural specificity. It suggests, rather, that such work cannot be legitimated by virtue of incantatory invocations of time and place that fall back on the dream of empiricism.[11] What is interesting about Rowe's work is that it has the measure of such insights, which loosely go by the name of poststructuralism, while remaining fiercely wary of the most rigorous and clear-sighted thinker of that "tradition."[12] Why does Rowe's "cultural hermeneutics" look instead to the work of Deleuze and Guattari?

Witness the two major themes that recur across Rowe's book. First, the insistence on the different temporalities that intersect in Latin America and that, disqualifying universalizing exegesis, precisely demand *cultural* hermeneutics. Thus, for instance, there may be three types of *dolor* in Vallejo (the cosmic-Andean, the colonial, and the modern), but none of these could come to light without the critical work that consists in reconstructing the specific Peruvian historical configuration. Second, the belief that this *po(i)ēsis* is as much sociopolitical as linguistic, that "la inteligencia poética" can have a bearing on "el imaginario social," to borrow the terms of the subtitle to the piece on Westphalen. The majority of Rowe's book is taken up with the issue of how poetry can participate in the making of a new social imaginary, but there is an early example of the way in which poetry may "reveal" the contours of an existing one. It is an example that goes to the heart of questions of tradition and modernity. Although he is constantly vigilant with regard to the concept of representation, Rowe is prepared to suspend disbelief at strategic points and to argue, in a strictly traditional way, but precisely in relation to strictly traditional cultural production, or at least to a cultural production imagined as conforming strictly to a certain conventional idea of the traditional, that symbolic production can neatly represent the social context out of which it emerges.

Referring to José María Arguedas's 1930s' essay "Carnaval de Tambobamba," in which the latter analyzes a traditional song performed in a Peruvian Andean region remote from the urban centers, Rowe sees in the essay a demonstration of the close relationship between cultural practice and perception of the landscape. The sound of a river is transformed into a collective voice in the song, which becomes not simply a representation of the noise but a cultural practice embodying a "collective mentality" and a peculiarly Peruvian Andean auditory way of giving on to the world. Rowe leaves in abeyance awkward questions about schizoid subjects and representation, in favor of a traditional approach whose underlying premise is that of a heightened, near-synaesthetic mimesis. In Arguedas's analysis of the song, "se ponen en juego las continuidades subjetivas, de creencias, y objetivas, de monumentos sociales." Arguedas offers "una contestación descentrada, que recompone el campo cultural desde una experiencia andina" (p. 30). Here cultural studies truly meets hermeneutics, in an effort to "rescue," in Lienhard's phrase, "the buried indigenous voice" (p. 60). In keeping with the traditional configuration (and lexicon) of hermeneutical inquiry, Rowe's brief analysis preserves the subject's predisposition toward belief in the authenticity of the object, and necessarily rests on the unearthing of the typical and the general (what if one of the participants in the carnival does not share the same mentality?), while eliding the conventional difficulties posed by the circularity of hermeneutic argumentation (how do we know the song articulates a collective mentality when we only have the song to go on?). And yet, the a priori assumption that a collective indian identity stands behind the song is certainly no worse, and may be politically both more necessary and more ethical, than the neoliberal a priori assumption of individual differences that disqualify the notion of collectivity.

However, Rowe's real coup is to recruit Deleuze and Guattari (arguably the most "modern," i.e., most apparently ruptural of thinkers) to the cause of hermeneutics. For poetry to reveal the landscape of a social imaginary or participate in the making of a new one, it must be thought of, *pace* Deleuze and Guattari, beyond the strictures of semiology (for Rowe, Derrida is precisely still tied to semiotics). Pain in Vallejo, light and earth in Roa Bastos, masks in Donoso, or landscape in Zurita, all escape the purview of a narrow semiotics. Words are not mere signs of something else. But neither is that something else simply "in" words (in what follows, at stake is pain):

> El lector es llevado hacia un lugar donde hay una máxima penetración de los sonidos, de las palabras como sonido, y de los sonidos de las palabras como una puerta a una zona que se puede llamar preconceptual. Se trata de un umbral del lenguaje que se relaciona con la capacidad (fuerza) penetrante de las palabras-sonidos.[13] (P. 109)

Echoes of Heidegger's faith in the Greek Logos, here Rowe develops not so much a philosophy as a cultural poetico-politics anxious to restore originary power to the word, which in the beginning was diglossic. The subsequent Fall into "authoritarian enunciation" is Rowe's point of departure. It is also where his concern with the question of critical position comes into its own. Why, he asks, do we see or hear one thing rather than another in Vallejo's words? Rowe is at his best in reconstructing the cultural context so that other, subaltern things might be seen and heard. But what kind of politics is in play here and where exactly is the place where this politics is in play?

The Politics of the Question of Context, or, Avant-Garde Subalternism and the Problem of Tradition

If politics cannot be divorced from context, it remains the case that the context of textual politics is always multiple. At the very least, we may posit two contexts where Rowe's book is concerned, one called "Latin America," the other something like "U.K. academia." Taking the two contexts in reverse order, in the case of U.K. academe the politics of a radical poetics, or of a cultural hermeneutics, lie principally in the critique of universalism. What Rowe argues tellingly in relation to pain in Vallejo is that to speak of pain as if it took but one form is to incur in a universalism that simply obliterates the phenomenon's different cultural expressions, not least its cosmic, that is, Andean dimension. However, as far as this kind of textual politics is concerned, to privilege politics at the expense of other—more explicitly academic—values is unsatisfactory. One can imagine a scenario in which Rowe's teachings regarding the intersection of temporalities in Vallejo's poetry harden into received wisdom. For it would always be possible to cite Rowe's argument elsewhere, to put it between quotation marks and reinscribe it in a new context in which its political radicality would be lost. The process of deradicalization can happen very quickly. It is the fate of most academic radicalisms. This is why Rowe's emphasis on "intellectual adventure" is so important, especially in a context that is currently witnessing what he sees as the institutionalization—and banalization—of cultural studies. He is insistent upon the necessity, if truly critical work is to be carried out, for intellectual adventure to entail sustained intellectual rigor. This is not to say that intellectual rigor stands above politics, that it somehow safeguards politics from a position outside or before politics. On the contrary, and to take just one of the more influential traditions of thought on this matter, the point about the classical Greek conceptions of philosophy and politics is that they have in common a series of shared values—not least the qualities of friendship and justice. The question of the politics of reading Vallejo's poetry thus already includes the questions: Does it do justice to the original, is it a good friend to the original (supposing the original deserves such justice and such friendship)? One cannot ask the question of institutional context without posing the question of the other context, that of the "object."

This brings us back to the first context, the Latin American one. For the demand for specificity that lies at the heart of cultural studies expresses a desire to be faithful and to do justice, not merely to an avant-garde poem (by placing it in context), but to the context in which it is produced. This demand and this desire entail a dethroning of the aesthetic object (what matters is the field), which at once accords it an exemplary and expanded role (the avant-garde object is recruited to reveal, and perhaps even subvert, something altogether vaster than literary history). The fundamental issue here revolves around the long-standing dispute between synchronic and diachronic approaches. By virtue of the very concept of the field, and notwithstanding caveats concerning temporal slippage, Rowe signals his strategic appropriation of a broadly synchronic approach. Although he is no structuralist, the insistence on divining the *processes* coursing through a given cultural field owes a huge debt to the structural revolution (which was precisely an attempt to grapple with Einsteinian and quantum insights). This synchronicism, which is probably inscribed at the heart of cultural studies itself (though not one with which Raymond Williams would concur), is a strategic choice taken against the prevailing orthodoxy of literary study (those interpretations that see Vallejo's work participating in a strictly poetic dialogue uninterrupted across the centuries). That the synchronic approach must sacrifice things en route, that its adventure will be a limited one articulates a banal objection that could be leveled at any approach. But what, more specifically, does Rowe's synchronic methodology sacrifice?

To construct a field is to sacrifice willingly the specificity and putative autonomy of the aesthetic object but also, paradoxically, to attenuate its radicality. This is the key issue in relation to the question of tradition and modernity. At its simplest, Derrida's point about iterability is that no context, no matter how specific it may be, can ever delimit or exhaust the meaning of an utterance. This is due not only to the fact that it may be cited and thus signify in a new context, breaking with the original context in the direction of the future; it is also because, even in its "original" context, that utterance may already be a citation, that is, a word, metaphor, symbol, or concept taken from an anterior time and place. This is not to deny the importance of the context of enunciation; it is to query its originality. For Derrida, all texts, all events in the history of thought, are negotiations with—and alterations to—other texts and contexts (past and contemporary), and thus their meaning cannot be reconstituted by a synchronic approach, no matter how keenly it multiplies the relational elements.[14] Texts collude in perpetuating the illusion that they issue from a uniquely specific place. By means of a plethora of rhetorical stratagems, nowhere better illustrated than in the deictic markers of the opening words of *Pedro Páramo* ("Vine a Comala porque me dijeron que acá vivía mi padre . . ."), texts themselves create the *effect* of touching the soil, of speaking from the place they speak about. But the *radicality* of a poetics is not best grasped by multiplying the relational elements of a field. For if the radicality in question describes a linguistic and conceptual deracination, the uprooting of an era's conventional habits of speech-thought, it must be noted that the latter is frequently achieved by means of the cultivation of other—perhaps suppressed—prior traditions. It is the reaffirmation of long-established popular traditions (which predate the advent of mass culture but which are then reformulated in it, preserving a reservoir of popular, collective, subaltern meanings) that animates the work of Jesús Martín-Barbero. It is precisely the recovery of deep-rooted, popular, collective traditions that forms the challenge to modernity in Arguedas. The methodological presupposition of the field, in contrast, privileges the iconoclastic avant-garde object that exceeds or fractures the field in the direction of the new. "Subversion" (the word has been rendered banal in contemporary discourse) is thus restricted to the modern ideal of a rupture with the past effected by the new understood as the never-before-seen. It is an idea that contradicts one of Rowe's—one of García Canclini's—key tenets, namely, the persistence of other cultural temporalities at the heart of the Latin American present, which henceforth becomes difficult to conceive of as a synchronic present at all. To admit that radicality may well be an effect produced by the recuperation of older traditions is to jeopardize the very concept of the field.

For all the profound similarities with Walter Benjamin's work at the level of method and pathos, Rowe's concept of the field distances him from Benjamin. For Benjamin, modernity—by which he means the time of the Second Industrial Revolution in Western societies—is a socioeconomic and technological reality qualitatively different from previous epochs. For that reason, modernity calls forth qualitatively different ways of experiencing reality. To the extent that this experience is his object of study, his method entails tracking this experience across wide-ranging and diverse cultural materials, "descubriendo 'oscuras relaciones' entre la refinada escritura de Baudelaire y las expresiones de la multitud urbana, y de ésta con las figuras del montaje cinematográfico."[15] High culture ("the refined writings of Baudelaire") forms part of these manifold cultural materials, not by virtue of its internal value, but because of the ways in which it is received and used by the public. Benjamin's aim is to register the altered sensory perceptions of modernity that constitute a necessarily *collective* experience. As Martín-Barbero says, the story of the work of art in the age of mechanical reproduction is thus not a melancholic account of cultural decline but a spur to the development of a new, egalitarian relationship to art and the fostering of a completely new level of sociability (Martín-Barbero, p. 58).

It is true that Rowe is close to Benjamin, inasmuch as the latter emphasizes change in the direction of the new. "A completely new level of sociability" corresponds to the creation of a new experience (that of modernity) rather than to the affirmation of an anterior traditional one. But because this modern experience is precisely a mass or collective one, it is by the same token already extant, that is, a mode of sensory perception that has already been created. The critic's task is to register this accomplished change, the phenomenon of a modern experience that has already arrived. This is why Rowe's book swerves away from Benjamin, and from the Martín-Barbero whose affirmation of collective, popular culture—of the memory inscribed in modernity—lay at the heart of one of Rowe's earlier works.[16] Because Rowe's literary object will consistently be the cultural prow (the modernist novel or avant-garde poem), and because his work is driven by the desire to uncover what breaks with the status quo, what creates something new, his theory and practice in this book will always sound like Adorno's hymn to modernist dissonance, whereby genuine art necessarily fights shy of the collective experience, taking its distance from the world around it. If in *Memory and Modernity* it is memory that disturbs modernity's desire to forget the past, in *Hacia una poética radical* the modern Nietzschean will-to-forget continually reasserts itself.

Cultural studies' problem with tradition resurfaces in Alberto Moreiras's critique of Western aesthetics. This critique is in part a rejoinder to Beatriz Sarlo. Sarlo argues that the sociology of culture's critique of aesthetic value has coincided with a generalized crisis of literacy and, by extension, *cultura letrada*, the latter coming under attack as the principal means by which the modern nation-state imposes its own ethnic and cultural values. Because the school is constructed as the coercive arm of a centralized authority, the way is left open for the embrace of mass media and information technologies as noncoercive sources of knowledge and culture that one is free to choose. School is the police; Nintendo, freedom.

The result is the triumph of a market-driven relativist pluralism in which an impoverished education and lack of intellectual discipline disables the nation's citizen-consumers from being able to counter the values of the marketplace.[17] Railing against the values of elite culture, the sociology of culture conspires with this devaluation of art, disqualifying in advance any analysis of the "resistencias propiamente artísticas que producen la densidad semántica y formal del arte" (p. 156). Moreiras argues that to maintain the importance and value of high literature, and hence the value of value, is to reproduce a Schillerian notion of the aesthetic that, in Paul de Man's words, "sets[s] up the aesthetic as exemplary, as an exemplary category, as a unifying category, as a model for education, as a model even for the state."[18] For Moreiras, this thinking of the aesthetic is based on a thought of universal or communal values that turn out to be nothing more than the values of the hegemonic order, which leaves out the values of the subaltern. The subaltern here is not to be thought of as an empirical subject, but rather as a function or possibility; the possibility of an unconditional rupture that would shatter all hegemonic norms and values—including, we would add, the possibility of university discourse on the subaltern.

On the surface of things, Moreiras's position is Derridian. If value thinking were to expand to accommodate the subaltern (in a thought of transculturation or hybridity perhaps), it would bring the subaltern within the remit of the hegemonic and leave the cultural order more or less intact (monsters would be pets).[19] Why not hold out then for "savage hybridity," for the unconditional irruption of the subaltern that would not be tied to the nation state, and thus be neither representable nor commodifiable? But there is an important difference between Moreiras and Derrida. When Derrida uses the phrase "democracy to come" instead of plain "democracy," he speaks of a democracy that is not certain to happen tomorrow, a democracy that is not a preprogrammed given, but that would nonetheless have to come out of an already extant democratic tradition with its attendant norms, conventions, and values. In other words, democracy cannot come out of nowhere; but nor does democracy have to become a regulative idea in the traditional sense, replica of an Ur-form or exact copy of the currently existing democratic order.[20] The idea of democracy that Derrida draws on but leaves open to modification belongs to a determinate political heritage stretching back to Ancient Greece and including specific institutions, texts, and values. In contrast, in speaking about the subaltern rather than democracy in an attempt to clear the way for the possibility of an alternative tradition of values, Moreiras uses a concept of the subaltern that is an abstract function defined only by what it is opposed to, and thus finds himself unable to say what that tradition and those values might be. Because, after the fashion of Hardt and Negri's notion of the multitude, Moreiras wants to hold out against Empire, because he wants to avoid all possibility that the monstrous-subaltern will become a pet in some transculturative or hybrid project of hegemony, he must posit a subaltern to come that looks dangerously like an impossible subaltern, or at best like an avant-garde subaltern. That is, he must posit a subaltern that, in order to emerge, would not only have to owe nothing to Western democracy (to borrow its terms would be to risk domestication by it); this subaltern capable of arriving unconditionally would also have to sacrifice tradition itself, that is, all values, all norms, and all collective identity. The irruption of such a subaltern could only ever be singular. If it is true that Sarlo makes few overtures to the duty of "respecting differences, idioms, minorities, singularities" (Derrida, *Aporias*, p. 19), a thought of an aesthetics to come need not end in the regulative idea of value, and at least recognizes that no thinking that draws on the European heritage of an idea of democracy can responsibly escape the values of that heritage.

Articulation versus Homology

> Articulation [. . .] stands as the name of the central theoretical problem or conceptual core of Cultural Studies.[21]

If cultural studies builds on the "progress" made by structuralism in opening up "the possibility of establishing a whole range of new relationships between materials of divers kinds," it does so in order to show the ways in which such materials are articulated with larger social and political processes.[22] Nevertheless, for Stuart Hall, articulation is a problem rather than a given:

> The unity formed by this combination or articulation, is always, necessarily, a "complex structure": a structure in which things are related, as much through their differences as through their similarities. This requires that the mechanisms which connect dissimilar features must be shown—since no "necessary correspondence" or expressive homology can be assumed as given. It also means—since the combination is a structure (an articulated combination) and not a random association—that there will be structured relations

between the parts, i.e., relations of dominance and subordination. (Cited in Jameson, "On 'Cultural Studies,' " p. 32)

In contrast, William Rowe does not "show" the articulations between the poem and the power structure. This is because there are none. There are only "processes" that run through the two and that the poem itself reveals. By deploying the concept of the plane of immanence, together with that other postulate of contemporary thought, the irrelevance of authorial intention, Rowe bypasses the need to show the articulations, opening the way to have the text reveal unlimited "obscure relationships." These operative principles are notably close to what Jameson, in a passage of great insight, identifies as Lévi-Strauss's method of the *homology*:

> Lévi-Strauss, anticipating postmodern social thought, evades the establishment of some fictive totalizing entity such as Society itself, under which more local and heterogeneous entities [. . .] used to be organically and hierarchically ordered. But he can do so only by inventing a different kind of fictive (or transcendent) entity, in terms of which the various independent "texts" of kinship, village organization, and visual form can be read as somehow being "the same": this is the method of the *homology*. As distinct as they are from each other, these various local and concrete "texts" can nonetheless be read as homologous with each other insofar as we disengage an abstract *structure* which seems to be at work in all of them, according to their own specific internal dynamics. In principle, the "theory" of structure, which justifies the practice of homology as a method, then allows one to avoid the establishment of ontological priorities. The structure of kinship is then, at least in principle, no more fundamental or causally prior than the spatial organization of the village [. . .]. But in order to secure that indifference or nonhierarchy of the various subsystems, an external category is required, that of "structure" itself. My own sense is that the influence of "structuralism" (and the extraordinary richness of new analyses that it opened up) is rather to be attributed to the possibility of making homologies than to the operative pretext—the concept of structure—which was its philosophical presupposition and its working fiction (or ideology). At the same time, it must be said that the notion of the homology rapidly proved to be an embarrassment and turned out to be as crude and vulgar an idea as "base and superstructure" ever was, the excuse for the vaguest kind of general formulations

and the most unenlightening assertions of "identity" between entities of utterly distinct magnitude and properties. (*Postmodernism*, p. 187)

Where the French structural-anthropologist uses "structure" as his working fiction, in Rowe it is the apparently more dynamic idea of "processes" that lends coherence to the field. That the avant-garde literary object can reveal the processes of a field suggests, as I argued earlier, that the conceptual framework here is a mixture of classical synchronicism and modern libertarianism (the critic will discover in the text whatever he desires). It suggests also a "culturalist" attempt to preserve the value of the literary text.

Rowe's project involves a wager that consists in asking how far cultural studies will allow him to get out of a traditional aestheticism without sacrificing, in the joint names of a cultural antielitism and a sociological finalism, the specific density of the literary object itself. This is why I am inclined to see Rowe's "culturalism" as a fending off of a certain type of multi- or interdisciplinarity in which what is believed to be the fruitful coming together of two or more disciplines turns out to be the annexation by one discipline of the others. Looking again at Hall's definition of articulation, does one not understand the degree to which the end of cultural studies is the pursuit of the logic of the social, that is, the degree to which the view of culture expressed therein is already a sociology and thus perhaps the end of cultural studies? It is for this reason that Rowe, whose interest is in an avant-garde art that cannot easily be articulated either with society or with cultural studies itself, takes a measured distance from cultural studies, assuming an approach that is neither multi- nor interdisciplinary but rather anti- or in- disciplinary.[23] As Rowe weaves between formal analysis and observations on the social imaginary, this distance manifests itself in the stress he places on reading and intellectual adventure, a stress that accords literature a correspondingly privileged political value while being unable to think its literariness.

Our first responsibility to the avant-garde literary object is to understand it. The insight which teaches that literature is not fashioned from an absolutely distinct semantic and conceptual system is important. However, that there is no relationship of exteriority between society and literature does not license their conflation into a cultural space–time soup. What are the codes and conventions that mediate between the two, especially when it is a matter of avant-garde writing, which tries so hard to dislocate the process of referentiality? The absence of hierarchization and dualism cannot be taken to signal the presence of a materially and semiotically undifferentiated field that would dissolve at a stroke the autonomy and distinction (albeit provisional) of objects, genres, cultural forms, and processes. The intellectual adventure entailed in reading the avant-garde will necessarily take us into a cultural and political field, and perhaps even open up a new one, but a certain specificity belongs to the adventure and politics of reading. If intellectual work entails being political, it cannot legitimize itself solely in relation to immediate political ends and may at times represent a means of defending the political against a specific form of politics. This was my point in the last chapter about the García Canclini of *Culturas híbridas*: that reading and poetics may represent a resistance to cultural studies; that a "slow aesthetics" may be a form of the political against that form of politics that reduces the logic of the text to the logic of the social. In the opening on to the future of which Deleuze and Guattari speak, where "to think is to experiment, but experimentation is always that which is in the process of coming about" (p. 111), cultural studies would have to take on board the chance that intellectual "adventure" (from *advenire*, "to come") might happen upon things other than those for which it was theoretically and politically programmed. Politics, too, would be a politics to come—which does not mean it would be a stranger to repetition, memory, or tradition.[24]

CHAPTER 4

Modernismo, Positivism, and (Dis)inheritance in the Discourse of Literary History

> Modernity, which is fundamentally a falling away from literature and a rejection of history.
>
> —Paul de Man

History and Modernity

A time and a place: the turn of the nineteenth century in Spanish America. Together this time and place comprise a context. A context, no doubt, of "deficient" socioeconomic modernization, but also, of books and ideas and other things besides (such as a political and economic model) that do not originate from that time and that place. A context is always an intricate weave, not just a scenic "background" to be taken as read. In that dense context of turn-of-the-century Spanish America, what has come to be known as *modernismo*, the first (relatively) autonomous artistic movement of any note to take hold in the subcontinent, makes two of the founding moves of European modernity. First, it names itself (the Enlightenment was the first to do this); and second, in naming itself as modern it insists on the break that it represents in relation to the past, which it desires to wipe out. "Modernity exists in the form of a desire to wipe out whatever came earlier, in the hope of reaching at last a point that could be called a true present, a point of origin that marks a new departure." The quotation is from Paul de Man's exemplary essay, "Literary History and Literary Modernity", in which he steers a course through Nietzsche's primarily philosophico-aesthetic concept of modernity, or what Nietzsche called "life."

We recall that in Nietzsche's luminous critique of the philosophical tradition and the dominance of historical thinking (which is also an indictment of the stolid mediocrity of German social democracy), humankind is pictured dragging the past behind it, remembering too much, devoid of spontaneity. To live truly, to be capable of experiencing the present in its uniqueness, man must live without historical awareness. "Moments of genuine humanity thus are moments at which all anteriority vanishes, annihilated by the power of an absolute forgetting":

> We are touching here upon the radical impulse that stands behind all genuine modernity when it is not merely a descriptive synonym for the contemporaneous or for a passing fashion. Fashion (mode) can sometimes be only what remains of modernity after the impulse has subsided, as soon—and this can be almost at once—as it has changed from being an incandescent point in time into a reproducible cliché, all that remains of an invention that has lost the desire that produced it. [. . .] But Nietzsche's ruthless forgetting, the blindness with which he throws himself into an action lightened of all previous experience, captures the authentic spirit of modernity. It is the tone of Rimbaud when he declares that he has no antecedents whatever in the history of France, that all one has to expect from poets is "du nouveau" and that one must be "absolutely modern"; it is the tone of Antonin Artaud when he asserts that "written poetry has value for one single moment and should then be destroyed. Let the dead poets make room for the living . . . the time for masterpieces is past." Modernity exists in the form of a desire to wipe out whatever came earlier, in the hope of reaching at last a point that could be called a true present, a point of origin that marks a new departure.[1]

"And this can be almost at once." According to this philosophico-aesthetic understanding of modernity—which certainly differs from the concept of modernity as a socioeconomic reality, but which, as I argued in chapter 1, is in no sense alien to the emergence of that reality—it is difficult to envisage how anything or anyone could "capture" the authentic spirit of modernity. An incandescence caught is already a fire. But that is de Man's point. To be modern is a "desire."

De Man writes of Nietzsche's essay "Of the Use and Misuse of History for Life" that the text "is a good example of the complications that ensue when a genuine impulse toward modernity collides with the demands of a historical consciousness or a culture based on the disciplines of history" (p. 145). Notwithstanding the nominally modern founding moves outlined above, the Spanish American *modernistas* appear much less modern to us than does Nietzsche. The complications of *modernismo* are less acute than those that beset the text of Nietzsche (or Rimbaud or Artaud). This is not because *modernismo* was merely "a descriptive synonym for the contemporaneous or for a passing fashion." It had its incandescence. But the protagonists of *modernismo* were much more attached than the figures mentioned above to the demands of a historical consciousness and an erudite culture based on the disciplines of history. In what follows, I show the extent to which the "literary history" of *modernismo*, which proclaims the latter's modern condition at every juncture—and which, in truth, comprises manifestos and other forms of discursive reflection above and beyond the narrowly academic sense of literary history—runs counter to the impulse toward modernity taken in its philosophico-aesthetic sense.[2]

Of course, the conflict between history and modernity is not unique to *modernismo*. History has always had a problem with modernity. Modernity is born as a rejection of the past and of history. In order to continue being modern, modernity must ceaselessly destroy itself, ceaselessly reinvent itself as that which resists sedimentation into a reproducible cliché. "The spontaneity of being modern conflicts with the claim to think and write about modernity" (de Man, p. 142). But if de Man is correct to say that there may well be an "inherent contradiction between modernity, which is a way of acting and behaving, and such terms as 'reflection' or 'ideas' that play an important part in literature and history," this cannot be taken to mean that all ways of giving in to history are of equal value. What counts, rather, is the degree of resistance that a reflection on modernity musters against history. In truth, in their historical meditations on what it means to be modern the *modernistas* succumb meekly to historical prerogatives, their own self-justificatory texts struggling to approach the condition of modernity they advocate. Intoxication with the thought of disinheriting themselves from the legacy of positivism is dissipated by a sobering, deeply conventional—not to say "positivist"—affiliation to the traditional rituals and concepts of literary history, not least the language and idea of historical progress.

If anything, *modernismo* exhibits two different understandings of modernity. On the one hand, there is the "aesthetic" concept outlined above: modernity as a ruthless forgetting, a ceaseless desire for the new, an incandescent impulse. On the other hand, stands the Enlightenment concept of modernity in which knowledge and symbolic production are developed in opposition to all forms of superstition and benightedness. As Néstor García Canclini has argued, this latter concept is that of the museum or collection. Modernity sorts its cultural production into discrete places, differentiating sharply between the high and the low, the elite and the popular. For its part, *modernismo* gathers into its folds the names, and the names of the objects, of classical as much as contemporary elite culture. *Modernista* literature is replete with emblems drawn from Classical Antiquity and has a deliberately anachronizing strain—most obviously in its (Symbolist-inspired) persistent thematization of the Platonic time of eternity. Thus, when it comes to wiping out whatever came earlier, in line with the first concept of modernity, the past in question is not Tradition understood as *traditio*. It is not a matter of Modernity seeking yet again, this time in one of the "peripheral" zones, to vanquish Tradition. On the contrary, *modernismo* mobilizes the topoi and figures of *traditio* in order to erase the memory of a specific tradition nearer to home. The *modernistas'* ambition was to build their own tradition—a kind of antimodern modernism—by laying waste to the dominant positivist legacy that exerted a huge influence on Spanish American intellectual life at the end of the nineteenth century.[3] The tactic of dismissing positivism on the grounds of its supposed oldness is a familiar move of so-called modern historical discourse and thought. Such a discourse had until recently met with little resistance in the Hispanic tradition of criticism. Its seemingly implacable, chauvinistic will to compartmentalize lived on most notoriously in debates surrounding the question of who belongs to *modernismo* and who to the Generation of 1898, as though it were a matter of separate planets each governed by an absolutely distinct lexical and conceptual system. Even if one would not bestow the proper name "positivist" upon every manifestation of this will, such manifestations give witness to the longevity of the positivist bequest.

Autonomy Domine

Interpretations of Spanish American *modernismo* have with good reason viewed it as a response to a period of oppressive socioeconomic change ("ruines tiempos," in Martí's phrase) resulting from the fuller incorporation of the region into the world economy;[4] as the product of a new, intensified psyche, itself the outcome of the sensory bombardment that is the modern metropolis;[5] and as a properly aesthetic manifestation of independence and resistance to traditional, especially peninsular, artistic discourse, "que sufría anquilosis," as Darío put it.[6] Angel Rama conducts a rightful defence of Rubén Darío on the last grounds, writing of the latter's invaluable contribution to an "orbe cultural propio que pudiera oponerse al español materno."[7] Darío himself spoke in similar terms: "Nuestro modernismo, si es que así puede llamarse, nos va dando un puesto aparte, independiente de la literatura castellana."[8]

This last interpretation has been extended in recent years by Julio Ramos, who sees in *modernismo* a Latin America avatar of Max Weber's thesis concerning the modern formation of autonomous spheres of knowledge.[9] For Ramos, *modernismo* is the first Latin American literary movement to be just that: literary. If there had been literature before, there had not been a specialized field called literature. In the work and in the times of Andrés Bello, the concept of *Bellas Letras* postulated "literary" writing as a medium for working on language in order to achieve *non*literary, *non*aesthetic effects. Literature, and more especially the prized classical virtue of eloquence, had its own social authority as an exemplary means of schooling oneself and others in the art of reason. Eloquence was an essential tool in the civilizing mission of building a rational social order. Literature did not, then, "thematize" or "reflect" politics; "las letras *eran* la política." Until the last quarter of the nineteenth century, to write was a rationalizing practice, authorized by the ongoing project of the formation of the nation-state. This relationship is problematized in the last decades of that century. As the nation-states are finally consolidated, there emerges a specifically *political* discursive field, tied to the state administration but autonomous from the republic of letters. More than a question of the professionalization and mercantilization of writing, the emergence of a properly aesthetic field is the result of a restructuring of the network of social communication (*el tejido de la comunicación social*), which reconfigured the old systems of authorization:

> Lo que ha cambiado fundamentalmente no es sólo (aunque también) el lugar de los escritores ante el Estado, que ya comenzaba a desarrollar administradores "orgánicos"; se ha transformado la relación entre los enunciados, las formas literarias, y los campos semióticos presupuestos por la autoridad literaria, diferenciada de la autoridad política. El sentido y la función social del enunciado literario ya no están garantizados por las instituciones de lo político, sino que ahora comienzan a producirse desde un lugar

de enunciación que ha diferenciado sus normas y autoridad. (Ramos, p. 65)

What is interesting for our purposes is that, in Ramos's opinion, the *enunciado literario* does not manage to create an autonomous field as such. The *modernistas* may *desire* autonomy, there may well have been a fierce *will* to autonomy (in Julián del Casal and José Martí alike), but this does not mean that autonomy was achieved. Ramos maintains that no such autonomy was secured, no "pure" literature created, on account of the fact that the *modernistas* were too conscious of their duty toward society and thus climbed down from the heights of autonomy to let their work be contaminated with social, quotidian concerns. It would be more correct to say that autonomy as such is never possible, but that the *modernistas* did more than most to secure the space and conditions for a notable semi-autonomous literary practice.

The notion of autonomy is no incidental attribute of modernity; it goes to the heart of what it means to be "modern." In order to give due recognition to a shift that has taken place between the early and later parts of the nineteenth century, Ramos says of the *modernistas* that they were the first "modern" Latin American intellectuals. They were modern, he says, by virtue of the fact that their practice was constituted "outside" politics (*fuera de la política*) and the state apparatus. They were modern, that is, by virtue of their autonomy from the formal sphere of politics and the machinery of the state. Ramos understands more than most the difference between the politics of the state apparatus and what is now commonly called simply "the political." Politics takes place in legislative chambers, among designated representatives. "The political," in contrast, is the name we give to affairs that bear on the workings of social relations within the polis—specifically on power relations within it—but that do not pass through the recognized channels of politics. The division of labor within the household is not subject to government dictate, but is a fundamentally political question since it bears on the relations of power between individuals. As the 1960s' feminist slogan put it, the personal is political.

The cultivation of a highly specialized, effete aesthetic practice by the *modernistas* is a form of the political. Ramos says as much. The development of an auratic notion of culture is designed to counter society's prevailing utilitarianism. That is, the fashioning of an a- or anti-political literary system was "political" to the core. In a sense, it was the only option open to them. Since they were isolated from politics, and since the republic of letters was outside the inner sanctum where

MODERNISMO, POSITIVISM, AND (DIS)INHERITANCE 73

the central affairs of the republic in general were decided, resistance comes from the cultivation of a "separate" realm deemed superior to politics and the mundane concerns of material society. But if, as Ramos argues, someone like Martí sees the authority of modern literature deriving from its resistance to the processes of modernization, and if it is legitimate to call this resistance political, such a resistance is not outside the walls of the polis. The only question that remains to be determined is whether the political is outside politics, in other words, whether it is valid to conceive of the two orders as separate. Would it not rather be the case that politics, that is, the formal sites, procedures, and language where, by and in which the direction of the state is determined, is always traversed by the political? The political may always encroach, perhaps has always already encroached from the beginning, on politics. This does not mean that each and every form of the political, each and every domestic or intellectual resistance to politics, can have significant impact on the direction of the latter (we must avoid such an idealization). If politics is shot through with the political, it also manifests its own resistance to it, most notably in the form of simple indifference.

This understanding of the political renders suspect the classificatory impulse of Ramos's historical discourse. Broadly speaking, we understand what he means when he claims, for example, that José Rodó's authority is more aesthetic than political, in a way that Sarmiento's never was. But what Ramos actually says is that Rodó's authority was "specifically aesthetic" (*específicamente estética*). However, if the aesthetic were specific, if the aesthetic were specifically itself, it could not be political or indeed anything else other than itself. It could have no commerce with politics and would indeed be outside the city walls. But this is not the case, as Ramos has argued, since aesthetics is political. This is what would define the modernity of the *modernistas*. They make aesthetics political in a very specialized way. However, if the notion that aesthetics has political freightage is new, if it is characteristic of our modern era, the same cannot be said of another notion that underpins Ramos's argument. If, following Martí, the authority of literature lies in its resistance to the processes of modernization, it remains the case that the notion of authority, the willingness to bestow authority on men of letters, as much as the willingness shown by an educated elite to accept the authority bestowed upon them, is neither new nor modern. If the designation of the *modernistas* as modern names something new, neither their authority nor their aesthetics correspond entirely to the condition of autonomy, which would mark them out as modern. We must take care with the classifying, periodizing drives of the discourse of history.

El cuchillo divisor

Questions of the name and of temporal periodization will lie at the heart of my analysis of what is arguably the dominant interpretation of *modernismo*, to which I now turn. This interpretation maintains that *modernismo* (and here the distinction between the Peninsula and the old colonies is eroded) represents a profound spiritual and philosophical transformation. Ivan Schulman highlights the consensus that took hold around this view in a famous 1907 inquiry published in *El Nuevo Mercurio*. He cites one of the contributors, Roberto Brenes Mesén: "El modernismo en el arte es simplemente una manifestación de un estado de espíritu contemporáneo, de una tendencia universal, cuyos orígenes se hallan profundamente arraigados en la filosofía trascendental que va conmoviendo los fundamentos de la vasta fábrica social que llamamos el mundo moderno."[10] For his part, in the first documented use that he makes of the word *modernismo*, Darío binds it closely to an "espíritu nuevo." Testimonies to this effect are legion.[11] However, as a plethora of critics have observed, *modernista* discourse defined this new spirit more precisely, seeing it as a rejection and subversion of a past dominated by positivism.[12]

Positivism is based on a belief in the process of scientific investigation and empirical observation (which is not enough to make positivism itself scientific). Crucially, in Comte's "lois des trois états," man evolves through the theological and metaphysical states, until he reaches the positivist one. In this last, man renounces the effort to know the absolute and most intimate causes of phenomena and turns exclusively to discovering their "lois effectives, c'est-à-dire leurs relations invariables de succession et de similitude."[13] (For his part, Taine distances himself from Comte, since for him causes form part of sensory experience and are therefore knowable.)

In his essay "Traducción y metáfora," Octavio Paz outlines the historical and psychological relationship between positivism and *modernismo* in the context of Latin America.[14] Paz argues that the variant of positivism embraced by the dominant classes in the second half of the nineteenth century functioned as a "cut," a *corte tajante* to reinforce the separation between Latin America and the Spanish tradition: "El corte, el cuchillo divisor, fue el positivismo. En esos años las clases dirigentes y los grupos intelectuales de América Latina descubren la filosofía positivista y la abrazan con entusiasmo" (p. 104). Positivism performs a *tabula rasa* on Christian mythology and rationalist philosophy alike, the result of which is "el desmantelamiento de la metafísica y la religión en las conciencias" (p. 105). Strictly speaking, the *desmantelamiento* is not total. Indeed, Paz will immediately add that even if the visible signs of metaphysics disappeared, a certain longing for the old guarantees remained, together with a feeling of "vértigo ante la nada." Enter *modernismo*:

> El modernismo fue la respuesta al positivismo, la crítica de la sensibilidad y el corazón—también de los nervios—al empirismo y el cientismo positivista [. . .]. El modernismo fue nuestro verdadero romanticismo [. . .]. La conexión entre el positivismo y el modernismo es de orden histórico y psicológico. Se corre el riesgo de no entender en qué consiste esta relación si se olvida que el positivismo latinoamericano, más que un método científico, fue una ideología, una creencia. Su influencia sobre el desarrollo de la ciencia en nuestros países fue muchísimo menor que su imperio sobre las mentes y las sensibilidades de los grupos intelectuales [. . .]. Los superficiales han sido los críticos que no supieron leer en la ligereza y el cosmopolitismo de los poetas modernistas los signos (los estigmas) del desarraigo espiritual. (Pp. 105–106)

Schematically speaking, according to Paz, the advent of *modernismo* marks the sign not just of a cutting of roots, but of an uprooting (*desarraigo*). In other words, the original instrument of separation—the positivist "cuchillo divisor"—which was to engender a properly Latin American cultural heritage and psychology is subjected in turn to a later, *modernista* disavowal. As Paz suggests, the rejection of the positivist world is not a purely academic affair; it is the refusal of an entire cultural vision that managed to impose itself among intellectuals and the ruling classes in Latin America. Whence the symbolic importance for the *modernistas* of a figure like Taine, who stood for everything that had to be purged simultaneously from and by the new cultural configuration.

It would be folly to pursue this powerful desire for rupture further than the notion demands. Scanning the mass of critical material on the subject, it is clear that the will to cut is more selective. Indeed, testimonies abound which suggest that although *modernismo* was engaged in an exercise of deracination where philosophy was concerned, it actively prolonged certain prior *artistic*, especially Romantic, traditions. Pedro Salinas writes astutely of the *modernistas*' indebtedness to previous art, which constitutes a thematic stockpile often put to rather superficial use: "Atributo capital del modernismo es su enorme cargamento de conceptos de cultura histórica, por lo general bastante superficiales.

Gran parte de esta poesía, en vez de arrancar de la experiencia directa de la realidad vital, sale de concepciones artísticas anteriores."[15] The relationship between this positive legacy and the negative one of the immediate philosophical past is not fortuitous. The two positions were, *pace* Paz, mutual preconditions, North and South of a "dialéctica contradictoria." The rise of a highly cosmopolitan, effete art represented a backlash against (positivist) philosophy.

There is a convenient selectiveness here (it must be said that an ancient division still accompanies us): *modernismo* sprang positively from prior art but negatively from philosophical positivism, lifting up its conceptual skirts and fleeing the domain of the philosophical patriarch. These versions of *modernismo* paint a radically modern, antideterminist movement able to slough off the weight of prior cultural knowledge by dint of sheer will. The simple question is: how adequate is this portrayal of radical disinheritance?

LEMA: Arte y progreso[16]

Let me state the central premise of this chapter without equivocation. It is this: in its more formally academic literary-historical avatar, as much as in its manifestos and public pronouncements, the "new," *modernista* discourse exhibits a pronounced kinship with the language and founding concepts of positivism, not least its attachment to the idea of progress, which, while clearly indebted to the Enlightenment, stands as a specific variant of post-Enlightenment historical thought.[17] Comte builds his system on the premise that the progress of humanity can be traced across stages of evolution that culminate in the positive state. In this third state, the historical method constitutes, for him, "le principal artifice scientifique de la nouvelle philosophie positive" (Charlton, p. 30). Comte's objective is to determine, with absolute, scientific precision, the place of social phenomena in the process of social development. Social development is understood as evolution in a specific direction and presupposes "that what comes later in the process is an unfolding of what was at least implicitly present in its earlier stage."[18] An observable transformation in the arts, for instance, is the symptom of some other more fundamental process of development "in the culture as a whole, or in the spirit of a people, or in Humanity, or Reality" (Mandelbaum, p. 46).[19]

I offer below a handful of examples to illustrate a certain attachment on the part of the *modernistas* to what Collingwood calls "the evolutionary metaphysics of the late nineteenth century" (p. 99).[20] When

José Enrique Rodó invests in *modernismo* in his *Rubén Darío* (1899), the form and content of the study mark it as legal tender in a familiar system of exchange:

> Yo soy un modernista también, yo pertenezco con toda mi alma a la gran reacción que da carácter y sentido a *la evolución del pensamiento* en las postrerías de este siglo; a la reacción que, partiendo del naturalismo literario y del positivismo filosófico, los conduce, sin desvirtuarlos en lo que tienen de fecundos, a disolverse en concepciones más altas.

Commenting on images from Baudelaire and Gabriel D'Annunzio in *Corte de amor* (1902), Ramón del Valle-Inclán says that such images are just "una consecuencia lógica de *la evolución progresiva de los sentidos*," which means that we perceive gradations of color doubtless missed by our ancestors of centuries gone by.[21] Darío himself furnishes no shortage of examples. Reflecting on poetic form, he uses a quintessentially nineteenth-century concept of historical development in "Dilucidaciones": "La forma poética no está llamada a desaparecer, antes bien a extenderse, a modificarse, a *seguir su desenvolvimiento en el eterno ritmo de los siglos*," which he deploys again in *España Contemporánea* (1901), referring to the "producción enclenque y falsa, desconocimiento del progreso mental del mundo" in Spanish intellectual circles.[22] This historicist posture is maintained in the "Palabras liminares" from *Prosas Profanas*, this time with an American nuance:[23]

En el fondo de mi espíritu, a pesar de mis vistas cosmopolitas, existe *el inarrancable filón de la raza; mi pensar y mi sentir continúan un proceso histórico y tradicional*. (Phillips, "Rubén Darío," p. 125)	à chaque moment on peut considérer le caractère d'un peuple comme le résumé de toutes ses actions et de toutes ses sensations précédentes, c'est-à-dire comme une quantité et comme un poids. (Taine, p. 40)

Finally, when Darío takes the rostrum at the headquarters of the magazine *El Ateneo* in Buenos Aires, his words fuse body politic and cultural spirit into a single organic process:

Mientras nuestra amada y desgraciada madre patria, España, parece	Une civilisation fait corps, et ses parties se tiennent à la façon des

sufrir la hostilidad de una suerte enemiga, encerrada en la muralla de su tradición, aislada por su propio carácter, sin que penetre hasta ella *la oleada de la evolución mental en estos últimos tiempos,* el vecino reino fraternal manifiesta una súbita energía, *el alma portuguesa* encuentra en el extranjero lenguas que la celebran y la levantan, *la sangre de Lusitania florece* en armoniosas flores de arte y de vida: nosotros, latinos, hispanoamericanos, debemos mirar con orgullo las manifestaciones vitales de ese pueblo y sentir como propios las victorias que consigue en honor de nuestra *raza*. (Darío, cited by Rafael Alberto Arrieta, "El Modernismo 1893–1900," in Litvak, pp. 275–276)

parties d'un corps organique. (Taine, p. 50)

ce qu'on appelle *la race*, ce sont des dispositions innées et héréditaires que l'homme apporte avec lui à la lumière, et qui ordinairement sont jointes à des différences marquées dans le tempérament et dans la structure du corps. (Taine, p. 39)

According to an almost algebraic logic, the discourse that sanctions the new spirit perpetuates the organic historicism of the old order of Taine and Comte. A disdain for positivism does not prevent the *modernistas* from slipping into the same discourse on the evolution of a species and the destiny of a people whose time has come. It is not a question of reprehending the *modernistas* for their incapacity to break with the past; their failing lies, rather, in being too quick to embrace the heady aesthetic discourse of modernity that underestimates the difficulty of breaking with the past. It is the classic paradox of historicism: a historical method that ends up bracketing out history, time, movement.[24] The momentum ascribed by *modernista* notaries to mental and racial evolution is denied in the analysis that would describe a new, uncontaminated spirit or psyche that has somehow emerged from nowhere, as if by magic. This magic finds support in the proper name, which is charged with the task of affirming ownership, belonging, propriety, cleanliness. Uncontaminated, the proper name testifies, quite properly, to the presence of the self-same, the identical, the unique. But a literary history dazzled by the proper name can no more account for previous change than for the possibility of future transformation. And whereas it purports to reveal the origin, univocal development and annihilation of a phenomenon in its absolute positivity, it necessarily betrays traces of the repression of the *moment* of the *milieu*, so to speak.[25] The tropological figures of trenchant cut, generational disinheritance, and genealogical discontinuity repress that which, at a certain level, was already within *modernismo*'s own formation, attempting to invest the latter with a false aura of originality.

This is not to argue, let us be clear about this, that the reason why the *modernistas* offered little or no resistance in their literary-historical mode to this crude version of positivist progress was simply because they were positivists. I indicate the traces of a repressed similarity, not in order to collapse the two movements into one, but rather to disturb the supposed trenchant difference that separated the new from the old spirit, signaling in the process a historical filiation that would not take the form of a genetically inherited psychology. The conclusion to be drawn from this is that a complex discursive and cultural economy is at work, in which one solves nothing by simply calling *modernista* thought "positivist": first, because certain aspects of the philosophy of *modernismo*, and above all its artistic practices, were counter-positivist in significant respects; but second, for the good reason that positivism "itself" cannot be construed as self-identical.

History and the Proper Name

The revealing thing about Angel Rama's sociological analysis of *modernismo* is that, despite pointing to the "contamination" of *modernismo* by things material, at a certain level the security of the proper name remains unbreached. It is as though the interaction with various— social and philosophical—materialisms determines to a large degree the early phase of gestation, but has no significant bearing on the final product. For all his well-honed criticism of the creationism that pervades *modernista* discourse, Rama follows positivism's own atomism in attributing an independence, or "positivity," both to the phenomenon called *modernismo* and to the concept of the latter. Like it or not, there is something called *modernismo* (which is not positivism). Everything then happens in the discourse of literary history as though one's relationship to the past can only consist in saying a categorical yes or no to an ideal, self-identical legacy, as though to be a successor of positivism meant either receiving or rejecting the inheritance absolutely.

This atomistic, faintly platonic positivism finds support in a historicism that restricts the inheritance exclusively to the tangible legacies to which a given body of knowledge was most immediately indebted.

History, the discipline that takes the passing of time as its primary concern, thus freezes out time by imposing a restricted chronology, together with another proper name ("the late nineteenth century"). It is quite logical to look to the end of the nineteenth century for an understanding of *modernismo*. In the most obvious, commonsensical view, the family tryst between *modernismo* and positivism in Latin America properly "belongs" to that era. It is an abuse of history, an inadequacy of historiography, however, to limit the temporal inheritance of the movement to that period alone. An important strain of *modernista* artistic production owes a debt to earlier artistic traditions, and positivism can certainly be viewed as a variation on the Enlightenment discourse of modernity, which, as Jonathan Israel has shown, does not begin in 1789. If it is the case, following Rama's vulgar concept of time, that "Nadie elige fuera de su tiempo," it is no less true, in line with a more complex notion of temporality, that we all choose outside our time. According to a differential understanding of both time and space, nobody is in a hermetically sealed locale. If this is so for all historical epochs, it has special resonance in the era of modernity, and even more so in a "peripheral" zone of the world marked by the experience of colonialism.[26] In the context of the jarring temporalities of turn-of-the-century Spanish America, there is particular reason for fighting shy of the simplifications of positivist historiography. Positivistic organicist metaphors of progress suggest a single, giant "oleada" that moves in one direction and at one rhythm, while the larger discourse makes it plain that not everyone has managed to catch the wave. As if there were only one wave; as if there were only one shore . . .

Rituals

> le rituel définit la qualification que doivent posséder les individus qui parlent (et qui, dans le jeu . . . de la récitation, doivent occuper telle position et formuler tel type d'énoncés); il définit les gestes, les comportements, les circonstances, et tout l'ensemble de signes qui doivent accompagner le discours.
>
> —Michel Foucault[27]

I argued in my original essay that there is something ritualistic and self-serving about such a positivistic discourse, but that it is unsatisfactory to explain such rituals as mere rhetorical posturing, suggesting instead that they be viewed as a policing of the frontiers of culture.

Late-nineteenth-century Spanish America was bedeviled by pernicious forms of positivism and Social Darwinism, and it is easy to see how the literary history on and of *modernismo* amplifies further this rather crude discourse of progress. *Modernismo* was hardly the Argentine Conquest of the Desert, but it did nevertheless play an active part in reproducing a certain Eurocentric conceptual apparatus. This is the basic lesson of semiotics, which makes all textual cultural politics possible: viz., discursive production not only "reflects" differences but actively produces them, or, let us say, moderating the hard semiotic line, that it (re)produces them as one component within a larger system of transmission.

What I also said in that first attempt was that it is perfectly possible to understand how the very logic of positivist discourse—based on a series of atomistic differences plotted onto a Western scale and supported by proper names—can be turned against those (Latin Americans) who use it. Thus, when Max Henríquez Ureña, echoing Menéndez Pidal, evinces a Tainian concern for the fundamental aptness of a spiritual orientation to a particular race—"El modernismo no se avenía, en su esencia misma, con el temperamento español, esto es, con el espíritu literario español" (p. 519)—it is but one short, albeit wholly logical, step to Díaz Plaja's Tainian-inspired racial-geographical law of excess. The latter consists of a dichotomy between the Generation of 98 and *modernismo*, which rests largely on the expeditious relegation of the latter to a system of nonrational, nonformal discourse: "El Modernismo es la proyección contemporánea del Mediterraneísmo." The peninsular *modernistas* soon tired of the style, *ergo* it was a rogue, marginal, Mediterranean deviation. If this deviation was undeniably a sign of Hispanic accession to the upper echelons of Humanity, what was being accessed was really only one side of a fundamentally double-sexed, dichotomous Humanity: "Este abandono de lo racional-activo a la pasividad-sensible ¿puede ser calificado con el signo femíneo?" (Díaz Plaja, p. 213). The "evolución mental" in Latin America—where the movement did take hold—is neither denied nor disparaged; it is simply situated as the logical unfolding of a proven historical propensity toward the mystical, the feminine, the exotic, the excessive, the nonrational.

But there is one important respect in which I now diverge from the early essay. If we can acknowledge that *modernista* discourse is entangled in a larger social apparatus and is therefore capable of producing political effects, this does not legitimize the abuse of the police metaphor. For two reasons. First, to describe literary history as a means of policing culture overstates the power of artistic and literary-historical discourse, which has a heavily circumscribed role in modernity.[28]

Second, the metaphor overlooks the ways in which art and knowledge produce things of value in addition to producing political effects. In the early essay, I pointed to the ways in which *modernista* literary-historical discourse is "contaminated" by the economic materialism against which it hoped to define itself. However, highlighting such contamination does not license us, did not license me, to insinuate that *modernismo* is homologous either with the polis or with material economic life. In the attempt to indicate a certain intercourse between art and economic life, between two things considered distinct by a tradition of thinking indebted to German idealism, I fell back on an imprecise formulation of their relationship, suggesting that *modernismo* was the "signo cultural del liberalismo." If *modernismo* was the sign of cultural liberalism, does this mean that other cultural manifestations contemporaneous with it were not signs? What does it take to be a sign? And if *modernismo* is a cultural sign of liberalism, precisely what kind of sign? Are the highly codified signifying practices of *modernismo* transparent signs of economic free trade? And would their transparency wipe out all other value? This reduction of the literary sign to some other, more fundamental process of social development is nothing less than the specter of a residual positivism, which assumes each motif of *modernista* poetry to be the transparent sign of something grander—a soul, a psyche, an essence, an ideology, Western imperialism.

If we are to muster some kind of resistance to positivist historiography, we must take seriously the ritual nature of discourse. Certain propositions follow from such a decision. First, one does not belong to a ritual position positively, essentially, without remainder. Ritual suggests instead a more provisional or strategic attachment to certain *gestes* and *comportements*, which always allows for the possibility of rejection, or at least the non-interiorization, of the doctrine. Second, one does not follow a ritual purely out of a (negative) sense of obligation. The police do not always hover over the concept of ritual. Rituals involve the pleasure of incantation, the seduction of known formulae, a sense of belonging, and a means of self-expression.[29] Third, to think the "ritual" nature of discourse is to understand that different *gestes, comportements, circonstances* and *ensembles de signes* animate different discourses. Of course, different discourses may well share some of these *gestes*, but each is likely to deploy them in a certain specialized mode that marks out the ritual called literature, for instance, from the one called literary history. Rituals entail different linguistico-conceptual codifications, differently inflected ways of configuring language and thought. Because there is no natural or absolute division between the rituals of literature and those of literary history, it would always be possible for the one to adopt the primary function conventionally reserved for the other. However, this possibility is much more available to literature than it is to history. Modern literature's capacity—and liberty—to incorporate other discourses into its midst, indeed to give itself over to another discourse, either for serious or parodic purposes, is one of its defining features, precisely part of its ritual. It is the privilege of literature, it is the liability that is literature, to be the more open and transgressive. The open, transgressive character of literature does not belong to it as an a priori quality (most literary production is as hide-bound as its historiographical counterpart) and may more often than not turn out to be a negligible openness or transgressiveness precisely because it is an accepted, and therefore inoffensive, part of the ritual.

The final proposition that follows from an attempt to think seriously about the ritual nature of discourse is that because there are plural discursive rituals, there are as a result different discursive positions within a movement such as *modernismo* or within the writing of a single poet. The broad, though in no sense absolute, difference between the rituals of literature and literary history explains why *modernismo* can produce, on the one hand, a highly conventional, rather closed discourse of history and, on the other, a literature able to be creative and (semi-)independent in certain life-affirming ways. It is true, of course, that many of the discursive positions of the respective rituals are mutually reinforcing—precisely because, one might say, they are intimately connected to a time, a place, and, even, a race. But only when we take seriously the possibility that different discursive positions can inhabit the same movement, do we understand how a poet with clear *modernista* and even *posmodernista* tendencies such as César Vallejo can, just a year before Darío's death, present to the University of Trujillo a literary-historical dissertation that bristles with references to Haeckel's theory of the inheritance of acquired characteristics. That is, a dissertation whose texture is indistinguishable from nineteenth-century positivism.[30] A context is never a positivity folded in upon itself, never the time and place of a closed book.

CHAPTER 5

Vallejo, Semicolonialism, and Poetemporality

How meaningful is it to think of César Vallejo as a representative of a non-Western tradition, a tradition opposed to the Western tradition and certainly to Western modernity? Two subsidiary questions immediately arise: what do we understand by the phrase non-Western and what would it mean here to be a "representative"? I shall approach these questions by drawing in turn on two traditions of criticism that have acquired prominence in the Western academy in recent decades and at the heart of which lies an overt political concern to redress the intellectual as much as political misrepresentation of those areas of the globe that fall outside the main Western powerbloc. The respective traditions are those of postcolonial theory and Latin American cultural studies.

In order to answer these questions, the chapter begins with some more or less raw geopolitical data in respect of the historical positions of Latin America and Peru, and some no less raw biographical data in the case of Vallejo himself. The purpose of such data is to highlight the strategic misprision—the conflation of two different understandings of colonialism—that allows postcolonial theory to speak of a Latin America that might more faithfully be characterized as a colonial postcolonial place. The chapter then moves to consider two modes of writing in which Vallejo explicitly deals with either questions of cultural difference (*Los heraldos negros*) or issues concerning the power relations between Latin America and what has come to be known as the developed world (his journalism from the late 1920s). Both before and after *Trilce*, and in two different modes, Vallejo positions himself discursively on the side of a modern Western (albeit differential) temporality, without thereby simply vindicating the West qua political bloc.

The second part of the chapter deals with an alternative "model" of the subcontinent's different temporalities. William Rowe's work on Vallejo is the first major attempt to apply the insights of Néstor García Canclini regarding the region's "multitemporal heterogeneity" to poetry. Rowe elects not to go down the conventional "postcolonial" road of construing Vallejo as an explicit native informant. Instead he unearths a more oblique non-Western knowledge in Vallejo's poetry: namely, an Andean indigenous concept of time. In following Rowe's interpretation of Vallejo, two doubts come to the fore. The first is familiar from the early part of the chapter and has to do with whether it is licit to construe *Trilce* as harboring significant elements of an indigenous, pre-Colombian worldview. *Trilce* VI certainly contains words from the Andean area and the poem may be understood as a Peruvian reworking of a traditional ritual. However, the ritual concerned is not an Andean-indigenous communal one opposed to Western modernity, but the ritual that surrounds the highly individual act of poetic creation. The second doubt emerges from the former and has to do with the fact that choosing between temporalities (modern Western or indigenous Andean) presupposes that Vallejo's writing must be the symptom or expression of a determinate historical temporality or intersection of temporalities plural. What if the unconventional, nonlinear "temporality" that flickers across some of Vallejo's poems is intimately bound up with the conventions and materiality of lyric poetry? This question does not take us somehow "beyond" history (the conventions of the lyric poem are not forged in a vacuum). It merely takes seriously the idea that the historical appurtenance of a text is never a straight line.[1]

Postcolonial Theory on Semicolonial Times

The model of colonization/decolonization posited by the major figures of what has come to be known as postcolonial theory (namely, Edward Said, Gayatri Chakravorty Spivak, and Homi Bhabha) has as its object the era of capitalist territorial colonialism and imperialism that began at the end of the eighteenth century and drew to a close with the first stirrings of decolonization in the mid-1940s.[2] What, in broad terms, is new about postcolonial theory, what marks a clear theoretical and political departure from, say, the work of Frantz Fanon, is the theory's understanding of the process of decolonization. Fanon ruled out the possibility of transition. He was a revolutionary, not a reformist. He advocated a *tabula rasa*, "a total, complete and absolute substitution" of the colonizers by the colonized. In his view, "Decolonization, which sets out to change the order of the world, is, obviously, a programme of complete disorder."[3] The conceptual violence of Fanon's prose is the rhetorical corollary of the political violence that is the "naked truth" of decolonization: "The naked truth of decolonization evokes for us the searing bullets and bloodstained knives which emanate from it. For if the last shall be first, this will only come to pass after a murderous and decisive struggle between the two protagonists" (p. 28). It is worth remembering, as Stephen Henighan writes in a sensitive piece on Fanon and Alejo Carpentier, that the Fanon acclaimed by postcolonial theory was a writer on colonialism, not postcolonialism.[4]

Postcolonial theory developed in a changed political and theoretical context. The dominance of Marxism as the Left's principal alternative political model to capitalism had been eroded, and the apocalypticism of theoretical Marxism that fed Fanon's text subjected to the critique of poststructuralism, even if apocalypse resurfaces in the language of some of the latter's key figures. Particularly in the work of Spivak and Bhabha, whose debt to Jacques Derrida is acknowledged, it becomes theoretically impossible to countenance either a *tabula rasa* or a program of complete disorder. In the hands of Spivak and Bhabha, the word *postcolonial* comes to name not a condition that would come after a colonial time yet owe nothing to it; it designates, rather, a condition of temporal transition, a difficult process of decolonization in which an indigenous culture regains control after a period of colonialism but has to struggle with the legacy of the departed—albeit precisely not entirely departed—colonialist culture.

The phrase *indigenous culture* stands as a glaring generalization entrusted with the task of covering the entire social spectrum from an elite class hugely influenced by colonial culture to those sectors largely untouched by colonial mores. But, for someone like Spivak, the phrase remains important and is not to be abandoned just because it becomes difficult to think of a pure autochthonous culture uncontaminated either by the culture of the colonizer or the conceptual prism of Western knowledge. At the heart of Spivak's project lies a wish to recuperate what she variously calls a "third-world subject" that is not Western, "the unnamed subject of the Other of Europe," "the Other of Europe as Self."[5] In the last sentence of the last endnote of her essay "Can the Subaltern Speak?" she sets Peter Dews's analysis of poststructuralist thought "quite apart" from her own concerns, on the grounds that "the Subject within whose History he places Foucault's work is the

Subject of the European tradition" (p. 313). Her postcolonial theory is driven by a desire to explore representations of cultures that, though touched by Europe, are non-European in significant ways. Although there are important differences between Spivak and Fanon that should not be minimized, the two are united by a basic concern to criticize the overreachings of Western thought and to affirm those cultures that are non-Western. The above, cursorily summarized, describes the object and objective of the dominant form of postcolonial theory. It is worth holding onto two main points: first, the complex temporality of the postcolonial condition; second, the affirmation of non-Western, indigenous, formerly colonized cultures.

The colonialism that beset Latin America has a different profile from the one outlined above. Its beginnings date back to the end of the fifteenth century; its endpoint is more debatable. According to historiographical convention, there is an endpoint, called "independence," which supervenes somewhere between the second and last decades of the nineteenth century. From this perspective, colonialism as such was brought to an end: The colonies became ex-colonies, broken up and reconfigured into a series of new nation-states that were not Spain and not Portugal. That much is a matter of historical fact and is not in dispute. But there is another perspective, which is no less a matter of historical record. From this alternative perspective, decolonization never happened, or, as Jorge Klor de Alva puts it, "the postcolonial condition, strictly speaking, has yet to occur."[6] Indigenous groups continued both in the nineteenth century and in Vallejo's day to be colonized subjects of a political, economic, and cultural order that was not their own. If the British left India to the indians in 1947 (if it is possible to "leave" what one never really had) and France ceded Algeria to the Algerians in 1962, in the nineteenth century Spain and Portugal were forced to leave Latin America *to their own descendants*, the *Criollos*, who subsequently fought among themselves and against the indigenous populations to achieve domination. In a remarkably frank passage from his *Carta de Jamaica*, Simón Bolívar has no illusions about the Creoles' need to fight both the Spanish "usurpers" and the indigenous population, or "legitimate owners of the country":

> We [creoles] are neither indian nor European, but a species in-between the legitimate owners of the country and the Spanish usurpers: in short, *because we are Americans by birth and have inherited the rights of Europe*, we have to dispute these with the country's original inhabitants, while standing against the invasion of the

usurpers; thus we find ourselves in a most extraordinary and complicated situation.[7]

The intra-Creole battle for domination was played out between conservative Creoles looking to restore the most traditional elements of Hispanic society and their liberal counterparts bent on replacing the latter with Enlightenment alternatives. In both cases, Western Europe continued to act as an important point of reference. In the case of Peru, even after "independence" the social order remained little altered. This continuity from colonial times does not simply have to do with "structures," but with people. What Bolívar describes as the Creoles' in-betweenness cannot pass for a position of neutrality. As Nelson Manrique writes, in an excellent analysis of the Peruvian case:

> It is customary to underline the importance of the maintenance of the structures of colonial domination, evident in a number of practices: the restoration of the tributes paid by indigenous people to the state after independence (re-established in Peru under the term "personal contribution"), the retention of free labour services for the state (the old colonial *mita* transformed into "Labour for the Republic," public works for the state and the municipal councils, and, between 1920 and 1930, the "road conscription"); and the different legal status of indigenous peoples, enshrined in the legislation of the 1920s that treated indians as minors, placing them outside of the nation, into which they had to be "integrated." Indeed, indigenism played a significant role in this infantilisation of indigenous peoples.
>
> But it is not just that these structures remained in force until the beginning of the twentieth century, for there is a further continuity: *that of a social subject who embodied the continuity of colonial domination and who had led the thrust for Latin American independence— the Spanish American.* [. . .] Benedict Anderson has repeatedly emphasised the identification of this sector with that of the peninsular Spaniards with whom they were to break. The original creoles were sons and daughters of Spaniards, spoke Castilian Spanish, dressed, ate, thought and lived according to Spanish custom, and their aesthetic tastes and ethical preferences were the same as those of peninsular Spaniards.[8]

Although one can find justification for speaking of the "Latin" population of Latin America as postcolonial, a more accurate designation would be "colonial postcolonial."

However, the above is but one understanding of Latin American colonialism. There is another, arguably more widespread understanding, which posits a slightly different object. Take, for example, what Vallejo says of Peru in 1933, which appears at first sight merely to confirm what has been said about the maintenance of a colonial order beyond the moment of decolonization: "[Los] descendientes [de los conquistadores españoles] y los blancos de las inmigraciones posteriores, no han hecho sino conservar, reforzándola, aun bajo la República, esta misma estructura social bosquejada hace tres siglos."[9] In reality, the meaning of colonialism adumbrated by Vallejo has undergone a change. The colonialism to which he refers corresponds more closely to Lenin's model of imperialism, premised on the existence of an international division of labor between capitalist-imperialist center on one side and international proletariat in the peripheral countries on the other (the Peruvian elite would be just local agents of the center). For this reason, Vallejo writes not of a "post-" but of a "semicolonial" condition, all the while conceding that, in reality, Peru's fate is barely distinguishable from that of a "verdadero dominio colonial":

> Ciertamente, no es ya una colonia ni un protectorado, ni hay al menos ni residencia, ni admiración extranjeras constituidas oficialmente. Pero es sólo este sombrero lo que le falta a su carácter pleno y típico de verdadero dominio colonial. Porque el resto, es decir, la sustancia social colonial está allí, real, evidente, innegable. ¿En qué consiste esta sustancia social colonial? Principalmente en esto: que la clase o las clases dominantes están compuestas por razas diferentes a las razas indígenas que integran, en su mayor parte, las masas sometidas a servidumbre.[10] ("¿Qué pasa?," p. 183)

If there is temporal transition here, it is not attributable to a resurgent indigenous culture dismantling colonial power structures; it is the phenomenon of modern capitalism being grafted onto a colonial legacy. In the case of Peru, this graft amounted to what has been called "traditionalist modernization," which brought few of the advantageous social changes that can accompany economic modernization.[11] Although Vallejo sketches the internal relationship between the dominant classes and the "razas indígenas," or "las masas," in the following paragraph he fills out the picture to include the international dimension, the "centros extranjeros que intervienen en esos países [de América]": "Son los imperialismos, inglés o yanki, el segundo elemento que completa el carácter semi-colonial del país: su sujeción financiera a los imperialismos anglosajones" (p. 183). This second, twentieth-century colonialism to which Latin America is subject is what the Leninism of 1960s' dependency theory would instead call "neocolonialism"—recognition that the dominance in question proceeds not from direct rule but from the exercise of political, economic, and cultural influence at a distance.[12]

The Ghost of Lenin

There are thus two different understandings of Latin American colonialism, neither of whose object conforms to the object posited by postcolonial theory. In the first, Western colonialism is de jure all but laid to rest in Latin America in the nineteenth century, only for it to resurface de facto as an internal colonialism orchestrated by the sixteenth-century colonizers' direct descendants; in the second, colonialism comes to mean the neocolonialism outlined by dependency theory. My principal contention is that postcolonial theory can only begin to legitimize its embrace of Latin America by virtue of a misprision: by strategically conflating aspects of both of these understandings of colonialism. From the first comes the basic fact of colonialism and decolonization, which produces a new, postcolonial temporality (Spivak's first criterion); from the second, the premise of capitalist exploitation of dependent countries, which permits the recuperation of Iberian descendants, otherwise "colonial postcolonialists," as victims (and hence satisfies Spivak's second criterion). The result is a postcolonial narrative, whose objective is to cast Latin America (not just indigenous America) as the subaltern Other of the West, struggling to throw off a colonial legacy which comes from a West that it is not.

Leninism itself has a part to play in this narrative, which otherwise belongs to the history of Western liberalism. By reducing protagonism to a series of geopolitical antagonisms (First World/Third World, developed/underdeveloped, Western/non-Western), Leninism tends, first, to overlook the profound cultural ties that exist between certain groups in the dependent country and their antagonists in the countries of the center, and second, to homogenize cultural and ethnic traditions within the dependent country (the different races in Peru are ultimately reduced to the single factor of class in Vallejo's essay). In this schema, the adjectives Western or European are reserved for the "imperialists," consequently becoming inappropriate as designations for Latin America–born descendants of Iberia. This important difference of *position* is what legitimizes Iris M. Zavala to cite Alexander von Humboldt to the effect that "The creoles prefer to be called Americans."[13] The logic is compelling and has truth on its side: a different position and identity demand a different name. But this affirmation of difference can also peddle gross simplifications. Thus Zavala can say of Latin American Modernism that it helped create a "third world," "which was neither the past nor a satisfying present, but an open possibility which would be neither European nor North American" (Zavala, pp. 1–2). Suddenly the Western contents of Latin America are conjured away and replaced by the antagonisms of the politico-juridical realm: either we govern ourselves or we are ruled by "Europeans" or "North Americans" (it being understood that "we" are neither of those things). The choice, for José Martí, was clear and principled. So principled that Zavala sees the value of allowing his spirit to hover, anachronistically, over all the continent's colonial struggles. As a result, all New World descendants of Spain and Portugal are positioned as either colonial victims of a West that would be categorically different from them or voices inaugurating a postcolonial era. Despite his own residual Leninism (see chapter 2), Néstor García Canclini's "model" of Latin America's "multitemporal heterogeneity," which with good reason he does not name postcolonial, has the virtue of acknowledging the persistence of colonial forms beyond a strictly colonial moment and can potentially leaven the cultural traditions that Leninism tends to flatten out, such that the antagonisms of the politico-juridical sphere do not obscure the *cultural* continuities (which are themselves political) between Latin America and the West.[14]

Hence, and to return to our central subject, it is with a certain caution that one broaches the question of César Vallejo and *post*colonial theory. By accident of birth and by virtue of his education, aesthetic preferences, and even dress code, Vallejo was complicit in what was at best a semicolonial and at worst a colonial situation. To be *mestizo*, or a *cholo* as was Vallejo, is not ipso facto to have the totality of Andean indigenous and modern European cultures at one's fingertips, a point made by José María Arguedas when he says of Peru, quite simply, that "hay infinidad de grados de mestizaje."[15] As a *mestizo* from the northern sierra of Peru, Vallejo participated in certain non-metropolitan traditions but was greatly Europeanized.[16] Assimilating him to the position of the subaltern native informant, and making him in the process the spokesman of a postcolonial order, is intellectually and politically ingenuous. It is not a matter of denying the "Peruvianness" of Vallejo's writing, but of grasping the historical fact that European logico-semantics already form part of that Peruvianness to which they are being opposed.

Symbolist Imperial Nostalgias

How, then, does Vallejo position himself in relation to the respective temporalities of traditional indigenous culture and Western modernity? I shall take just two "moments" of Vallejo's production—one poetic, the other journalistic.

Vallejo's first collection of poetry, *Los heraldos negros*, makes space consciously, indeed self-consciously, for traditional indigenous Andean culture, though only by confining it largely to a section revealingly named "Nostalgias imperiales." In that section, in which the *modernista* exoticization of the pre-Colombian is unmistakable, indigenous Andean temporality is figured either as something predominantly past and remote or as that which stands outside time, "el reino de lo sin historia."[17] In the second of the four sonnets that comprise the poem "Nostalgias imperiales," the "anciana pensativa" ponders the past in a manner redolent of the way in which the aged mariner of Darío's "Sinfonía en gris mayor" contemplates distant lands. Where he meditates through a haze of tobacco smoke, she, cipher for pre-Colombian Andean cultures, muses while spinning, that is, while practising one of those cultures' great crafts. Vallejo depicts the *anciana* as actively elaborating a thread of continuity with pre-Colombian cultures, but also as petrified, "cual relieve / de un bloque pre-incaico"—as though she were a fossilized relic-detail of another, celebrated Andean technological past.[18] In the third sonnet, the oxen are compared to kings weeping over defunct domains (*muertos dominios*). The atmosphere is melancholic, senescent, decadent; in the oxen's "widowed pupils" the dreams have no memory of the time they are supposed to revivify, not because they are gloriously timeless, but because the past is so remote ("se pudren sueños que no tienen cuándo").

The three sonnets that comprise "Terceto autóctono" strike a different note, that of festival time. They process the festival's sights through the sound of the traditional song form, the *yaraví*, and distill both sights and sounds through the conventional visual and rhythmic form of the *modernista* sonnet. The *fête galante* of Darío's "Era un aire suave" becomes an autochthonous festival. The second line of the Darío poem, "el hada Harmonía ritmaba sus vuelos," is syllabically reworked in the third line of Vallejo's opening sonnet such that the source of music is not Greek Harmony, but the humble, telluric plough: "Es fiesta! El ritmo del arado vuela." The synaesthesia continues in a conceit that binds together color and music, sight and sound in the idea of an ancestral connection (blood) to the Incan worship of the sun (sacrifice): "En las venas indígenas rutila / un yaraví de sangre que se cuela / en nostalgias de sol por la pupila" (p. 62). The conceit is taken up in the last line of a final stanza that gives full recognition to the processing of Christian materials by pre-Colombian beliefs:

> Luce el Apóstol en su trono, luego;
> y es, entre inciensos, cirios y cantares,
> el moderno dios-sol para el labriego. (P. 62)

The stanza acknowledges the temporality that dominates the hybridization (it is a *modern* sun god) *and* takes its distance from the traditional (the modern sun god is *for the other*, "para el labriego"). The second sonnet abounds in *couleur locale* raised to epic proportions (the shepherdess's traditional clothing wraps her in a "humildad de lana heroica y triste"); while the last one depicts a river as drunk as the festival-goers as it simultaneously celebrates and mourns a time before time ("el río anda borracho y canta y llora / prehistorias de agua, tiempos viejos"). The three poems attempt a species of indigenization of symbolist topoi, "aquenando hondos suspiros" as Vallejo puts it in the first sonnet, in a stanza that sounds like a distorted echo of the opening verse of "Era un aire suave," replacing the violins with indian *quenas*. Ultimately, however, the poems clothe the indigenous in a symbolist aesthetic, such that the quotidian quechua words require italicization whereas the high-literary tropes of personification and hyperbaton remain the norm ("Y al sonar una *caja* de Tayanga, / como iniciando un *huaino* azul, remanga / sus pantorrillas de azafrán la Aurora").

The poem "Aldeana" continues the use of synaesthesia, mimicking the mournful monotony of the *yaraví*. In it the time of the indian is again figured alternately as the non-time of eternity or the time of death and the past, of "idilios muertos." But it is in "Los arrieros," from the section "Truenos," that we find the most explicit and most revealing statement of cultural difference expressed as temporal disjuncture. There the poetic persona watches an indian *arriero* heading slowly for the sierra with his donkey. As the *arriero* distances himself in space, the "I" distances him in time:

> Arriero, con tu poncho colorado te alejas,
> saboreando el romance peruano de tu coca.

> Y yo desde una hamaca,
> desde un siglo de duda,
> cavilo tu horizonte [. . .]. (P. 106)

The two subjects may live in the same place, the poem seems to suggest, but they do not live in the same time. I take seriously the expression "desde un siglo de duda" that Vallejo uses to position himself discursively as one removed from the representative of traditional Andean culture. Vallejo is conscious of his own modernity, of the legacy of doubt bequeathed by the death of God, and caution should attend efforts to make him into a prophet of multitemporal heterogeneity. For temporality is just what is denied to the *arriero*. The poem ends by making the place of the indian into the locus of the non-time of eternity. The neologism "los Andes / oxidentales de la Eternidad" highlights the temporal difference (the Iron Age versus the Modern Age) at the same time as it suggests, strictly speaking against the idea of eternity, the deterioration (the rusting, the oxidization) of the latter.

The conclusion that Vallejo is a modern, cut off from tradition and uncontaminated by it, is to be avoided. It is untenable to draw a clear distinction in the case of Vallejo's production between an ancient subject matter (i.e., pre-Colombian culture) and a modern aesthetic form (symbolism). Not only is the ancient culture resignified in the modern era, as we saw in "Terceto autóctono"; symbolism itself, as Raymond Williams observes, is at once symptomatic of its own historical time *and* expressive of an ancient, traditional temporality. Synaesthesia may well have invoked the contemporary moment through its appeal to immediate sensory experience, but it also sought to tap into a timeless spiritual realm: "Characteristically, in the Symbolists, as clearly in Baudelaire and again in Apollinaire, [the] form of poetic revelation involved a fusion of present synaesthetic experience with the recovery of a nameable, tangible past which was yet 'beyond' or 'outside' time."[19] In other words, symbolism can only be erected as a representative of the modern on condition that it bear witness to the porous, differential character of modernity.

"Nostalgias imperiales" and certain contiguous poems demonstrate that it is not enough to provide a taxonomy of the lexical and larger discursive elements of Vallejo's poetry that appear to articulate a specifically Andean indigenous vision of things. The most hackneyed tourist guidebook can effortlessly accommodate such a lexicon, the presence of which may betoken not the speaker's familiarity with the material but the distance from that reality with which he tries to populate his pages. It is noticeable in Vallejo's later poetry just how often the cultural and topographical references to things Andean are accompanied by the presence of exclamation marks (see "Gleba," "Los mineros salieron de la mina," and "Telúrica y magnética"), as though the author could only mention these things with a voice pitched precariously between a Marxist hyperbole celebrating the workers as Promethean force and a discourse that cannot quite have faith in them as realities rather than hyperboles.

The (Peruvian) Western Discourse of Modernity

Vallejo's journalism affords another insight into his relationship to the West. In an article entitled "Oriente y occidente," written in Paris in April 1927 and published the following month in Lima, Vallejo comments on a debate provoked by a Paris newspaper apropos of the relationship between East and West. Is "the Orient" waiting in the wings to destroy Europe or merely reasserting itself in the wake of European attempts to liquidate its economy and culture? Vallejo sides with French academician Louis Massignon, in whose eyes Europe has exploited the Orient to the point of destruction, precipitating the "ruina absoluta del espíritu oriental."[20] The piece is marked by an apocalyptic discourse (Vallejo himself writes of Massignon's "voces apocalípticas, corneta de juicio final"), which overlooks the persistence of traditional forms of Oriental life that not even a rapacious West was powerful enough to annihilate. The last paragraph of the article says as much, though not without repeating, this time in relation to Latin America, the discourse of ruination and the figure of an oversimplified collective victim-subject:

> ¿Quién podría denunciar, una vez por todas, que en América hemos perdido también nuestra alma y que la hemos perdido por Europa? Porque en América (hablo de América Latina) los europeos nos han arruinado todo, filosofías, religiones, industrias, artes y, del mismo modo que en el Oriente, hay desde el arribo de Colón, un terrible vacío en nuestra vida. "Al Oriente sólo le queda ahora la raza y el país,"—dice Massignon. ¿A América le quedará también la raza y el país, al menos . . . ? (P. 210)

The "emptiness" is, of course, not so complete. But then neither is Vallejo's attempted identification with a "nosotros," which would be absolutely different from a European subject.

What is interesting about "Oriente y occidente" is that in denouncing the ravages caused by European colonialism, it musters many of the topoi of European Enlightenment thought: the preeminence of spirit, modernity as self-critique, and the importance of disinterested knowledge (Vallejo is at pains to stress the fact that Massignon is a "free writer," in the pay of no one, speaking simply "as a man"). Moreover, Vallejo identifies the need for industrialization, for technological and socioeconomic modernization in accordance with a European model of capitalism, as a prerequisite for Oriental resistance to Western colonialism. In sum, in questions bearing on spiritual and material concerns, Vallejo's anti-imperialist perspective is notably shaped by the language and logic of the Enlightenment, which thereby becomes something other than European, becomes something Peruvian. Vallejo participates in—and in so doing redescribes—the European trajectory of Enlightenment and modernity, appropriating the idea of rational critique and turning it back against Europe itself to denounce the latter's barbarism. Unlike the Romantics, Vallejo advocates industrialization, and thereby instrumental reason, together with progressive reason, as a pragmatic means by which the East can put itself in a position of strength from which to counter the West. It is a project with a clear sense of direction: forward and onward, leaving superstition and obscurantism behind, leaving Europe's own prejudices and despotism behind.

For Vallejo, at least in the late 1920s, and once more at variance with the European romanticism that otherwise left an indelible imprint on his writing, it is not, generally speaking, a question of returning to a past or autochthonous tradition that would be the crucible of a non-Western worldview. Nor does he frame the resistance to Europe in terms of a lateral movement into another, already extant, indigenous temporality running parallel with a modern variant. He will tend, rather, to depict the struggle for cultural resistance in terms of the need to create, to create a future. The insistence on artistic freedom, on the avoidance of mimicking European models, and on the principle of creativity are constant leitmotifs of Vallejo's journalism (in this he is nothing if not pre-post-*modernista*, echoing Darío's injunction from "Palabras liminares": "Y la primera ley, creador: crear").[21] Such themes guide to a considerable degree his rejection of surrealism and his later denunciation of the Latin American avant-gardes: In the case of the latter, the celebration of the new is, in Vallejo's harsh judgment, nothing other than the repetition of a project whose roots lie elsewhere and can thus be considered derivative. The main butt of Vallejo's invective is not then-contemporary Europe; he is at much greater pains to criticize those who do not have the independence and strength of mind to outdo Europe, or to out-Europe Europe. Without disguising his admiration for the European idea of autonomous fields of specialization and knowledge, he can say that if the European model of democracy has been imposed with terrible consequences, Europe's universities nonetheless remain creative powerhouses. By contrast, the Latin American centers of learning have failed to rival this creativity. Imitating European styles and ideas, they omit to copy the one principle—that of creativity—which would lead them out of the ghetto of derivativeness and set them free from "mesianismos de segunda mano."[22] It is perhaps for the same reason that, two years later in 1929, Vallejo can, first, pronounce that Latin America neither has nor will have for some time a "spirit" of its own;[23] second, set his face against the "continental megalomania" of those who maintain that the future belongs to Latin America;[24] third, and in the same article, harbor an admiring respect for both U.S. and Russian economic development, reserving his criticism, again, for those who disparage the achievements of both; and, finally, on hearing Latin American intellectuals arrive in Paris only to pronounce it déjà vu, attribute this to the fact that the capitals of Latin America are so Parisian.[25] These opinions do not predate Vallejo's conversion to Leninism. It is not the case that Vallejo was a naive Eurocentric until his consciousness was raised by Marxist thought and practice, which, in any event—and as Michel Foucault once said provocatively apropos of its understanding of historical time—was like a fish in water in nineteenth-century European thought.[26] Vallejo assumed the burden of Western thought (if burden it be) with good conscience. Because he understood the crucial point—which was subsequently obscured by dependency theory and has often remained so in contemporary critical discourse—that "Western" culture was not isomorphic with a geographical territory called Europe:

> La cultura occidental [. . .] no es un hogar doméstico y privativo de Europa. Es un organismo cuyos núcleos y brazos palpitan más allá de esa parcela geográfica y vertebralizan el espíritu de muchas otras sociedades contemporáneas, entre las que figura América Latina. ("La megalomanía," p. 328)

Although he does not explicitly say so in this piece, Vallejo's writings make it abundantly clear that the important thing for those in his position is not to reject Western thought but rather to appropriate it, using it where necessary against the West. My point is simple. There is a coherent solidarity between Vallejo's pronouncements on aesthetico-spiritual matters and those matters relating to economic and material projects. Formal experimentation in art is empty borrowing if it has no connection to sensibility, in the same way that the mere transplantation of European political or economic models is insufficient. In both cases, the injuncture is borrow and transform, borrow and create.

Poetemporality

I have taken time to guard against construing Vallejo as an indigenous Andean native informant and have striven likewise to suggest that Vallejo's journalism of the late 1920s is marked by European visions of modernity—not because Vallejo desperately wants Latin America to be Europe or the United States, but because he wants it to be more enlightened, more democratic, and more creative than those powerblocs. But what of the less explicit ways in which a traditional Andean temporality might find its way into Vallejo's work? The remainder of this chapter examines the alternative critical strategy deployed by William Rowe in relation to Vallejo's poetry written in Peru. Drawing on García Canclini's idea of multitemporal heterogeneity to produce one of the most original and stimulating contributions to criticism on Vallejo, Rowe shifts the debate away from the task of identifying a manifest indigenous subject and thematics. Rather, he explores what he believes to be a more oblique indigenous knowledge, which makes its presence felt in Vallejo's writing. Central to this shift is the recognition that Vallejo's refractory, avant-garde aesthetic necessarily prevents such knowledge from emerging in an explicit, conventional way. Rowe's strategy also takes me to the nub of the question left in abeyance. To what extent does the complex temporality of Vallejo's Peruvian poems belong to a non-Western culture or a postcolonial condition, and to what extent is it a conventional property of modern poetry itself?

In his inaugural lecture, "Trauma and Memory: César Vallejo and the Poetics of Time in the Peruvian Twentieth Century," Rowe addresses the idea of progress that animates the Western discourse of modernity, that is, the commonly held belief that history moves forward toward ultimate developmental goals. Rowe's claim is that Vallejo's poetics does not respect this discourse and temporal direction. Commenting on *Trilce* VI, he reads grammar anthropologically, applying the idea of different cultural temporalities to the different grammatical tenses confusingly at work in the poem's opening lines:

> El traje que vestí mañana
> no lo ha lavado mi lavandera:
> lo lavaba en sus venas otilinas,
> en el chorro de su corazón [. . .]. (P. 175)

For Rowe, the temporal incongruence is produced by time itself, by the presence of another, competing, specifically Andean conception of chronos: "In the Andean idea of time, the person imagines the past in front, as something known, whereas the future is behind one's back, unknown."[27] In support of this conception, Rowe cites the end of the poem, where Vallejo takes up the idea of "tomorrow" in the lines "Qué mañana entrará / satisfecha, capulí de obrería, dichosa / de probar que sí sabe, que sí puede / ¡COMO NO VA A PODER! / azular y planchar todos los caos." This is strictly undecidable. The Western conception of time is similarly unsure of the future and there is no clear sense here that the poem is gesturing to what is most different about the Andean conception, namely, its location of the past in front and of the future behind. (The larger issue here is whether the insistence on uncovering a uniquely Andean time does not rest on a Western philosophical prejudice, that is, the uncritical belief that a theory of time might accurately represent the experience of time.)[28]

Equally undecidable, though more convincing, is Rowe's explanation of the ironing image that ends the poem and that signifies more than the traditional idea of the female giving shape and order to the world:

> In Santiago de Chuco, there was a particular occasion on which a woman might be seen ironing in the street. When a woman's husband died, she had to stay indoors for ten days. On the tenth day the custom was that she would emerge from the house and iron the dead man's clothes in public. After that, she went to the cemetery, to pay respect to the dead man's grave. This ritual includes within it the Andean indian idea that the soul of a dead person remains in the vicinity of where they lived until some two weeks have passed. The mestizo ritual differs from the practices of the indians, who do not use irons—their hand-woven clothing does not need it; where indians wash the clothes of the dead person in a river, the mestizos of Santiago de Chuco make ironing into a ritual act. (Rowe, p. 5)

Rowe concludes:

> Inside Vallejo's image—in the way it is made and the way it works—there is a Peruvian time. The sense of time is generated through a particular, localized perception: the sound, sight and smell of a woman washing and ironing, and the feel of a woven cloth as it is smoothed. (Rowe, p. 5)

Aside from the question of whether the poem is about ironing or washing, there is a significant omission and a strategic generalization on Rowe's part, which allows him to iron out the chaos of other readings. Rowe opts for the broad cultural narrative: in this "Peruvian time," the image of the ex-lover washing and ironing "produces the future [. . .] generated by social ritual" (Rowe, p. 5). Again, the social, communal nature of Andean societies is invoked. But is it really "Peruvian time" that is in play here? I shall organize the rest of the chapter around two alternative ways of reading the temporalities that intersect in the poem.

Two Alternatives for *Trilce* VI

First reading: The word *traje* in *Trilce* VI refers literally to the persona's clothes and metaphorically to his soul. The word *alma* appears later in the poem ("mi aquella / lavandera del alma") precisely as that which is washed by the loved one. (Vallejo uses the same technique of describing the immaterial internal soul as though it were something physical to be worn externally in the expression, "Ponte el alma" from "Los desgraciados.") She washes his clothes and, in a reworking of the Christian idea of the host, she washes his soul in her veins. But there is another dimension, which Rowe elides by ignoring the second stanza, where it becomes clear that what the image produces is the possibility of a very personal, individual ritual, the ritual of writing:

> A hora que no hay quien vaya a las aguas,
> en mis falsillas encañona
> el lienzo para emplumar, y todas las cosas
> del velador de tanto qué será de mí,
> todas no están mías
> a mi lado.
> Quedaron de su propiedad,
> fratesadas, selladas con su trigueña bondad. (P. 175)

Now that the lover has left him, now that she no longer does his washing/cleanses his soul, his writing has dried up. She is his muse—more menial than the traditional muse but still the source of inspiration. The rituals of writing over which she used to keep vigil (including his mournful mantra "what will become of me?") have left with her and now belong exclusively to her like a seal of quality or copyright. With her departure goes the order and calm necessary for writing. Like the mother, the lover sets the world to rights, ensures that time is in place, guarantees that there will be a tomorrow. The poem is not about a Peruvian social time opposed to modernity; it is about the time of writing, and the male artist's dependence on female love and attention—even if, typically, the writer manages to fashion the poem out of the loss of those things that are supposed to be the source of poetry.

If the poem does thematize an Andean social ritual and conception of time, what does it do with them? In what sense does it take them seriously, accord them respect, and understand them on their own terms? The difficulty of knowing what the poem is drawing on is compounded by the avant-garde aesthetic, which works by condensation and obliquity, and does not elaborate *any* philosophy of cultural space-time in conventional propositional fashion. But does not that prove the point? If Andean ideas and practices are in play, they are not opposed, but are rather subordinated, to a thematics and compositional technique characteristic of Western modernity. Rowe ignores the question of resignification, which plays such a key part in García Canclini's work. In this case, the poet processes traditional materials into a modern symbolic and economic circuit attuned to the dictates of individualism, ripping the materials out of their traditional context with no attempt to recontextualize the imagery. If we return to that strange *mélange* of tenses in the poem's first line, and to Rowe's efforts to read grammar anthropologically as the sign of an autochthonous Andean temporality, we may counter that the temporality in question is first and foremost that of poetry, specifically that of modern Western lyric poetry, which, as Octavio Paz maintains, is itself conventionally opposed (or at least would like to see itself thus) to the linear time of the modern age:

> Abolition of yesterday, today, and tomorrow in the conjoinings and couplings of language. Modern literature is an impassioned rejection of the modern age. [. . .] Like their Romantic and Symbolist predecessors, twentieth-century poets have set against the linear time of progress and of history the instantaneous time of eroticism or the cyclical time of analogy or the hollow time of

the ironic consciousness. Image and humor: rejections of the chronological time of critical reason with its deification of the future.[29]

In the desire to challenge the hegemony of Western modernity, Rowe imagines that opposition to it could come only from outside. Thus, in the same address, he sees in Vallejo's poems of mourning further evidence that the poet has rejected the dominant modern concept of time. The temporality of the poems *in memorium* may be viewed as a sign of a childhood lived "in the non-modern world of Santiago de Chuco, in a different time-frame or temporality." In them "there is no progression from past to present: then and now are equally present, the dead brother is still there" (Rowe, p. 6). Yet, the implied opposition between the modern and the nonmodern, each located in a specific place, negates García Canclini's point about their intersection. Santiago de Chuco is already shot through with the modernity to which it is being opposed. The question concerns the degree of hybridization, not whether hybridization exists. Less trenchant but more persuasive is Rowe's statement that the poems of mourning suggest "*a fissure in the fabric of time*, specifically in the notion of time as moving toward the goals of maturity and progress" (p. 6; my emphasis). We can go further. It is not a cultural temporality radically opposed to Western modernity that fissures modern time in the poems; in play and at play, aside from the simulation of a very real psychological time (Rowe speaks of the "failure to complete the business of mourning"), is the temporality of the modern lyric. The poems harbor the Romantic desire to destroy the present while exploring the *other* time, that "time before time" (which is still a time), the time of childhood (Paz, p. 44). The crucial point about "A mi hermano Miguel," for example, is that there precisely has been a progression beyond childhood, toward that limit-point (that is death) which begets mourning. The poem may not prioritize either past or present, but it presupposes that there is a difference and dramatizes the pathos of one who both glimpses that basic fact of temporality and tries to deny it. These poems illustrate with poignant brilliance that there is, as Rowe says, "no sense of overcoming or transcending childhood" (p. 6). This does not mean that the poems suggest we remain in childhood, that we are not engaged in a process of becoming-adult. I would venture to say that only in Vallejo's poetry does one encounter the disruption of a linear temporality otherwise left untouched in his propositional writings. But we miss the essential if we do not also understand that disruption comes as standard in the personal lyric. It is a generic, conventional feature of lyric discourse, of the time of modern poetry. Of modern Western poetry. Of modern Peruvian Western poetry.

In one sense, nothing that has been said above threatens the socio-historical reading of Vallejo's work. To emphasize the conventions of poetry is not to see it somehow cut off from society. The time of modern Western poetry, which since the Romantics wants to be out of step with the socius, is marked at every turn by dialogue with the social sphere. That Vallejo draws upon the modern Western lyric tradition can be explained, *pace* García Canclini, by saying that the respective temporalities of Peru and the West intersect in important respects, even if they are by no means fully synchronized. Cultural forms enjoy a relative autonomy and do not necessarily move to the same rhythms as the broader historical temporality (Vallejo can be grappling with "modernist" aesthetic forms that are out of kilter with an otherwise relatively unmodernized socius). The connection between high-cultural production and historical temporality remains secure: victory to the cultural historian. In another sense, however, Vallejo's work cannot but threaten, as it is threatened by, the narrative of history. Is every grammatical lapsus, every instance of catachresis, an anthropological symptom or expression of a determinate historical time? Such is the causal reductionism of cultural history. García Canclini is absolutely lucid on this point. In his view, the reductionism merely puts high-cultural forms in their place, a very small place in the scheme of things. At stake, for him, is counterhegemony, not grammatical slippage.

The reductionism that consists in seeing every poetic detail as the faithful reflection of a larger, determining historical context leads to the curious prejudice that would exclude an author's own previous writings from a given text's history. This omission of the fact that literary texts process materials "internal" as well as apparently "external" to literature is exposed by the second alternative reading of *Trilce* VI. In a fascinating piece on intertextuality, Federico Bravo has shown the extent to which the meaning of *Trilce* VI becomes clear if one accepts the "autophoric" reading of its enigmatic central lines "en mis falsillas encañona / el lienzo para emplumar":

> Beyond what the poem "suggests" through its metaphoric, symbolic or iconic organization, and beyond the biographical facts which inevitably show through [. . .], the text is organized as an autonomous signifying system analyzable from within. Thus,

what is *plum(b)ed* [*encañona*] or looms *behind the paper* across which the poet's *plume* flows is, in fact, *another text* which, in the manner of a stencil, shows through the paper as it guides its writing. What is exceptional in this new decanting of writings is that the text does not here invoke an outside textual referent, if I may call it thus, but sends us back to the writing of Vallejo himself, who, citing himself, merely states what (that) he is doing (it).[30]

That other text, the stencil-text or "poema-falsilla," is "Idilio muerto" from *Los heraldos negros*. I cite just a sample of the numerous parallels between the two poems that Bravo so expertly teases out. To the left of each arrow are snippets from "Idilio muerto"; to the right, fragments from *Trilce* VI: " '*planchaban*' → '*planchar*,' '*cañas* de mayo' → '*encañona*,' '*qué será de* su falda' → '*qué será de* mí,' '*blancuras por venir*' → '*mañana entrará / a entregarme las ropas lavadas*' " (Bravo, p. 22).

Two observations. First, inasmuch as it is a reworking of an already deployed trope, *Trilce* VI does not thematize the act of composition as an original moment of inspiration; it dramatizes the polytemporality of literary composition. (Bravo writes of the poem as an "autonomous signifying system analyzable from within" but contradicts that claim in the very act of uncovering a past stencil-poem.) This is not due to a text's anchoring in a determinate historical moment marked by the copresence of radically different cultural space-times, but to the fact that writing— even a writing that would define itself as exclusively "modern"—is, in its very constitution, a multitemporal heterogeneity. Words, phrases, entire forms are borrowed from—but bear the trace of—divergent pasts. Modern texts may borrow materials, and use them in ways unknown to previous eras; but it was not necessary to wait for Cubism to appreciate that producers of texts cut and paste from other times. Second, it is not just a matter of multiplying historical times, for poetry takes place both in and out of time. A text is patently marked by real historical events, by ideas and beliefs—not to mention other texts—which recognizably occur in real time; but it is not tied to them and, in a no less "real," no less "empirical" sense, could not function without cutting itself off from the time and place of its birth. We do not need to reimport a universalizing, transcendental theory of art as that which takes place somehow *outside* time. The poem is neither in nor out of time, but out of joint. To dismiss the transcendental argument *absolutely* is to repeat that move of modernity's that consists in leaving behind the past (or tradition) as obsolete.

The Peruvian (Western) Discourse of Modernity

In the strictest sense, there is no text that is not a multi- or polytemporal heterogeneity, or whose temporality is not aporetic.[31] This assertion does not invalidate the anthropologico-historical understanding of temporality. It merely warns against the historicizing excesses of the latter, which ends up freezing out historicity. What García Canclini and the narrative of cultural history can nevertheless help us to understand is that Vallejo's challenge to the colonial order comes not from a postcolonial, Andean indigenous temporality but from what, for want of a better term, one might call a "progressive discourse of modernity" (if the problematic temporal schema of that discourse is accepted, so too is its principle of critique and emancipatory ideals). But to speak thus can only begin to make sense if we depart from modernity's image of itself as a great moment of temporal rupture, applying to the text of modernity what we have said about writing in general. Modernity, too, would be a multitemporal heterogeneity. Modernity would not simply denote a time after the age of tradition that might have the European scientific revolution as its starting point and be considered an exclusively Western affair, with Vallejo yet another sad epigone of misplaced ideas. Modernity hosts ideas that go back at least to Ancient Greece; which are not exclusively Western in origin; and which are taken up *and reworked* by "semi"-Europeans. In Peru, and in the hands of Vallejo, they become not simply Western ideas, but Peruvian Western ideas.

Are such ideas "progressive"? Octavio Paz writes that the newly independent countries of Spanish America "went on being the old colonies; social conditions remained unchanged, but now reality was hidden under layers of liberal and democratic rhetoric."[32] We do not have to concur with Paz's hyperbolic pessimism (the old colonies did change in that they became republics) to appreciate the sentiment that motivates it: Spanish America is no ordinary postcolonial society. Paz's remark has the added merit of returning our attention to the specific aspect of that society in which Vallejo intervened: namely, "rhetoric." Vallejo's intervention was doubtless a strange one, which can only be said to "represent" an already existing terrain, native informant, or postcolonial subject if one adopts a language mired in the invasive mimeticism—with its deep roots in Western philosophical soil—that such an intervention is trying to resist. If there is any value in labeling Vallejo's writing postcolonial, it would be as a way of describing its displacement of colonizing rhetorical forms, such as a Spanish-derived *academicismo* and a fossilizing *modernismo*. Insofar as Vallejo's work could not have been articulated without these forms Vallejo was unavoidably complicit in semicolonial times.[33] The phrase semicolonial times is not just to be understood in Vallejo's sense (of neocolonialism), but as a historical conjuncture characterized by the perpetuation of a colonial order on the part of a postcolonial Latin population. In such a conjuncture, Vallejo's modernism neither represents nor liberates all. And yet it remains legitimate to qualify his work as progressive. The emancipatory ideal is strong in his journalism and in his poetry there is already a departure from the Enlightenment's view of the popular classes as a drag-factor on a country's progress. In a different essay, Rowe cites William Carlos Williams's harsh view that Eliot's *The Waste Land* was catastrophic for American letters in "making it difficult to bring local American experience and the local spoken language into poetry."[34] I can sacrcely think of a better way to encapsulate one of Vallejo's poetic achievements than to say that what was apparently made difficult by Eliot became easier with Vallejo. His poetic embrace of the "vulgar, childish, peripheral" (Rowe) is not at adds with the Western tradition, but with "the dominant Western tradition" (the phrase, without comma, is Rowe's).

CHAPTER 6

Borges and a Differently Colored History

¿Tocar a nuestro concepto del universo por ese pedacito de tiniebla griega?

—Jorge Luis Borges

En el instante en que se presenta esa idea [del Eterno Retorno], varían todos los colores—y hay otra historia.

—Friedrich Nietzsche

Borges wrote repeatedly—obsessively—about the stubborn contradiction between conventional linear time and the (Greek) time of eternity.[1] The present chapter relates this "habit" to the broader question of Borges's understanding of tradition and modernity. Or, rather, traditions and modernities. For in Borges, both tradition and modernity may be taken in two main ways. Tradition is the popular cultural forms, figures, and social relations of the nineteenth-century Southern Cone, but also the order of revealed knowledge about the world that held sway before the advent of secular modernity. Modernity is the (problematic) name given to a historical phase of socioeconomic development, but also an aesthetico-philosophical condition characterized by a questioning of received knowledge and authority, and by the production of novelty. The interest of the relationship between tradition and modernity, and between eternal and linear time, lies in their messy entanglement, not in their separateness. Modernity may be dominated by *el tiempo que pasa*, but it is not reducible to it; tradition may have been dominated by *la identidad que perdura*, but is not oblivious to the river of successive time.[2] In Borges, the time of eternity is one "habit" among many used to criticize modernity and affirm tradition, even if, as Pierre Menard came to understand, the direct recitation of fragments of tradition necessarily alters it.

Though I refer freely to poems and short stories alike, the chapter is structured around a series of essays, from *Historia de la eternidad* (1936) and *Otras inquisiciones* (1952), which foreground the question of time. The essays allow me to illustrate two of my arguments explicitly. First, their insight into the development of contemporary thinking on time both confirms the importance of linear chronology and highlights how unsatisfactory the notion of linearity is. On at least two occasions, in essays on time from 1936 and 1944, a lengthy passage from Borges's earlier *El idioma de los argentinos* (1928) is abstracted from its "original" context and grafted onto "later" work. These punctiliously dated essays convey a real sense of historical situation at the same time as their explicit graftology exemplifies, at least to a degree, Borges's point about circular time: namely, that any given present time, *and hence the very idea of modernity understood as a going beyond of a premodern historical phase*, is perpetually haunted by ghosts from the past—not least Greek ones. Borges knew better than most that the relationship between a text and a context is always a strange one, that his use of the Greek abstraction is a limit-case of the general condition suffered by all writing and intellectual production. If this condition is graphically illustrated by essays from the 1940s, which incorporate a fragment from a decade and a half earlier, it is no less true of the 1928 text itself: even in its original context, a text may already be a citation taken from an anterior time and place. All texts are negotiations with—and alterations to—other texts and contexts. As such, to attempt to reconstruct a text's meaning by appealing narrowly to the historical moment of its production is to exhibit a dearth, rather than an abundance, of historical sense.

Second, the uncharitable reading of Borges's graftology affirms thus: so many years, so much change in the world, yet so little intellectual development. Beatriz Sarlo's hypothesis is that Borges's recourse to nineteenth-century Argentine culture is a flight from the rapidly modernizing Buenos Aires of the 1920s and 1930s.[3] According to this logic, his recourse to the *pedacito de tiniebla griega* would be the most hyperbolic instance of historical evasion, a flight not just from a determinate historical moment, but from historical time itself. At least momentarily.[4] To dismiss Borges's use of the time of eternity as a mere "flight" from the present (a trope Borges himself deploys, as we saw above) is to overlook the connection between his graftology and (Southern Cone) modernity, and miss the degree to which his fascination with Greek time, and with other forms of traditional deterministic thought (most notably the three religions of the Book), has serious ethico-political resonances *in a specific historical context*. As well as constituting a typical modernist reaction against literary realism, Borges's use of the time of eternity is a flight from and a critique of certain "modern" habits of thought that formed part of the fabric of 1940s' Argentina. Following Borges's nomenclature, these habits may be gathered under the rubric of nominalism. Borges takes issue with modern nominalism on the grounds that its desire for particularity ends in a self-regarding affirmation of uniqueness. Nationalism narrowly conceived would be the extreme face of this nominalism. Nationalism foregrounds the question of what counts as belonging to, and what falls outside the confines of, a so-called given national context. We recall that 1940s' Argentina, though officially nonaligned in the Second World War, was unofficially strongly proaxis. In response to nominalistic nationalism, Borges's recourse to eternal time and other topoi of tradition is an affirmation of supranationalism. The little piece of Greek darkness manifestly brings with it the risk of Platonic universalization. But one does not begin to get the measure of this risk until it is understood that what is called Platonism to a certain extent cannot be avoided, and, second, that a risk is risky precisely insofar as it carries positive as well as negative consequences. If no good could come of a risk, it would be a wholly predictable (negative) affair and thus no risk at all. The point about Platonism is that it may at times, especially in dark times, just be worth the risk.

The History of Eternity

The essay "Historia de la eternidad" begins with Plotinus's *Enneads* and with a gambit designed to emphasize the incommensurable distance between Ancient Greece and modern Western ideas of time. In order to understand the nature of time, the Greek text affirms, one must first understand eternity, given that eternity is, "según todos saben," the model of time. The essay proceeds schematically ("en cinco o seis nombres") to chart the history of the idea of eternity from Platonism to Christianity. What all variants of the idea share, Borges affirms, is the notion of simultaneity. In Plato, past, present, and future are laid out in the timelessness of the "inmóvil y terrible museo" of Platonic archetypes (p. 18).[5] Eternity and simultaneity presuppose one another in that they both abolish the arrow of time. In the Platonic doctrine of Forms, the Idea of the just, for example, which exists in the Form of the Good, is not subject to time and must therefore be such that it can be apprehended in an instant—though only, of course, by the supreme Form of the Good.

The second section of "Historia de la eternidad" moves from the Good to God, from Plato to Christian theological disputes and the part played by the doctrine of eternity ("our eternity") in combating gnostic heresy. The gnostics had cast doubt on the unity of the Trinity by questioning the logic of its temporality. If the Word is engendered by the Father, and the Holy Ghost by the Father and the Word, it follows that the Father is anterior to the Word, and both of these to the Holy Ghost: the Trinity is dissolved. In the face of this dissolution, Bishop Ireneo "inventó un acto sin tiempo." For this defender of orthodoxy, the double process whereby the Father generates the Son, and both the latter emit the Holy Ghost, does not happen in time. Rather, it exhausts past, present, and future once and for all. In one fell swoop, God is able to register every moment that is, has been, and will be, every possible and every impossible permutation. The world can thus take on temporal dimensions, breaking free of the immobilizing Platonic Idea. Eternity now belongs with God and is God; it is the attribute of God's boundless mind.

Borges's history of eternity turns out to be a battle between the two great doctrines of Western theological and philosophical thought: on the one hand what Borges calls realism, that is, Platonism predicated on the primacy of the generic or ideal world of Forms, and on the other hand nominalism, that is, Aristotelianism, which grants more space (and time) to experience and worldly detail. Plato makes a sharp division between the sensible and the intelligible worlds. The sensible world is the world inhabited by humankind and particulars. Particular things partake of the universal idea (say, of the just), but they are fallible and changeable. Only in the intelligible world of the Good, only in the realm of ideal Forms, is there to be found the permanent and unchanging essence of the just. In Aristotle's view, reality is not two but one. We can only understand the opposition between the sensible and the intelligible if there is some means of going from one pole to the other. For Aristotle, the world is a self-enclosed sphere in which there are only differences of degree. This view of things moves Aristotle to accord greater value to particulars and the dynamism of matter.[6]

Borges's account of the two traditions attracts the following *mise au point*, a seemingly gratuitous observation concerning "our" own unconscious nominalism: "Ahora, semejantes al espontáneo y alelado prosista de la comedia, todos hacemos nominalismo *sans le savoir*: es como una premisa general de nuestro pensamiento, un axioma adquirido. De ahí, lo inútil de comentarlo" (p. 28).[7] And yet *comentarlo* is just what Borges will do. He will insistently criticize this "premisa general" of the modern age, which we know better as empiricism. And it is as part of his critique of an empiricist modernity that Borges's embrace of eternal time may usefully be understood. Before considering the ways in which Borges uses the time of eternity to criticize the nominalist axiomatic of modernity, it is necessary to refute the suggestion that Borges was himself a nominalist. This will have the added advantage of specifying the kinds of modernity and tradition that are in play in Borges.

The Question of Modernity (and Tradition)

In the final analysis, Beatriz Sarlo presents Borges as a nominalist. Or let us say she intimates that, at the level of both philosophy and sensibility, Borges is a modern. Sarlo, it should be remembered, stands in the vanguard of a form of sociocultural criticism that is itself a present-day avatar of nominalism. Sociocultural criticism is not interested in Borges the "universal" writer. Its focus is on the Borges who belongs to a particular time and place, and who can responsibly be understood only in that context. In Sarlo's view, Borges is an *orillero* working on and in the border between a modernity and tradition that are specifically Argentine. The modernity in question refers to a period of accelerated modernization consolidated in the 1920s, while the tradition is that of the Argentine nineteenth century. The "Landscape for Borges" that she sketches out is that of a Buenos Aires undergoing huge transformation:

> Buenos Aires in the 1920s and 1930s. Every attempt at periodization is controversial, but these decades undoubtedly witnessed spectacular change. At issue is not just the aesthetic avant-gardes and economic modernization, but modernity as a cultural style permeating the fabric of a society that offered little resistance, either politically or socially. The socioeconomic processes set in train in the second half of the nineteenth century altered not only the urban landscape and ecology of the city, but also the lived experiences of its inhabitants. (P. 9)

Sarlo quickly adds that Buenos Aires is a scion not only of socioeconomic modernization but of the intellectual projects of modernity elaborated by Domingo F. Sarmiento and Juan Bautista Alberdi respectively. Her major point is that while the overwhelming majority of twentieth-century Argentine intellectuals sided with the Sarmiento paradigm of the city, Borges embraced both the Sarmiento project and the celebration of rural life encapsulated in José Hernández's poem *Martín Fierro*. However, in the urge to put Borges in context, Sarlo's text paints a misleading landscape, eliding the extent to which Borges's engagement with tradition entails a tradition older and substantially different from that of nineteenth-century Argentina, which nevertheless remains crucial in his literary imaginary. The problem may be formulated thus:

1. On the one hand, Sarlo's periodic assertions of the ambivalence of Borges's project are crystal clear. Thus she locates Borges as one of a younger, parricidal generation of modern writers opposed to the sclerotic traditionalism of the literary establishment (represented by the Centenario, *Nosotros, La nación, modernismo* and, above all, Leopoldo Lugones) at the same time as she recognizes that Borges is not unremittingly modern:

> Still very close to Borges stood the nineteenth-century gauchesque literature of the River Plate, the writings of Sarmiento, the almost family saga of the civil wars that preceded the organization of the nation state, the battles between indians and whites throughout implacable, bloody and unjust decades. These traces of the Argentine past never disappeared from Borges's work. Rather, one of his goals was to gather up the scattered fragments of that tradition and to rearticulate within his own writing the writing of other Argentines who had now disappeared. (P. 4)

As a consequence, the Borgesian metropolis is simultaneously the place of change and the site for a mythopoesis that invents a corner of the suburb untouched by modernization.[8] In Borges and others besides, there is a clear refunctionalization of the past, a strategic reinvention of cultural and literary tradition.

The reasons for the character that this refunctionalization assumes in Borges are fleshed out by Sarlo across many pages. It is clearly (and thankfully) no straightforward task to accommodate Borges within a history whose generic propensity to simplification he always warned against. But the manner in which Sarlo attempts to accommodate

Borges is scrupulously fairminded. Borges's rather classical aesthetic she views as an aristocratic reaction to (she does not say it is simply determined by) "a disorderly world that in the 1930s seemed to be tottering on the edge of irrationality [. . .]: the irrationality of fascism, communism—and of mass democracy" (p. 53).[9] Of course, and as Sarlo is swift to point out, mass democracy in Argentina was hardly in the ascendancy in those years. The September 1930 coup put paid to the first real experiment in Argentine democracy and led to the backlash of the *década infame*. However, Sarlo is right to draw a distinction between the hiatus in social reform that happened at the level of formal politics, and the dynamism of the larger process, that of socioeconomic modernization, which continued, albeit unevenly, to transform parts of the country. What concerned Borges and his friends in the intellectual elite was the massification of culture and society resulting from a catch-up modernization that, in the space of twenty years, had turned Buenos Aires into a modern city. Faced with the emergence of a working-class and popular culture shaped by a rapidly developing culture industry, and confronted with a more complex, more democratic, but more heterogeneous and threatening cultural system,

> Borges's response could be seen as the imposition of a principle of order in a world where immigration, multilinguism [sic], the new order constructed by the Radical Party which had governed from 1916 to 1930, the social unrest which followed the crisis of 1929, seemed together to spell the end of criollo hegemony over culture and society. (P. 54)

It may seem odd for Sarlo to interpret Borges's "abstract discipline of a philosophical and narrative situation" (p. 70) as a symbolic overriding of demographic and social change, when what had preceded this modernization was a postindependence period characterized by a violent quasi-feudal struggle in which disorder and the absence of an independent governmental and legal apparatus were the norm. It is explained, however, if we understand that there was *another species of order* in place, a premodern order that took the form of "personal ties of dependence, concrete services or obligations secured by traditional vows, and loyalty to the *patrón* or to other leaders." This alternative kind of bondage explains, for Sarlo, why the elite—including Borges, whose family ties bound him to the modernizers among the elite— were suspicious of modernity's tendency to substitute abstract relations for the traditional ties that, in their view, had secured order throughout the years of turbulence. Even if the preservation of privilege looms large in the equation, the elite's sense of insecurity was not solely the product of a reactionary viewpoint:

> Although the elite seemed satisfied with the modernization process (which opened up what appeared to be almost limitless economical opportunities), intellectuals found that the very process that had created modern Argentina was flawed by the absence of strong cultural bonds. Society was firmly entrenched, secularized and autonomous; but, as with all modern societies, its institutional and formal basis was deprived of the strong echoes of tradition and myth.
>
> Borges stated this sense of loss (or absence) in one of his first essays: what Buenos Aires needed badly, he wrote, was ghosts. [. . .] "Ghosts" imply a common ground and a sense of harmony with the past. In a society where modern institutions founded on written law had eroded traditional beliefs and "natural" bonds, the fact of sharing the same "ghosts" opened up, symbolically, the possibility of retrieving the sort of deep cultural awareness threatened by a modern republic itself riven by conflict. (Pp. 83–84)

2. On the other hand, two aspects of Sarlo's book confuse the debate surrounding Borges and modernity. First, and for reasons that bear on the book's hybrid condition as the scion of a series of grafts from other texts whose focus is Buenos Aires in the 1920s and 1930s, the book's discourse of the new (Sarlo writes of the "new physical spaces, and material and ideological processes" of the new metropolis) hovers insistently over its discussion of Borges and the avant-garde, even when its propositional content fully acknowledges their not-so-newness. Through syllogistic contamination, the city is synonymous with modernity;[10] the avant-garde with the city; ergo the avant-garde with modernity. This, despite the fact that contributors to the avant-garde literary magazines of the 1920s (*Martín Fierro, Prisma,* and *Proa*) were reformists rather than refuseniks; that their reformism was confined to "literary mores" (p. 99); and, finally, that their *raison d'être* lay in proclaiming a difference from *modernismo*, which amounted to promoting an internal difference within *criollismo* and thus in a sense reaffirming rather than rejecting the latter.

Martín Fierro's condemnation of the social realism and *lumpen* sentimentality of the literary group Boedo, together with its hostility toward the growing mass culture industry, was prompted by a concern with social class. By contrast, the avant-garde attack on specific Creole *modernistas* was anything but a blanket rejection of *criollismo*. What Borges and the avant-garde attempted, rather, was a "purification" of *criollismo*, curbing its bombast in favor of a more modern idiom, "the language that we truly speak, unencumbered by the frills of rhetoric," as Oliverio Girondo put it (p. 105). Sarlo writes of a new language ("avant-garde urban *criollismo*") and a new space before once more catching at herself. Language and space were new and very old. The "unresolvable contradictions" within *Martinfierrismo* are latent in the journal's name: a hero of traditional gauchesque poetry is mobilized for a program of avant-garde aesthetic renovation. Sarlo says all these things and more. In the meantime, the book beats out its rhetorical incantation to the modern.

Second, the effect of this hymn to a modernity in tension with *criollismo* is to misrepresent a crucial element of Borges's work, namely, his resistance to the nominalist fabric of modernity. According to Sarlo, what we have with Borges is two times in tension: a desire for the new and a nostalgia for the (*criollo*) past. Although the two attitudes may be ambivalent, their coexistence is not in doubt. Note that Sarlo is writing about Borges's poetry:

> His poetry was part of an aesthetic, a sensibility and an urban landscape experiencing a rapid process of change. His system of perceptions and memories linked him to the past; his poetic project, on the other hand, was linked to "the new." He worked under the influences of aesthetic renewal and urban modernization to produce a mythology which contained premodern elements but which was filtered through aesthetic and theoretical avant-garde principles. (P. 122)

If her picture of a gently ambivalent balancing of new and old is broadly true for the polemics of the 1920s and 1930s, it is not so a decade later, the decade of Borges's canonical short stories that form the substance of Sarlo's meditation (if she refers above to the aesthetic of his poetry, it is to the short fiction that she turns for textual support). Sarlo half-fits Borges into a Bermanesque paradigm of modernity without crediting the degree to which he repudiated the discourse of the new. It was not simply that he modified his praise of the new by complementing it with a gesture to the past; rather, he disowned in significant ways the juvenile celebration of novelty. And he did so for good reason, since his attachment to the past does not bind him exclusively to nineteenth-century Argentina. The reaction against modernity is more far-reaching, even if it takes place from within a certain modernity. Embracing an "era" altogether more premodern than Sarlo acknowledges, Borges "returns" us to Tradition with a capital T. When he takes us back to 1880s Uruguay, Funes is reading not just Locke but Pliny.

There is little doubt that Borges was a modern writer. He was profoundly attached not only to "aesthetic renewal" but also to Enlightenment modernity and, by extension, the general "philosophical" sense of modernity as secular nominalism—the savoring of the world's infinite variety, the production of endless novelty. The essential point, however, is that Borges was skeptical of the unholy alliance between the absolutist version of philosophical modernity, which wants to cut itself off definitively from the worthwhile learning and values of the past, and a no less absolutist (precisely because relativistic) "bourgeois" or even Peronist modernity, which makes a virtue out of some of the more crass elements of socioeconomic modernization. In opposition to that alliance, Borges follows much modernism in being in important respects antimodern.[11]

Sarlo may well be right when, exploring the reasons for Borges's return to nineteenth-century tradition, she entitles one of her chapters "The Question of Order." But the order in question is more premodern than she concedes. Borges participated in tradition. *Tradition as a critique of modernity made from the vantage point of a modernity that is not to be thought as a historical phase divorced from tradition.* Tradition in which, according to its most hyperbolic, most Platonic expression, knowledge is the revelation of the always already there. We recall the epigraph, from Francis Bacon, to the title story of *El Aleph* (1949): "Solomon saith: *There is no new thing upon the earth*. So that as Plato had an imagination, *that all knowledge was but remembrance*; so Solomon giveth his sentence, *that all novelty is but oblivion.*"[12] "Ni veré ni ejecutaré cosas nuevas," Borges writes in a poem from 1925.[13] The refusal of novelty is a denial of succession (and vice versa) and an opening up of another time.

A Personal (Platonic) Theory of Eternity

> Qué importa el tiempo sucesivo si en él hubo una plenitud, un éxtasis, una tarde.[14]

To see how Borges's critique of linear time dovetails with his critique of nominalism and, by extension, modernity, we must return to the first section of "Historia de la eternidad." On the face of it, things do not begin well. Borges appears hostile toward the Platonic version of eternity, pronouncing it more impoverished than the world it purports to encapsulate. He does not let it go, however, without leaving a footnote that suggests the intimate relationship between the temporality of Platonic thinking, the idea of the generic (*lo genérico*), and desire:

> No quiero despedirme del platonismo (que parece glacial) sin comunicar esta observación, con esperanza de que la prosigan y justifiquen: *Lo genérico puede ser más intenso que lo concreto*. Casos ilustrativos no faltan. De chico, veraneando en el norte de la provincia, la llanura redonda y los hombres que mateaban en la cocina me interesaron, pero mi felicidad fue terrible cuando supe que ese redondel era "pampa," y esos varones, "gauchos." Igual, el imaginativo que se enamora. Lo genérico (el repetido nombre, el tipo, la patria, el destino adorable que le atribuye) prima sobre los rasgos individuales, *que se toleran en gracia de lo anterior*. (*OC*, vol. I, p. 357, fn. 1)

The *adieu* is an *au revoir*. Borges's claim is that "glacial" Platonism might actually be the form of (hot) desire itself. The child's interest in the men and plains becomes passionate only when he learns their generic names *pampa* and *gauchos*. The individual traits of men and plains recede in importance as the generic category takes their place. From this point on, the fact that the first (childhood) experience was an experience of particulars is forgotten; instead, the experience of the particular seems now to come after the experience of the generic, such that every individual becomes a type. To that extent, knowledge is never contemporaneous with itself, but is always marked by a strange anteriority.[15] Roland Barthes calls it the Book of Culture—that storehouse of general categories, commonplaces, and stereotypes, which seem to precede and frame the apprehension of the object. The importance of *lo genérico* is a reminder of the part played by the subject's foreknowledge in the encounter with the other. Seven pages later, Borges expands on the idea that the intensity of the generic ("*Lo genérico puede ser más intenso que lo concreto*") is the psychology of desire. The key lies in the temporality of nostalgia. Nostalgia, above all the nostalgia of the exile, freezes a fondly remembered preterite moment such that the many and varied experiences of the sun setting become in the memory a single sunset. More awkwardly, Borges claims the same for the future, suggesting that the most incompatible hopes for the future can coexist simultaneously in our anticipation of them. In short, past, present, and future exist in a kind of intemporality. Or, as Borges says, "el estilo del deseo es la eternidad" (p. 364).[16] Immediately after the above, the final section of the essay contains Borges's "personal theory of eternity." It also contains, or rather it *is*, the first example of the grafting I mentioned earlier, a two-page excision from "Sentirse en muerte" from *El idioma de los argentinos* (1928) in which Borges recounts a nocturnal stroll in Buenos Aires that produces an ecstatic, difficult-to-define "experience" of eternity. Walking at night through unfamiliar quarters, deliberately *au hasard* (the premeditation involved in ceding to chance is tangible), he ends up in his childhood *barrio*, which he confesses to having possessed more through words than in reality. Standing on a street corner, his vision, which, the text says, is simplified by tiredness, is "irrealized" by its very typicality (*tipicidad*). What we are about to witness is the hybrid product of Platonism and expressionist nostalgia, a *personal* theory of eternity that is a personal *theory* of eternity: on the one hand, the individual experience; on the other, the theorization of that experience, which must necessarily pass by way of the generality of concepts and which is the fate of all thinking of the particular (this is why we are never done with Plato).[17]

Borges reflects that the place is the same as thirty years earlier, adding that whereas thirty years may not seem much in some countries, it is a long time "en este cambiadizo lado del mundo." The thirty years in question correspond closely to the years of Argentine modernization about which Sarlo writes. And yet, precisely at the point where a sense of lived history appears to distance the earlier epoch even further, the thought of being in that earlier time becomes a reality. A moment of "death," an ecstatic instant opens up an experience of eternity:

> Me sentí muerto, me sentí percibidor abstracto del mundo: indefinido temor imbuido de ciencia que es la mejor claridad de la metafísica. No creí, no, haber remontado las presuntivas aguas del Tiempo; más bien me sospeché poseedor del sentido reticente o ausente de la inconcebible palabra *eternidad*. Sólo después alcancé a definir esa imaginación.
>
> La escribo, ahora, así: Esa pura representación de hechos homogéneos—noche en serenidad, parecía límpida, olor provinciano de la madreselva, barro fundamental—no es meramente idéntica a la que hubo en esa esquina hace tantos años; es, sin parecidos ni repeticiones, la misma. El tiempo, si podemos intuir

esa identidad, es una delusión: la indiferencia e inseparabilidad de un momento de su aparente ayer y otro de su aparente hoy bastan para desintegrarlo. (P. 366)

I shall comment shortly on the importance for Borges's thinking about eternity of the nexus between night/"death" and abstraction. My principal concern at this point, however, is with the logic of Borges's text, a logic that is precisely more, or less, or more and less, than "thought." It is the logic of mathematical paradox. The "indiferencia e inseparabilidad" of moments describes the paradox concerning the impossible divisibility of an instant. If the difference between two moments could be located midway between the two, it would either still belong to both moments (in which case there would be no division and no seriality) or fall in an interval between them (and thus somehow fall outside time).[18] Borges uses this logic to claim that time is therefore a delusion.

The leap from that argument to the affirmation of eternal time is easily made. Given that life's experiences are limited in number, it is always possible that the same permutation of emotions, thoughts, and so on may coalesce to produce the same experience. As Borges puts it, "la vida es demasiado pobre para no ser también inmortal." What is interesting here is that a certain intellectual reserve marks the meditation, which Borges identifies elsewhere with Nietzsche's doctrine of the Eternal Return. Borges concedes that whereas the senses and emotions may well have been persuaded by this insight, not so the intellect, from whose "essence" the concept of succession would appear inseparable. In view of the logical reserve that recognizes the claims of linear time, the idea of eternity must remain at the level of "emotional anecdote." And, by the same token, the moment of ecstasy and the glimpse of eternity must remain in an account fully conscious of its own undecidability ("en la confesa irresolución de esta hoja").

It is symptomatic that in "Sentirse en muerte" it should be nightfall that makes space for the abstraction that is the prelude to eternity.[19] Strictly speaking, the *textual subject's* meditations on eternity are not the fruit of the diverse theologico-philosophical traditions or the contemporary advances in science and mathematics that left their mark on Borges, but rather are attributable to the work of a certain abstraction that interdicts history and chronology. These meditations will frequently be "caused" or activated by nightfall, "death," or "blindness," by an ecstatic moment of abstraction that, generally in the form of an irruption, precedes an uncanny event or hiatus in the flow of conventional linearity.[20] It is this moment of abstraction that, keeping the multiform world at bay, opens the way for thought, memory, and literature.[21] In "Sentirse en muerte," the critique of serial time and the irruption of eternity are vehicles for self-indulgent nostalgia. The wall is seen through a prism formed by Pythagoras, Anaxagoras, and the rose-, or celestial-colored spectacles worn by the nostalgic. Night, Ancient Greece philosophy, mathematical paradox, and Proust combine for nostalgia's sake to cleave the fabric of unrepeatable time, and with it the axiomatic of modern nominalism. Elsewhere (one is tempted to reintroduce history and chronology by saying "a decade later"), the critique of seriality has sharper teeth. Before elaborating on its relationship to nominalistic nationalism, I would first like to bring the story of Borges's essayistic engagements with time up to date.

The Eternal Return: '44, '46, '43, '44, '46 . . .

The essay from 1936 provided a potted "history of eternity" that went as far as Saint Augustine before ending on a personal note of nostalgia, which was at the same time an extrapolation of Platonism. In "La doctrina de los ciclos," written in 1934 and published slightly before "Historia de la eternidad" in 1936, the schematic history of philosophical inquiry into eternity is updated.[22] The essay begins with the latest avatar of the doctrine, Nietzsche's theory of the Eternal Return, before swiftly moving to refute it by means of, among other things, Cantor's set theory. "La doctrina" exhibits a skepticism toward the time of eternity that, with the notable exception of "Historia de la eternidad," will become more pronounced in subsequent essays. But it does not dispense with the Greek idea. In fact, the exposition and refutation of the idea consume a mere three pages of an essay that extends for a further five. What else remains to be said, one might wonder, once the truth of the doctrine has been disavowed? The question contains an impatience and a teleology that it is the essay's purpose to challenge. Borges does not have to subscribe absolutely to the "doctrine of cycles" to use it as a lever against the teleology, and violence, of a linear notion of time. He writes in "La doctrina" of a Saint Augustine who, refuting the ignoble suggestion that the world returns eternally, turns to Jesus as the *vía recta* allowing us to escape from the "laberinto circular de tales engaños" (p. 388).[23] The Augustinian metaphor harbors a violence and a certainty that Borges eschews in favor of the labyrinth as a more fitting metaphor of the mystery and complexity of the world. Blindness, too, will serve as metaphor for a searching that is not led by a dogmatic theo-teleology. The blind man can ill afford Augustinian certainty.[24]

As if to illustrate the point, "La doctrina de los ciclos" shapes as though to end with a "certidumbre final" but in fact ends in paradox. If we accept Zarathustra's thesis about the Eternal Return, Borges muses, why do not two identical processes (the present moment in which I type these lines and the future moment in which, after the finite number of permutations has been exhausted, I once more type these lines) agglomerate into one? What licenses us to continue speaking of them as two? Is it not the case that to speak of two, to resort to seriality, is to reinscribe successive time into the heart of the doctrine of eternity?[25] The paradox is much used by Borges. The real interest lies in what he says about the refusal to take on board the paradox. Since, he says, none save an archangel could possibly bear witness to the seriality in question, the doctrine can only be dogmatically affirmed, only validated by fiat. Such a state of affairs may in this case have little practical importance; but that the intellect should turn a blind eye to logical contradiction is more serious:

> ¿Basta la mera sucesión, no verificada por nadie? A falta de un arcángel especial que lleve la cuenta, ¿qué significa el hecho de que atravesamos el ciclo trece mil quinientos catorce, y no el primero de la serie o el número trescientos veintidós con el exponente dos mil? Nada, para la práctica—lo cual no daña al pensador. Nada, para la inteligencia—lo cual ya es grave. (P. 63)

This thinking of paradox is replayed in two of Borges's later meditations on time from the 1940s (which are precisely not altogether posterior). Both essays incur deliberate anachronisms and contradictions that complicate the image of thought as *vía recta* advancing steadily toward its goal (an image already complicated by the fact that the "update," "La doctrina de los ciclos," is followed by an essay, "Historia de la eternidad," which all but ignores the update). In "El tiempo circular" (1941–1943), Borges expands his purview to include not only the Platonic and Nietzschean strains, but also a third permutation of the Eternal Return, which Borges calls the least melodramatic and indeed the only truly imaginable conception of time. This third conception marks a pronounced shift in Borges's essayistic deliberations on time away from the principle of identity to that of similarity. It would be better, the essay implies, to construe the cycles of the Eternal Return as analogous rather than identical. In other words, the second experience of the street corner would not be the experience of 1800 and something; it would be *similar* to it.[26] At that point, good nominalists that we are, we can breathe a sigh of relief. And yet things are not so straightforward. Although conceding that the extreme version of the doctrine of circular time, even when premised on analogy rather than identity, remains hard to tolerate, Borges holds out for the general idea that there are a limited number of human perceptions, thoughts, and emotions that we will have exhausted by the time we die. And in his final major essay on time, "Nueva refutación del tiempo," with its two parts dating from 1944 and 1946 respectively, Borges complicates the picture still further, explicitly contradicting both the earlier text, and, more pointedly, the major premise of "Nueva refutación" itself.

Ignoring the drift toward the idea of analogy in "El tiempo circular," both parts of "Nueva refutación" initially regress to a hard-line negation of linear time as they advance the cause of the doctrine of cycles. Both articles provide a synopsis of idealism before proceeding to criticize its attachment to the idea of serial time (if matter and spirit do not exist outside the act of perception, why should time exist outside each present moment?). In the second, Borges cites the example of Chuang Tzu, who dreamt twenty-four centuries ago that he was a butterfly. He proposes that we imagine that one of Chuang Tzu's readers dreams that he, too, is a butterfly, and then that he is Chuang Tzu. What if, "por un azar no imposible," this dream repeats the master's dream in every detail? Borges then repeats phraseology from the first article almost verbatim:

> Postulada esa igualdad cabe preguntar: Esos instantes que coinciden ¿no son el mismo? ¿No basta *un solo término repetido* para desbaratar y confundir la historia del mundo, para denunciar que no hay tal historia? (P. 195)

Such a postulate is, as Borges would say, easily refutable. The dream of the acolyte could never repeat the master's dream in every detail for the same reason that Pierre Menard's verbatim version of the *Quijote* could not *be* the *Quijote*. The acolyte's dream and Menard's text are produced at different historical times, and although history may be jumbled up and disrupted, it is not to be annihilated. Dream and text may be similar to their respective precursors, but never the same. Strictly speaking, it would not have been possible to repeat so much as a single term.

In the end, though, both parts of "Nueva refutación del tiempo" seem to opt for Schopenhauer's vision of a permanent lived present, a world in which past and future exist only as constructs to aid human reason. Time is like an endlessly turning circle where the downward arc is the past, the upward one the future, and the uppermost point is the now, the present that is the form of all human life. However, just after citing Buddhist avatars of the "same" metaphor of the wheel, Borges suddenly performs a volte-face, which produces a radical internal bifurcation and temporal anachronism. Article "A" ends with a ghost from the past, once again the graft from "Sentirse en muerte," which, spliced into the text without comment, appears to confirm the eternal return by virtue of its very presence. Article "B" concludes (almost) with the famous concessive penultimate paragraph that reintroduces the time of succession:

> *And yet, and yet* . . . Negar la sucesión temporal, negar el yo, negar el universo astronómico, son desesperaciones aparentes y consuelos secretos. Nuestro destino [. . .] no es espantoso por irreal; es espantoso porque es irreversible y de hierro. El tiempo es la sustancia de que estoy hecho. El tiempo es un río que me arrebata, pero yo soy el río; es un tigre que me destroza, pero yo soy el tigre; es un fuego que me consume, pero yo soy el fuego. El mundo, desgraciadamente, es real; yo, desgraciadamente, soy Borges. (P. 197)

Why the bifurcating endings? Why reproduce the little piece of Greek darkness when it is clearly refuted in article "B"? I would suggest two reasons, the first having to do with thinking in general, the second with thinking in a specific place and at a specific time.

1. The first reason is that Borges follows the light of the Enlightenment in believing that the critical use of reason, even in support of a little piece of Greek darkness, is an ethical act. The point is that successive time is not a fact that is done with; it still remains open to a Greek challenge, to an Argentine Greek challenge. As Borges says in "Historia de la eternidad," to suppose (as does the modern conception of time) that everything past gets swept away is no less incredible than to imagine that everything is saved. The *And yet, and yet* . . . is thus the refutation of the refutation, but is only to be taken as the annihilation of everything that has gone before (everything in both articles and in all his other work besides) on condition that the latter has neither philosophical nor aesthetic, nor political value, and providing

that it somehow falls outside, or before, the reach of memory, such that the refutation refutes nothing.[27] In a phrase from "Una oración," from the prose version of *Elogio de la sombra*, Borges puts together two of the virtues of classical thought—justice and reason—which make up the ethics of philosophy. Although we are ignorant of the universe's designs, Borges writes ("Borges" prays), we know that "razonar con lucidez y obrar con justicia es ayudar a esos designios, que no nos serán revelados" (*OC*, vol. II, p. 392). To refuse to think lucidly poses an ethical danger, which is why "La doctrina de los ciclos" ends with a (very modern) defence of the ethics of the intellect, unhappy that seriality should be proclaimed by fiat. Ethics is a way of doing, not simply a doctrine.[28]

2. The second reason for Borges's decision to include the two endings of "Nueva refutación" has to do with the historically specific dimension of thought, and with the relationship of thought to the polis. In the above question of the ethics of thought, in the yoking together of justice, reason, and virtue, there is an opening onto politics. The philosophico-literary politics in question are not readily assimilable to the conventional politics of parties and constitutions. Eschewing programmaticity, they enjoy the benefits of a freedom not found in conventional politics, but frequently sacrifice the ability to exert meaningful influence. Yet if this textual politics is not reducible to conventional politics, it does not for all that take place outside the polis. Even if the act of thought itself alters the parameters of a context, the idea of which is used in classical thinking to surround, delimit, and determine thought; even if thought produces an anachronistic scandal in the heart of the present, thinking does not take place outside of any and every context.

The Context of Nationalism

Does it really matter that a story such as "Funes el memorioso," a *conte philosophique* about the impossibility of nominalistic totalization, dates from 1942 and is set in 1880s Uruguay? Let us recall the gist of the story, with the proviso that, on the surface of things, "Funes" is not an auspicious place to look for the time of eternity, since the moment of ecstasy gives on to abstraction and memory, though not eternal time.[29] But that is the point. Funes's inability to comprehend "la identidad que perdura" condemns him to a plethoric but ultimately impoverished appreciation of the world. Funes has memory in abundance, but his capacity to retrieve infinitesimal particulars from the world's sensorium is both the product of pathology (he is thrown from a horse) and is itself pathological.[30] The memory of the dog seen side on is unrelated, in Funes's mind, to the memory of the same dog seen head on a moment later. An infinity of memories, then, but no dog as such, and certainly no dogness.

In this gentle satire on a nominalism taken to extremes there lurks not only the empiricist Locke, but also Nietzsche, commonly thought of as the essential philosopher of modernity (Funes dies the same year, 1889, Nietzsche suffered his breakdown).[31] Nietzsche's second essay from the *Genealogy of Morals* (1887) discusses the importance of forgetting as that active power allowing a temporary shutting of the doors and windows of the mind so as to make room for the more noble functions of foresight and calculation. Funes cannot forget; ergo, he cannot think. "Pensar es olvidar diferencias, es generalizar, abstraer. En el abarrotado mundo de Funes no había sino detalles, casi inmediatos" (p. 490).[32] The portals of his mind are always open. He is incapable of cutting himself off from "los detalles," hence incapable of thought (*abstraere*, "to cut"). The constant openness to the world's infinite "details" leads to the impoverishment, not to say abolition, of thought. Better night, *sombra*, blindness. While Borges appears here to diverge from an ocular-photocentric tradition of metaphysics (that of Plato), from the imbrication of truth in a metaphorical system that accords maximum privilege to those values grouped around light, vision, clear and distinct perception, it is possible to interpret the value that Borges confers upon the capacity of thought to abstract itself from external reality as a confirmation rather than a displacement of idealism.[33] The discourse of Borges is not against light as such, against light as truth and truth as light. It is against a certain kind of light, against the light of empiricism and the privilege accorded by empiricism to the eye and the doxa of the uniqueness of particulars.

However, to return to my question above, why does the context of "Funes" matter, not just the context in which it was written, but the time and place that provide its setting? The hinge that links the importance of context to otherwise abstract philosophemes of nominalism is the question of nationalism. Nationalism lies at the heart of Borges's production in the 1930s and 1940s. An instructive way in to the hinge-question of nationalism is offered by the essay "El escritor argentino y la tradición" (1951), which, for our purposes, may just as well be called "El lector uruguayo y la tradición."[34] Though Borges does not say it, the essay stands as a critique of Boedo, the old *criollos, and* that part of the journal *Martín Fierro* that had signaled its affiliation to *criollismo* by revisiting the debate, initiated by Lugones, concerning the canonization of Hernández's poem as the expression of the nation's essence. What all three share is a fateful yoking together of nationalism and nominalism. On the one hand, Borges will call this a peculiarly modern error. The idea that Argentine poetry should abound in "rasgos diferenciales" and "color local" is a relatively new idea that would have left Shakespeare perplexed. By the same token, the idea's novelty is tellingly circumscribed: the apparently Argentine cult of local color is itself an import, "un reciente culto europeo," which any self-respecting nationalist should reject as foreign. On the other hand, Borges points out that this error has a long history. The problem of tradition is merely a contemporary form of the "eterno problema del determinismo" (p. 273). We may extrapolate from this critique to say that the point of criticizing Boedo's social realism is not to swap one form of local color for another, that is, to end up laying claim to the specificity of a Creole nineteenth century. Rather, it is to get beyond the impoverishment born of the conceptual solidarity between nominalism and a series of other terms (nationalism, regionalism, *criollismo*, etc.), which thrive on strategies of delimitation and claims to specificity.

In short, it matters profoundly that the story's setting is Uruguay, and that its subject is a humble *compadrito* from Fray Bentos. On the one hand, that this modest (fictional) Uruguayan should be a Nietzsche, a Locke, and a Pliny exemplifies Borges's point about nationalism, and indeed about the Southern Cone nations that are the product of modernity. Funes is neither simply Uruguayan nor simply modern, if by those adjectives one understands unique conditions that bear no relation to any other: Funes is a Uruguayan German, a Uruguayan Englishman, a Uruguayan Ancient Greek. However, the matter does not end there. On the other hand, then, although the story wears away at any simple idea of national identity, nowhere does it suppress the singularity—certain incurable limitations—of the local. On the contrary, at the same time as it takes its distance from positivistic notions of national identity, the story affirms (a complex) Southern Cone condition: Funes is more than German, more than English, more than Ancient Greek; he's Uruguayan. "Pedro Leandro Ipuche ha escrito que Funes era un precursor de los superhombres; 'Un Zarathustra cimarrón y vernáculo'; no lo discuto, pero no hay que olvidar que era también un compadrito de Fray Bentos, con ciertas incurables limitaciones" (p. 485). The story is at once critical of a narrow notion of national identity and affirmative of the singular name

"Uruguay" that is the crossing-point of diverse traditions. Funes is not simply Uruguayan; he is complexly so. He is neither Nietzsche nor Locke nor Pliny; he is all those things and more (and less): he's Funes.

A comico-satirical example of the convergence of modernity, nominalism, and nationalism is the story "El Aleph," which is nothing if not a fictional version of "El escritor argentino y la tradición."[35] The story is about a personal desire that, since the tale is a rewriting of Dante, is also and inseparably archetypal. In it the poet and pedant Carlos Argentino Daneri combines a "vindicación del hombre moderno" with a mimetico-nationalist writing practice bent on transcribing the unique contents of that modern world. Daneri's "vindication" of modernity as a break with tradition and the past is a debasement of Nietzsche in that it amounts to little more than an enumeration of the technical accoutrements of modern life (*telégrafos, fonógrafos* . . .). This enumeration irritates and pains "Borges" in equal measures since, as we have seen, every reminder of novelty and change takes him further away from Beatriz. Daneri's no less irritating literary project of enumerating the detail of the modern world collapses under the weight of its own (arch-traditional) bombast. Having poured scorn on this attempt to transcribe the world according to the mimetic aesthetic favored by the Boedo group and denounced in "El escritor argentino," the story then trumps Daneri by revealing the presence of an aleph in the basement of Daneri's own house. As in "Funes," access to this would-be totality is preceded by a hiatus or blindness of sorts: "Borges" closes his eyes before fixing his gaze on the wondrous object.

The aleph shapes up as a wondrous, traditional figure of revelation, but is no such thing. Daneri holds it to be a cipher of eternal time, which reveals in an instant everything that has been, is, and will be: the perfect figure of mimesis that makes his own pompous verses pale into insignificance. Although the aleph reveals what will be as well as what has been, the future in question would in effect be an already-written future, the future as given or *fatum*. To that extent, the aleph joins a series of key figurative and thematic substitutions (immortality, circular time, the Eternal Return, Buddhism, Kabbalah, idealism, dreams, transmigration, the Book, the library, gauchos, and Greek literature as rumor), which are heavily impregnated with a sense of anteriority and predetermination (Kabbalah means precisely *received tradition*).

Before jumping to hasty conclusions about Borges's traditionalism, however, three caveats must be made. First, the contents of the aleph cannot be communicated in language (there can be no mimesis). Second, the aleph is an aporetic figure: though it promises absolute knowledge, it does not, after all, contain a stable world about which one could say that it was "given." The vision the aleph promises can never be complete, since it would have to include within it the viewer gazing upon the aleph, and within that second aleph the viewer gazing upon that aleph, and so on ad infinitum (there is no stable original object of mimesis). Third, the aleph in the calle Garay is not even the only aleph in existence (there is another total version of the world). This is the point in the story where the question of nationalism melds with those of nominalism and modernity. According to Richard Burton, there exists another aleph lodged in a column in Cairo. Is this other aleph an Islamic aleph, then? No, not even that "Islamic" aleph is simply and exclusively Islamic, since "las columnas proceden de otros templos de religiones anteislámicas." In other words, the story concludes, the other, that is the foreign, stands at the origin of the self-same, or the national: "Pues como ha escrito Abenjaldún: *En las repúblicas fundadas por nómadas, es indispensable el concurso de forasteros para todo lo que sea albañilería*" (p. 627).

It is worth recalling that the collection in which "El Aleph" appears begins with the earlier-cited arch-Platonic epigraph to "El inmortal," ends by promising but ultimately frustrating the traditional dream of a world given in advance and given up to omniscience, and then allows the spirit and letter of the last story to stand as title for the whole collection. One may choose to draw from this the conclusion that Borges is not an exponent of Tradition, but a critical, or modern, traditionalist.[36] Without subscribing to it absolutely, Borges is wont to let the overbearing determinism of the idea of the Book, for instance, take full flight for aesthetic and aesthetico-political reasons, for what it has to say to an age of overweaning individualism. Borges uses the figures and themes of tradition but does not treat them traditionally.[37] Whence the significance of the Kabbalah in Borges. Moments of a lecture like "The Kabbalah" appear to see the Kabbalah as a reservoir of traditional traditionality (stasis and repetition of the known), as something anterior and firmly opposed to modernity.[38] However, in that same lecture, as in the lecture on the Kabbalah from *Siete noches*, and most importantly in his literary practice, Kabbalistic tradition is understood plurally and dynamically, in accordance with the view of Gershom Scholem, for whom the tradition of the Kabbalah is not the dogmatic orthodoxy which consists in paying homage to a single truth revealed once and for all.[39] Truth resides in the dialogue between the texts of the tradition, in the conflicts and contradictions of a community of writings, in the work of constant interpretation.

Reference to the Kabbalah highlights the fact that the above conclusion, for all its merits, is missing something. Something beginning with α. The name of the story whose spirit and letter stand as the title of the collection as a whole is the first letter of the Hebrew alphabet. Although in this chapter I have given priority to the Greek tradition, on the grounds that Borges's essays on time have a predominantly Greek matrix, *El Aleph* works and reworks the figures and themes of numerous traditions, not least the Jewish one. The collection draws on Ancient Greece, Judaism, Islam, the Mayas . . . and the Southern Cone. All in order to suggest that *en las repúblicas fundadas por nómadas, es indispensable el concurso de forasteros para todo lo que sea albañilería.*

Otra historia

All of the essays and stories considered above date from the 1930s, 1940s or early 1950s. In an era convulsed by the thematics of purity and the promise of a final solution as a new beginning, the question of the non-self-identity of the present, or of a national context's difference from itself, is not simply an abstract question—even if it is that, too, and must be defended as such. Borges's critique of the myth of absolute beginnings (in "La creación y P.H. Gosse," 1941), his reminder that the project of abolishing the past has a long history, which is itself proof that the past cannot be abolished (in "Nathaniel Hawthorne," 1949), and, finally, his disavowal of a "pure" language (in "Dos libros," 1941)—all carry a progressive political weight.[40] All make the same point that the nominalistic championing of absolute particularity is intellectually unsustainable and politically nefarious.

The political significance of the doctrine of the Eternal Return, in contrast, would still seem to be quintessentially conservative—a life-denying refusal of the possibility that humanity might develop and progress.[41] "La doctrina de los ciclos" appears to confirm this conservatism. In it, Borges argues that Nietzsche proposed the "intolerable hipótesis griega" as a trial of strength to distinguish the heroic overman from bearers of the slave mentality and social democrats. But, as Derrida has shown, Nietzsche's politics are not so straightforward. Nietzsche's aristocratic criticism of social democracy is that *it* is the tyrant, encouraging submissive obedience as it whispers its poorly thought out precepts into the ears of its citizens.[42] In this sense, the benighted doctrine of the Eternal Return is the possibility of a luminous alternative. Borges cites words from Nietzsche, which assume specific political significance only a decade later: "En el instante en que se presenta esa idea, varían todos los colores—y hay otra historia" (p. 390).

The concluding paragraph of "El tiempo circular," published in the midst of the Second World War, offers two responses to Borges's conjecture regarding circular time: the doctrine may be a cause for pessimism or a reason for hope. Borges refuses to suggest that the alternatives are a matter of subjective preference. What counts is the historical moment, the epochal time, the conventional chronology in which the conjecture is thought. I reproduce the final paragraph of the essay, completed, we recall, in 1943:

> En tiempos de auge la conjetura de que la existencia del hombre es una cantidad constante, invariable, puede entristecer o irritar: en tiempos que declinan (como éstos), es la promesa de que ningún oprobio, ninguna calamidad, ningún dictador podrá empobrecernos. (P. 69)

The modal shift from "puede" ("puede entristecer o irritar") to "es" ("es la promesa") signals the rhetorical call to arms, a specific gesture of defiance, which had formerly ("En el instante en que se presenta esa idea, varían todos los colores—y hay otra historia") remained an abstract possibility. The embrace of circular time affirms the possibility that things might always be otherwise than they currently are. It is an affirmation of hope, now, at this moment, in this irreversible, iron chronology. The gesture of hope is, of course, a curious affirmation of difference inasmuch as it is difference born of the return of the same (or the analogous): instead of Hitler, we would see the "return" of former civil times, of a differently colored history.

It is not without irony that, here as elsewhere, Borges should use Platonism to criticize a nominalistic nationalism in thrall to a sense of the uniqueness of its never-before-seen hues. One of the exacerbations of nationalism, that is, fascism, is precisely Platonic in its proclivity for transhistorical essences. Much fascist thought of the 1930s and 1940s willingly embraced variants of the Eternal Return to propagate the idea that their regimes were modern reincarnations of the great empires of the past. But that is Borges's point: namely, that zealous nationalisms are Platonic nominalisms. Which is to say, assertions of uniqueness that take a near identical form to other contemporary and anterior assertions of uniqueness . . . To that extent, and insofar as Hitler is a pleonasm of Carlyle, Borges writes, reality is always anachronistic ("Dos libros,"

p. 103).[43] Borges observes in the same essay that Platonic nominalism does not just belong to tyrants; in fact, it permeates the thinking of democrats, making them nazis:

> [H.G.] Wells, increíblemente, no es nazi. Increíblemente, pues casi todos mis contemporáneos lo son, aunque lo nieguen o lo ignoren. Desde 1925, no hay publicista que no opine que el hecho inevitable y trivial de haber nacido en un determinado país y de pertenecer a tal raza (o a tal buena mixtura de razas) no sea un privilegio singular y un talismán suficiente. Vindicadores de la democracia, que se creen muy diversos de Goebbels, instan a sus lectores, en el dialecto mismo del enemigo, a escuchar los latidos de un corazón que recoge los íntimos mandatos de la sangre y de la tierra. ("Dos libros," pp. 102–103)

Failure to recognize the conceptual and discursive similarity with Goebbels is "grave para el intelecto," but grave, too, for democracy. It is not that Platonism, rather than nominalism, should be our guiding light in modern times. The shortcomings of Platonism are already laid bare in the critique of the hybridity of Platonic forms in "Historia de la eternidad." Borges's Platonism stands, rather, as a strategic reminder, at a specific, tenebrous historical juncture, of the force of *lo genérico*. But no more than any other doctrine can the Eternal Return lead to Eternal Resistance.

CHAPTER 7

Rulfo and the Mexican Roman Trinity

Transculturation

The question of tradition has been at the heart of recent debates on the cultural production of Juan Rulfo, most notably the debate stemming from Ángel Rama's work on transculturation.[1] Rama's thesis concerning transculturation is that, in the wake of processes of modernization in Latin America, there emerges a new generation of writers rooted in a rural environment but receptive to modern artistic developments. It takes this new generation to do artistic justice to the traditional cultures of Latin America. The transculturators, as Rama puts it in the original 1974 essay, "built the bridges necessary to recover the cultures of the regions [. . .] by making use of the artistic potential of modernity in an unprecedented and original way."[2] Aside from myth, the principal material with which the transculturators worked was language. Regional speech was no longer relegated to the margins of a text, but instead woven into the main narrative voice through a process of "unificación textual." Transculturation is not confined to the question of language, since at stake are culture and *anthropos*. "Fidelity to the environment culminated in a fidelity to [. . .] the cosmology which held together the elements of a culture" (Rama, "Processes," p. 67). This is the real prize. Not just fidelity to rural speech, but faithfulness to an entire *cosmovisión*—that of the marginalized and the oppressed.

Published in 1982, Rama's book gathers up material that dates back to the early 1970s and, as a result, stands at the crossroads of two broad currents of cultural criticism in Latin America. On the one hand, it is nourished by the daily bread of 1970s' Marxist–Leninist dependency theory; on the other hand, it registers the 1980s' shift away from an economistic Marxism toward a more affirmative appreciation of the cultures of the periphery. Thus, Rama plays up the powers of appropriation displayed by novelists of transculturation from the periphery, while playing down their indebtedness to the West.[3] At the same time, the book affirms the popular, oral, traditional cultures of rural Latin America at the expense of the region's high, metropolitan cultural formations. To that end, Rama proposes a correlation according to which the greater a writer is inserted into traditional society, the greater the originality and unusualness of the "internal equivalents" found to rival foreign writing techniques.

There are three main difficulties with Rama-influenced critical work on Rulfo and tradition, each of which is explored in this chapter. The first relates to a problematic insistence not just on the traditional elements of Rulfo's work but on the non-Western provenance of some of them.[4] It is known that Rulfo photographed the art and architecture of indigenous culture, and indeed *indígenas* from various Mexican states, and that he went on to work for the Instituto Nacional Indigenista in the 1960s. But where his fiction is concerned, Rulfo insisted repeatedly that he writes exclusively about Creoles and mestizos; that Creole and mestizo life in his native Jalisco has virtually nothing to do with indian life; and indeed that he has no understanding of the indians. Jalisco, he remarks, was characterized by the absence of an indian tradition and the presence of an aggressively Spanish-leaning Creole population.[5] Strictly speaking, Rulfo's demographic assessment of Jalisco is inaccurate: there was in the 1950s and continues today to be an indian population in his home state.[6] What there is not and never has been, however, is the concentration of self-consciously non-mestizo people, speaking a language other than Spanish and possessing a significant degree of political and religious autonomy, that one finds in Michoacán, Chiapas, or Oaxaca. In the absence of a full record of Rulfo's cultural interactions, and notwithstanding the brief appearance of *indios* from Apango and the presence of Nahuatl words in *Pedro Páramo*, it is the thrust of this chapter that indian culture occupies the outer margins of Rulfo's literary production. In the main, his fiction deals with a popular, Creole and/or mestizo Jaliscan culture "sentada," in the words of historian Jean Meyer, "sobre la Biblia, la tradición oral cristiana, los libros de caballería y la poesía cortesana."[7]

The second difficulty has to do with a certain understanding of the traditional rural popular, and with a tendency to construct Rulfo as a quintessentially traditional-rural writer. This understanding and this tendency do not originate in critical work on transculturation, but the latter has done little to shake them. Recognizing at one level that movement between rural area and city is the engine of transculturation, at another level transculturative work lets the urban-cosmopolitan dimension fall from view. Despite the fact that he made his home in Mexico City, Rulfo becomes mythologized as the great traditional-rural writer. Behind this mythologization lies a familiar conceptual move, which aspects of Rulfo's work appear to license, that aligns the urban with modernity while framing the rural as the essential place of tradition. Everything starts from the fact that Rulfo's subject matter was rural Mexico. Look at his photographs: virtual absence of modern cities, no factories, often no people, the black and white images emanate a sort of rural degree zero, which belies their heavy stylization.[8] On the basis of this rural degree zero, the leap is made to the conclusion that Rulfo's subject matter is traditional Mexico. It is as though traditions were only found in rural areas and, by extension, rural areas only knew a traditional way of life. Even if Rulfo's photographic and literary work frequently colludes with a certain hypostatization of the traditional-rural, there are signs in it that suggest that rural and urban circuits already intersected in 1940s' Mexico, and hence that he writes not about tradition but about a tradition sutured by modernity.[9]

The third difficulty of transculturative work is closely allied to the second, and concerns the question of writing technique. It is symptomatic that Rama should write that the transculturators "ma[de] use of the artistic potential of modernity in an unprecedented and original way." The catch-all term "modernity" avoids any suggestion that the dominant force in Rulfo's compositional matrix may have been high-literary writing, and above all modernism. Because it issues from the West and from the domain of high culture to boot, modernism becomes an undesirable ancestor. Although it would be reductive to ascribe all of Rulfo's techniques to modernism, it is disingenuous to play down the role of modernism in the genealogy of Rulfo's work. Modernist techniques had by the 1940s come to constitute something like a communal resource bank that writers would draw on, not to undermine tradition per se (modernists frequently draw on traditional-popular materials), but to call into question the restrictive tradition and authority of the rationalist-realist aesthetic.

There is an obvious danger in checking fictional production against history. Texts produce meaning, they do not simply reflect a readymade historical formation. Even if we can scan such a formation for material upon which Rulfo may have drawn, in truth we will never know absolutely what motivates Pedro Páramo, or whether the *ánimas en pena* are moved by pre-Colombian or Catholic beliefs. In one sense, these characters have no psychological or historical depth beyond the surface of the text. In another sense, however, this truism belies the fact that these characters are woven in part from a text—called "history"— which is larger than the one in which they ostensibly find themselves. It is interesting that when asked about the gestation of *Pedro Páramo*, Rulfo should utterly fail to distinguish between literature and history, seeing the downfall of the fictional Comala as payback for its moral laxity and consistently reactionary role in real Mexican history.[10] Without going as far as Rulfo, I shall read Rulfo with a hermeneutic will to establish possible connections between his writing and history. This will can only begin to do justice to Rulfo's work, however, if it understands that his writing "gives to be read that which will remain *eternally* unreadable, *absolutely* indecipherable, even refusing itself to any promise of deciphering or hermeneutic."[11]

Pedro Páramo and the Mexican Roman Trinity

Consistent with his view that pantheons are the only interesting things in Mexican villages (*Autobiografía armada*, p. 66), Rulfo attempts in *Pedro Páramo* to novelize the Mexican cult of the dead. Bolstered by the widely accepted view that the major contemporary Mexican manifestation of the cult of the dead, el Día de los Muertos, is itself a product of Catholic and pre-Hispanic traditions, critics have seized on Rulfo's portrayal of the dead as the manifestation of a pre-Colombian worldview in which life and death are not as rigidly separated as they are in Western modernity.[12] Three reasons suggest that this assessment is untenable and that the link which the novel establishes between a pueblo of dead souls and a tyrannical *cacique* is grounded in a powerful Western element of Mexican tradition, an element that certainly includes Catholicism but is not reducible to it. First, supposing that it did put forth a nonlinear conception of the relationship between life and death, this would not in itself be enough to prove the presence of native American materials in the novel. As Octavio Paz observed in *El laberinto de la soledad* (1950), premodern Western Catholicism itself did not recognize any neat separation between life and death. If in the Aztec tradition death (through sacrifice) regenerated the creative forces of life, in the premodern Catholic view death was a "salto mortal" between two lives, the temporal one and the otherworldly.[13] To complicate further the genealogy of the novel's central conceit, the idea of dead souls haunting the living is a commonplace of pagan culture in classical Antiquity.[14] So when Rulfo says that, in Jalisco as in the novel, the Christian respect for the dead has been crossed with the pagan cult of ancestors (he does not say "crossed with the *pre-Colombian* cult of ancestors"), the word "pagan" may just as well refer to premodern beliefs of European origin as to a native American worldview.[15]

Second, the novel does not in any case offer up a cyclical philosophy of life, Toltec-Aztec or otherwise.[16] It portrays a world without regenerative energy, a world without transcendence (*transcéndere*, "to pass over" or "go up") populated by characters who are precisely going anywhere. It is a Catholic world (Comala does not resemble Mictlan: the Aztec idea of "Hell" had no moral significance, and hence no threat of eternal damnation[17]) in which the life in question, to hark back to Paz's schematization, is "individual" (a matter of personal salvation) rather than "colectiva" (as in the Aztec tradition).

Third, the characters are the product not just of popular Catholicism but of another mediation, that of literature of the fantastic, the effect of which is to personify the wandering souls as full-fledged, recognizable individuals. Although, ventriloquized through Harss, Rulfo speaks of *ánimas* (" 'la idea de que aquel que muere en pecado sigue vagando sobre la tierra. Son las ánimas de los muertos' que no encuentran paz ni reposo"), and although the novel also uses the word in relation to the dead, what has not been sufficiently remarked upon is the fact that the "souls" in the novel readily become "people." Explaining why they are in purgatory (they have not received the bishop's pardon), the incestuous sister of Donis says: "Y ésa es la cosa por la que esto está lleno de ánimas; un puro vagabundear de gente que murió sin perdón y que no lo conseguirá de ningún modo."[18] In a yoking together of modern mestizo Catholicism and literature of the fantastic, *ánimas* become a "puro vagabundear de gente" and behave in a suitably verisimilitudinous manner.

Insofar as the novel draws upon historical materials above and beyond the literary, however, these materials are not reducible to Mexican Catholicism. Establishing a connection between the *ánimas en pena* and *caciquismo*, the novel deals not just with Christianity, but with the larger legacy of the "Roman trinity"—the triumvirate of religion, authority, and tradition that underpinned Western society for centuries, and which, duly exported, becomes the Mexican Roman trinity. The contours of this complex cultural configuration will illustrate why the Western tradition looms large in the novel.

The Roman Trinity

Until challenged by the forces of modernity, the Roman trinity of religion, authority, and tradition was held together by the idea of foundation. Of supreme importance to the Romans was the belief that they should found something that would remain binding for all future generations.[19] The specific foundation in question is that of the city of Rome. To be engaged in politics is, for the Romans, essentially to preserve the *polis*. The foundation of the body politic becomes, in Arendt's phrase, "the decisive, unrepeatable beginning of their whole history." This is why religion in Rome literally means *re-ligare*: "to be tied back, obligated, to the enormous, almost superhuman and hence always legendary effort to lay foundations, to build the cornerstone, to found for eternity" (p. 121). If religion means a tying back to foundations, the idea of authority, or *auctoritas* (from *augere*, "to augment"), points to the activity of augmenting the foundation. The endeavor to augment the foundation accounts for the superiority of those said to be in authority. Authority is not the same as power. It was an article of faith for the Romans that those in authority did not have power, which resides instead in the people. The authoritative character of the "advice" offered by the elders derives from this apparent absence of power, from the fact that it neither takes the form of a command nor requires external coercion to make itself heard. This conception of authority entails a clear temporal direction toward the past. Earlier acts of augmentation—the deeds of ancestors—become exemplary guides for present behavior. Present life is driven not by the desire to forge new untrodden paths (as in modern individualism), but by the need to respect the founding templates of the past. This is why old age was considered by the Romans to be the pinnacle of human life—not because of the store of wisdom and experience accumulated by the old, but because "the old man had grown closer to the ancestors and the past" (p. 123). Growth is directed not, as in our modern conception, toward the future; one grows, instead, toward the past. Here, then, is the third pole of the trinity. For this exemplary past was sanctified by tradition:

> Tradition preserved the past by handing down from one generation to the next the testimony of the ancestors, who first had witnessed and created the sacred founding and then augmented it by their authority throughout the centuries. As long as this tradition was uninterrupted, authority was inviolate; and to act without authority and tradition, without accepted, time-honoured

standards and models, without the help of the wisdom of the founding fathers, was inconceivable. (P. 124)

The key point in relation to Rulfo is that the Christian Church inherits the political and spiritual legacy of the Roman Empire by repeating the foundational move of the Romans. The success of the Church as a public institution lay in its ability to give itself a foundation, a "decisive, unrepeatable beginning," which would allow it to take over the Roman trinity.[20] That foundation is achieved by making the life (and death) of Jesus into a historically recorded event. The Apostles become the founding fathers of the Church; and the Church derives her authority from the act of augmenting the foundations by handing down the Apostles' testimony by way of tradition (p. 126). To that extent, the Church also inherits from imperial times the Roman distinction between authority and power. Whereas the Church claims for herself the old authority of the Senate, she leaves power to the state. This separation of Church and state has the two-fold consequence of bestowing on the Church the kind of permanence that had been Rome's for a thousand years, while stripping politics of authority. Political structures may have a validity of sorts, but not lasting authority.

This goes some way to explaining the Cristeros War, which so obsessed Rulfo. A rapidly modernizing but fragmented state renews its assault on the Church and is met with a wave of popular resistance. As Enrique Dussel puts it, the Church had stayed close to the daily life of the people in a postindependence period of extreme volatility; "it was the only institution to provide a permanent point of reference," the only one "that could stand up to the state in the name of *traditional* and historical values."[21] At the risk of simplifying the novel's many layers, we can say that it deals with the very absence of foundations, and with the Church's failure to provide a permanent point of reference. That is why the Western dimension is so salient. The text deals with this tradition of European origin not out of some perverse Eurocentrism but because it constitutes its primary object of critique. *Pedro Páramo* depicts the breakup of the Mexican Roman trinity and its supplantation by naked power, while showing that it is the religious legacy of that tradition—and here Rulfo dissents from Dussel—which prevents the inhabitants of Comala from resisting the *cacique*. To that extent, and contrary to claims that Rulfo is the champion of traditional-rural culture, the text is tied to the modern tradition of a negative, Enlightenment view of religion and popular culture, which is only partially offset by the novel's transculturative qualities.

In the Name of Power

The absence of foundations underpins Rulfo's portrayal of the *cacique*. The name is the key. The Roman trinity is inscribed in the name of Rulfo's fictional tyrant ("Pedro", from the Latin *petra*-, "stone"). But Pedro Páramo is no foundation stone. His first name spills over alliteratively into the second (*páramo*, 'plain' or 'unproductive, inhospitable land'), leaving us with wild nature, and the historical traces of delinquency, rather than civic order.[22] The association between the *cacique* and crumbling foundations stretches from the novel's title to its final sentence: "Dio un golpe seco contra la tierra y se fue desmoronando como si fuera un montón de piedras." The only things Pedro Páramo augments are his landholdings and dominion over others. To that extent, although he is a father (his name also contains the word *padre*), he is not the *padre protector*:

> No es el fundador de un pueblo; no es el patriarca que ejerce la *patria potestas*; no es rey, juez, jefe de clan. Es el poder aislado en su misma potencia, sin relación ni compromiso con el mundo exterior. Es la incomunicación pura, la soledad que se devora a sí misma y devora lo que toca. (Paz, p. 74)

Paz is not in fact writing about Rulfo's novel in the above, but the parallels with the Mexican archetype of the Father are irresistible. Pedro Páramo is the 'macho' who conforms almost entirely to the negative image of *el Dios Padre*, which dominates popular Mexican representations of "el poder viril": "Jehová colérico, Dios de ira, Saturno, Zeus violador de mujeres" (Paz, p. 73). He exercises not authority, but unauthorized "feudal" power: "Una palabra resume la agresividad, impasibilidad, invulnerabilidad, uso descarnado de la violencia, y demás atributos del 'macho': poder. La fuerza, pero desligada de toda noción de orden: el poder arbitrario, la voluntad sin freno y sin cauce" (Paz, p. 73). Of course, the name Pedro is also an anagram of *poder*. The exception to his rule by naked power, and the reason he does not conform entirely to the negative image of *el Dios Padre*, is his love for Susana San Juan. The name Páramo also contains the word *amor*.

It would be tempting, on the basis of the above, to concur with those who have viewed the novel as the depiction of an essentially traditional-rural order, and to say that Comala's traditional way of life is destroyed by a "premodern" figure: half-warlord, half-Old Testament *Dios Padre*. Anthony Giddens has tabulated the general differences between "premodern" and "modern" cultures.[23] In Rulfo's novel, all the elements gathered together under the Giddens rubric of "Environment of Risk" in premodern cultures are in evidence. The threat from nature has killed Comala; the human violence from a local *cacique* has brought about the latter; the compromised moral conduct of the villagers leaves them haunted by their perceived fall from grace. In contrast, all the positive aspects that constitute Giddens's "Environment of Trust" in premodern cultures are either absent from or under mortal threat in Comala. Kinship relations have been extinguished; the local community has been all but annihilated; religious cosmologies persist, but offer no solace; tradition persists, but only as empty habit. Capricious and arbitrary, the *cacique* decimates all vestiges of tradition (on account of the fact that others fail unwittingly to observe the tradition of mourning) to the point where he fails even to secure the routinization and hence continuity of his own order. To judge solely by Giddens's characterization of the premodern, Rulfo's Mexico is an exclusively premodern affair, and the *cacique* an archetype drawn from the most conventional image-repertoire of the omnipotent warlord/God. After all, at first sight Comala is destroyed neither by the depradations of capitalism nor by the selling off of communal lands, but by the will of one man.

And yet, Giddens's scheme can blind us to the text's figurative quality, to the fact, for instance, that the text's central narrative situation is based on hyperbole. Just as García Márquez would later pass the grotesqueness of dictatorship through the esperpentic *El otoño del patriarca*, Rulfo lets the distortions of *caciquismo* contaminate the narrative form itself, such that the tyrant seems larger, even, than History. But Mexican history is the subtext that "causes" the cause, that produces the phenomenon of *caciquismo* that makes possible the individual *cacique*. The novel is a hyperbolic allegory of the depradations of *caciquismo*. To recognize the hyperbole, and to descend into the detail of the text, is to realize that the novel's fictional Mexico is not simply premodern, but has been traversed by secular modernity. Despite airily dismissing the law, and boasting that he intends to make the law himself, the *cacique* operates at the point where the premodern intersects with the rational-legal-bureaucratic order of modernity, epitomized by the system of law. Even though he threatens to burn all his legal papers—of which, supposedly being beyond the law, he has no need— the *cacique* knows better than to dispense with either *abogado* or *papeles*. Perhaps we can say that he participates in modernity—paying lip service to it—without ever belonging to it. To belong to modernity would involve being circumscribed by it. In the same way that he orders Fulgor not to worry about boundary walls (*lienzos*), Pedro Páramo is cognizant of but always excessive in relation to the strictures of modernity, much as he is aware of but invariably disregards the bonds and bounds of tradition.

Religion

The *cacique*'s excessiveness, his calculated indifference, with respect to both tradition and modernity is in marked contrast, however, to the text's overall stance, which conforms more closely to a typically modern attitude, and nowhere more so than in its treatment of religion. In an early generational showdown between the young Pedro and his *abuela*, the motivations behind the protestations of the godless young rebel with a cause ("Que se resignen otros, abuela, yo no estoy para resignaciones") are alternately and undecidably readable as expressions of either a modern thrusting individualism or a premodern, age-old will to power.[24] In contrast, the novel is characteristically less equivocal in locating the place from which the *abuela* speaks. She is the ageing upholder of tradition who rehearses the old Roman and/or pagan belief in the preeminence of seniority ("Por ahora eres sólo un aprendiz") but grafts onto it the Christian belief in the rewards that will come to those who wait. With the exception of Susana San Juan, who moves even Pedro Páramo to use a religious-transcendental idiom, the women in the novel conform to the traditional image of tradition by being the protagonists of religious ritual. And in its depiction of them, the novel is in turn tied to an Enlightenment (modern, Western, high-cultural) tradition of critique, which views religion as Marx's opiate of the people. The novel's marxisant depiction of women as upholders-cum-dupes of religious ritual offers scant support to the opposing view of religion and superstition as popular forms of expression, which seek the alleviation or easing of social tensions and provide a communal foundation-stone that the volatile nation-state cannot offer.[25] Rulfo had little time for the mindset of the Mexican peasantry that took up arms in the Cristeros War, frequently pronouncing on religion and belief with an Enlightenment idiom and impatience.[26] Anticlericalism comes through first and most obviously in the novel in the Church's moral bankruptcy. Despite voicing the obligatory criticism of the *cacique*, the Church colludes in his immoral behavior and in the maintenance of a vicious patriarchy. The priest's name, Padre Rentería, says it all: the *pater* of patriarchy is for hire (*rentar* in Mexican Spanish means "to rent out") to the most powerful paymaster. A similar anti-Catholic, pro-Enlightenment sentiment makes itself felt through the other main vector for criticism of religion in the novel, namely, its ventriloquism of the discourse of the Final Judgement by the (almost without exception female) characters. This second vector is more nuanced in that criticism is leveled at the Church and the doctrine, whereas pathos is reserved for the doctrine's followers. Here the transculturative dimension of Rulfo's writing comes to the fore as characters either humbly rearticulate orthodoxy in their own idiom, in order to bring it within their understanding, or else formulate their rejection of it.

On the face of things, traditional (Platonic) Catholic discourse dominates the women's lives, striking fear into their hearts and causing incalculable torment.[27] For the incestuous sister of Donis, the wandering souls who come out at night are a cause for fright, not celebration. As far as she is concerned, even the "living" live in sin and shame, without God's grace, and, moreover, without the means of achieving it:

> Si usted viera el gentío de ánimas que andan sueltas por la calle. En cuanto oscurece comienzan a salir. Y a nadie le gusta verlas. Son tantas, y nosotros tan poquitos, que ya ni la lucha le hacemos para rezar para que salgan de sus penas. No ajustarían nuestras oraciones para todos. Si acaso les tocaría un pedazo de Padre nuestro. Y eso no les puede servir de nada. Luego están nuestros pecados de por medio. Ninguno de los que todavía vivimos está en gracia de Dios. Nadie podrá alzar sus ojos al cielo sin sentirlos sucios de vergüenza. Y la vergüenza no cura. Al menos eso me dijo el obispo que pasó por aquí hace algún tiempo dando confirmaciones. (P. 119)

However, as the final sentence of the above makes clear, the discourse belongs to the representative of the Church. In keeping with the basic tenets of baroque Catholicism, it is clerical hierarchy, rather than a direct individual relationship with God, which is the source of truth (Voekel, p. 10). And yet, by the same token, in her performative ventriloquism, the "dummy," Donis's sister, cuts her own linguistic and conceptual way through the doctrine's fire-and-brimstone thickets. A tender simplicity surfaces in the interstices of the harsh Old Testament doctrine, as she processes the bishop's words in order to accommodate herself to them and vice versa. The image of quantitative inadequacy, the potentially leaden sense of the dead souls outnumbering and outweighing the living, is leavened by the language used: There are so few of us, and so many of them, she says, that our prayers simply won't go round.

Although the traditional Old Testament doctrine remains powerful, the novel shows that it is beginning to lose its grip on the townspeople because their fear of it has been surpassed by their fear of the *cacique*. When Eduviges speaks in traditional fashion of joining Juan Preciado's dead mother in the afterlife ("alcanzaré a tu madre en alguno de los caminos de la eternidad"), we realize that she intends to transgress Church law by taking a short cut ("acortar las veredas")—a clear metaphor for suicide. In another instance, Dorotea speaks the language of Plato at the same time as she bears witness to its extenuation. It is a passage worth quoting in full because, for all its terribleness, it has a similar poetic transculturative quality to the words of the incestuous sister:

—¿Y tu alma? ¿Dónde crees que haya ido?
—Debe andar vagando por la tierra como tantas otras; buscando vivos que recen por ella. Tal vez me odie por el mal trato que le di; pero eso ya no me preocupa. He descansado del vicio de sus remordimientos. Me amargaba hasta lo poco que comía, y me hacía insoportables las noches llenándomelas de pensamientos intranquilos con figuras de condenados y cosas de esas. Cuando me senté a morir, ella rogó que me levantara y que siguiera arrastrando la vida, como si esperara todavía algún milagro que me limpiara de culpas. Ni siquiera hice el intento: «Aquí se acaba el camino— le dije—. Ya no me quedan fuerzas para más.» Y abrí la boca para que se fuera. Y se fue. Sentí cuando cayó en mis manos el hilito de sangre con que estaba amarrada a mi corazón.
(P. 135)

It is noticeable in both of the above examples that, although the language of Christianity remains in place, the "priestly [. . .] mediation with the Divine" (Voekel) present in the earlier instances has gone, and the characters are beginning to step out of the shadow of ecclesiastical authority. The message of this distance-taking from Christian discourse is in one sense negative: that the women would rather risk the wrath of God than agonize further in Páramo's Comala betokens just how great the *cacique*'s capacity to visit misery upon earth has become. And yet, in a manner that will later find an echo in Susana San Juan's delirious rejection of the ghastly images of eternal punishment that Padre Rentería "estaba sembrando dentro de ella" (p. 184), the way in which

Dorotea articulates this negative state of affairs subtly opposes to it something more positive. It is Dorotea's body, not her soul, that speaks. And what it says, and says so beautifully—especially in that last image—is that it has found peace. The soul may still be tormented, but the body that is supposed to suffer eternal punishment has found peace in a moment of jubilee, even if this means giving up on life.[28] This warmth has already appeared two sections earlier, when Dorotea welcomes Juan Preciado into her grave. Reversing the natural order of things, Dorotea, the childless old woman who could have been his mother, is held like a baby in the arms of Juan, the motherless young man. Reversing the natural order of things (the dead don't speak), she nonetheless upholds and alters a certain tradition. Not the tradition of hellfire and damnation. But the tradition in which the elder offers the apprentice words of advice. The advice of a friend. Advice whose language derives its power, and its poetry, from the enunciation of the impossible, from the impossible enunciation: "Haz por pensar en cosas agradables porque vamos a estar mucho tiempo enterrados." In neither the rearticulation nor the rejection of the doctrine of the Final Judgement does pre-Colombian religion surface as a matrix of resignification; the work of transculturation is performed on written Western orthodoxy by a folk Catholicism of European origin, which has been processed in the speech of a marginalized Mexican mestizo peasantry.[29] Either way religion and Church law are no foundation stones.

"Luvina" and the Time of Tradition

The story "Luvina" occupies a special place in Rulfo criticism because it holds out the possibility of splicing *El llano en llamas* down the middle and inserting *Pedro Páramo* into its midst. That way, both books can be taken as depictions of a traditional Mexico at odds with the modern (Western) age.[30] Above all, it becomes possible to assimilate "Luvina" to the novel on the basis of their similar treatments of time.[31] Like the novel, the story thematizes time as the time of stasis, death, eternity. This is the time of tradition understood traditionally, a temporality turned toward the past as exemplary model that governs the present and future, condemning them to ritualized repetition.[32] The temporality in "Luvina" jars with the time of *desarrollismo*, the state-sponsored ideology of development, which had brought significant change to 1940s' and 1950s' Mexico. "Luvina" shapes up as the portrait in sepia of a pueblo left behind by modernization.

However, the presence of a cultural attitude, "which sees the present as the repetition of the past," does not mean that such a society actually repeats the past or is "static."[33] A distinction must be drawn between lived time, which moves forward even in traditional societies, and a conception of time that believes time to be static. Thus, the narrator of the story, who is a schoolteacher from the modern world, cannot be sure how long he spent in Luvina, but says: "debió haber sido una eternidad . . . Y es que allá el tiempo es muy largo."[34] The truth is that it is not that time does not pass in the town; it is that the inhabitants' primordial *conception* of time involves no sense of time being accumulated and progressing. For them, time entails the repetition of the same, like a wheel raised off the ground that goes round without ever going anywhere. In Luvina, the days begin, the days end, then night falls and so on until death:

> Nadie lleva la cuenta de las horas ni a nadie le preocupa cómo van amontonándose los años. Los días comienzan y se acaban. Luego viene la noche. Solamente el día y la noche hasta el día de la muerte, que para ellos es una esperanza. (P. 126)

The repetition of days and nights might almost be the annulment of time. The text seems to say as much: "todo se queda quieto, sin tiempo, como si se viviera siempre en la eternidad" (p. 126). And yet, the *como si* structure is telling, suggesting an *impression* of timelessness formed by one striving to communicate the strangeness of the place, and resorting to a traditional hyperbolic comparison to do so.

In reality, the narrator makes it clear that the time in question corresponds to the experience of the old villagers. Thus, what began as a general "nobody" ("Nadie lleva la cuenta de los años") is soon made specific, and it begins to look as though the temporality of Luvina is not an essential property of its premodern socioeconomic condition (traditionality), but is an effect produced by the perspective of the old:

> Estar sentado en el umbral de la puerta, mirando la salida y la puesta del sol, subiendo y bajando la cabeza, hasta que acaban aflojándose los resortes y entonces todo se queda quieto, sin tiempo, como si se viviera siempre en la eternidad. Eso hacen allí los viejos. (P. 126)

The added detail ("Eso hacen allí los viejos") warns us against describing the text as a portrait of "traditional" Mexico. If the portrait is traditional, it is in part because the portraiture is traditional. That is, the narrative that paints the picture takes pains to paint a traditional picture of tradition. The question of technique, and of the productive—as opposed to merely reproductive—power of writing, is paramount here. Rulfo was conscious that his work did not merely "register" the truth of traditional Mexico in accordance with the mimetic ideal, but was rather a "transposition" of rural Mexico.[35] In fact, the text's understanding of tradition is shot through with cliché and stereotype. Thus Luvina is inhabited by old people and women—at least those kinds of women traditionally classed as passive-helpless ("mujeres sin fuerzas," "mujeres solas, o con un marido que anda donde sólo Dios sabe dónde")—while the act of procreation receives its arch-traditional masculinist metaphorization in the form of the sowing of seed by the active male. The men return once in a while to "planta[r] otro hijo en el vientre de sus mujeres," disappearing for another year, or perhaps forever:

Es la costumbre. Allí le dicen la ley pero es lo mismo. Los hijos se pasan la vida trabajando para los padres como ellos trabajaron para los suyos y como quién sabe cuántos atrás de ellos cumplieron con su ley. (P. 126)

But this raises the question: Where are the children that issue from this seed sowing? The story mentions children several times, but on each occasion they are the narrator's own offspring, never the townspeople's. The children of Luvina and the activity of childrearing in Luvina are absent from the frame. One understands that the male activity of laboring in the fields does not figure, because that work is done outside Luvina. But young women's work, and children themselves are airbrushed out of the portrait by the portraiture.[36] It is as though childrearing, and by extension women, who are the principal transmitters of tradition, the principal physical, umbilical means of "connecting present and future" (Giddens), played no part in the maintenance and transmission of custom, law, and tradition. Women and the intense activity of childrearing fall below the threshold of significance. In the schoolteacher's arch-traditional description of tradition, practices that are manifestly perpetuated by labor and the expenditure of energy, receive a description that is instead premised on stasis.

The conception of traditional reversible time that the schoolteacher deploys is at one with an uncritical understanding of the relationship between tradition and modernity in which the two stand as opposing archetypes.[37] What the conception of traditional time really means, however, is not that there has been no quantitative chronological movement in such traditional societies. It means that there has been no *qualitative* development: that is, that the passage of time has brought no significant social change. The problem arises when commentators confuse concept and lived world, when the belief that the traditional world is static is taken for the traditional world itself. Blanco Aguinaga sees "Luvina" mesh seamlessly with *Pedro Páramo*, where Rulfo's reality ends up in a "verdadero mundo sin historia, sin tiempo, muerto." "Todo el tiempo," he continues, "es ya una sola eternidad sepultada."[38] Joseph Sommers, too, writes of the "timeless perspective of the afterlife," and of the "negation of history."[39] This way of speaking about the novel calls forth two clarifications. First, as Carlos Monsiváis has observed, all this talk of timelessness has myth as its common denominator. The net effect of reducing everything in *Pedro Páramo* to myth is that rural Mexico is primitivized and exoticized (Monsiváis, p. 36). It is not that myth cannot serve to understand time in the novel. As Lévi-Strauss recognized, myths are not timeless, but are at once historical and ahistorical.[40] They may transcend time or condense multiple times, but they are not timeless. What happens in the above critical readings of Rulfo and rural tradition is that allegory and hyperbole are taken literally. When Rulfo says in the late 1960s that "En México estamos estabilizados en un punto muerto" (in Harss, p. 312), he uses stock hyperbole as a comment on the lack of social progress in the Mexico of the time. And he does the same thing in writing about a "timeless," "dead" town in Mexico in 1955. Not because he thinks traditional society is timeless, but because Comala's apparent timelessness stands as a metaphor for a revolutionary society that failed to secure meaningful social reform in rural areas.

The second point is that it is difficult to conceive of a mythical place as timeless for reasons that have to do with the essential problem of portraying death and eternity without slipping back into the spatio-temporal logic and syntax of our own language and thought. Thus Juan Preciado shares a grave with Dorotea, which, the text tells us, is distanced in space from another occupied by Susana San Juan. Likewise, when Juan Preciado speaks, he does so in a manner that carefully respects the conventional passing of worldly time. It is symptomatic of a certain critical haste that Jean Franco should evoke the putative stasis of Comala by invoking the passage where Juan Preciado has to breathe in the air he has just breathed out, that is, by invoking the very activity (breathing) that dictates the rhythm and time of life.[41] *Pedro Páramo* is the "fantastic" performance of the (im)possibility of imagining the ultimate other.

Blanco Aguinaga gave the debate on Rulfo and the time of tradition an added twist by claiming that the traditional order finds its linguistic corollary in the verbal repetition that marks Rulfo's writing. When the narrator of "Talpa," or when Juan Preciado in the first fragment of *Pedro Páramo*, repeats certain phrases, it is in order to "hacer así que todas sus palabras queden suspensas en un mismo momento sin historia."[42] A static society that repeats the past is locked into linguistic repetition. However, it is possible to view this speech in a manner that recognizes the presence of traditional speech habits without conceiving of them, like the tradition that they would represent, as unerring markers of a static society sealed off from the future. Monsiváis writes of Rulfo's recreation of the peasants' reiterative logic as verbal *dynamic* (p. 36). Linguistic repetition may be the marker of orality, but orality cannot simply be equated with the absence of time or movement. Both Juan Preciado and the narrator of "Talpa" are involved in phatic acts of communication: Juan Preciado, because he is explaining things, and explaining himself, to Dorotea; the narrator of the short story, because he is locked into a form of repetition-compulsion in the narrative exorcism of guilt. Both characters reiterate and consolidate what they have said, in a manner that doubtless betrays ponderousness as they trawl falteringly through the material of memory. But this gaucheness indicates nevertheless that consideration and judgment are actively at work. Although linguistic repetition is indeed a key marker of orality in Rulfo, to speak of immutability and fixity is to rule out the possibility that the traditional mindset could ever diverge sufficiently from the doxa, and from itself, to protest. Let us recall that when the narrator of "Luvina" mentions to the old inhabitants the possibility that the government might help them move to better lands, it is the luveños who demonstrate cynicism. Despite the arch-traditional thing they say about needing to stay in Luvina to be with their dead, it is the traditionalists who are the skeptics and who question the authority of the *gobierno*, deriding the illegitimacy of its foundations. They know the government only too well, the text says: "De lo que no sabemos nada es de la madre del gobierno."

The Origins of Technique

It remains to consider the relationship between tradition and narrative technique. A useful starting point is again provided by Rama, who maintains that the form of Rulfo's novel derives from traditional

Mexican popular culture. The transculturators's re-immersion (*repliegue*) into traditional culture offered them literary techniques subtly different from the modernizing options, and made it possible for Rulfo to "oppose" the compartmentalized narratives of Dos Pasos and Huxley, born of the juxtaposition of "pedazos sueltos de una narración," with the "discurrir dispersivo" of the traditional "comadres pueblerinas." This solution provides narrative devices that "proceden de una recuperación de las estructuras de la narración oral y popular" (Rama, *Transculturación*, p. 44).[43]

Without denying the literary intertextuality that arises from erudite culture, Rama is interested rather in the intertextuality that issues from "a multiplicity of sources" including oral tradition, folklore, popular literature, journalism, and religious or political discourses ("Processes," p. 169). This expanded, less hierarchical sense of intertextuality moves away from the notion of a "literary" text to one defined more broadly as "cultural." To his credit, this shift is not a straightforward affair in Rama. There is a constant battle in his work between the idea that the writers of transculturation are engaged in a cultural practice, and the reminder that their work is specifically literary (see Rama "Processes," p. 169). Despite such caveats, and despite the fact that at one point in the book he writes of a coming together of indigenous traditions and modern Western thought in the exercise of mythical thought (p. 55), Rama's reflections on literary "structuration" do not tally with the thrust of his argument concerning transculturation. Why is it a question of "opposing" traditional forms of oral popular culture to the new "modernized" ones, of asserting that Rulfo's technique derives from the *comadres pueblerinas* rather than from Dos Pasos or Huxley? If the transculturators were involved in a retreat back or re-immersion (*repliegue*, literally "folding back") into traditional culture, is this not because they have been out of traditional culture and have returned to it on the back of the experience of modernity? Rama severely downplays the extent to which the "retreat back" is made possible by a venturing out.

Rama pursues his case in the section on "Cosmovisión," in which the key role is played by myth. The study of myth in the twentieth century, he recounts, was inspired by English anthropology, by psychoanalysis and studies of religion. The incorporation of myth into the work of an Asturias or a Carpentier could not disguise the fact that the origins and intellectual foundations of the interpretative system lay elsewhere. However, once the rationalist discourse of regionalism is more thoroughly brought into question, the re-immersion into traditional culture becomes possible:

> Este repliegue restablece un contacto fecundo con las fuentes vivas, que son las inextinguibles de la invención mítica en todas las sociedades humanas, pero aun más alertas en las comunidades rurales. Se redescubren las energías embridadas por los sistemas narrativos que venía aplicando el regionalismo, se reconocen las virtualidades del habla y las de las estructuras del narrar popular. Se asiste así al reconocimiento de un universo dispersivo, de asociacionismo libre, de incesante invención que correlaciona ideas y cosas, de particular ambigüedad y oscilación. Existía desde siempre, pero había quedado oculto por los rígidos órdenes literarios que respondían al pensamiento científico y sociológico propiciado por el positivisimo. [. . .] La quiebra de este sistema lógico deja en libertad la materia real perteneciente a las culturas internas de América Latina y permite apreciarla en otras dimensiones. (*Transculturación*, pp. 52–53)

A dispersed universe marked by free association of ideas, by inventive ways of relating ideas and things, and by ambiguity and indeterminacy: this is the rejection of the constricting rationalist—and literary realist—tradition of the West. Let us be clear about this: Everything that Rama says about the antirationalist quality of marginal oral cultures is true (although the barely disguised idealization of traditional rural life has had to reimport all those values of creativity and dynamism that had formerly been denied it); and everything that Rama says about this antirationalism is equally applicable to the efforts of Western modernism to contest the dominant Western rationalist tradition. This is the central duplicity of Rama's argument: on the one hand, it recognizes that the transculturators went out into Western modernity for creative sources; on the other hand, the extent to which the undermining of the dual poles of philosophical rationalism and literary realism belongs to the history of the West itself is passed over in silence and attributed instead to non-Western traditional cultures.

It will be objected that to concede that high-literary Western modernism has the same antirationalist impulse as the mythical narratives of traditional non-Western oral culture, offers no grounds to accord the greater protagonism in Rulfo's writing to modernism. Let me cite three reasons to foreground modernism. First, Latin American *vanguardismo*, which, as Rama says, was already antirationalist, had precisely been forged in dialogue with modernism. Second, and as Rama himself again says, in order to discover the subcontinent's interior, the new generation of writers had to draw on the technical resources of Western "modernity"—for which read "modernism." Rama argues convincingly that Rulfo's literary preference was for the nordic writers (Knut Hamsun, Halldór Laxness) and others such as Faulkner who belonged to rural areas on the periphery of industrial modernity. But these intertexts fall away with his suggestion that *Pedro Páramo* owes its form principally to popular oral narrative. Third, and most importantly, although many of the myths in Rulfo may derive from marginal cultures, the structure of *Pedro Páramo* does not derive from mythical forms. Mythical forms are characterized by their attachment to traditional narrative structures. *Rulfo's writing draws on the content of myth to produce a subversion of traditional narrative form.* He processes (largely) traditional antirational materials through a (largely) modern antirationalist technique.

By the early 1950s, modernism had become a vast processing-machine offering up a generalized technical "bank" available to cultural producers from the fields of high and mass popular culture alike. *Pedro Páramo*'s montage structure and technique of narration from the grave have clear precedents both in the domain of high modernism (Faulkner's *As I Lay Dying* or Eliot's *The Wasteland*) and in Hollywood cinema (Welles's *Citizen Kane*, 1941, and Billy Wilder's *Sunset Boulevard*, 1950).[44] The presence of this communal technical bank undoubtedly calls into question the existence of supposedly distinct cultural fields called high and mass popular culture respectively. However, it tells us little about the precise reasons why and the ways in which a Rulfo might be said to augment, rather than simply deplete, the bank's reserves. The nature and quality of a text is not determined solely by the origin of its subject matter, but more so by the way in which a text processes its material. The cultivation of formal complexity is important: it bears on Rulfo's desire not only to go beyond traditional narrative forms, but to take leave of the (Mexican) Roman trinity.

Demo(cra)tic Design

Rulfo joins a tradition of twentieth-century writing, which stretches back at least to Joyce, whose aim was to subvert the Roman trinity *by formal means*. *Pedro Páramo* is the result of intensive pruning carried out primarily to excise an overzealous didacticism—the "explicaciones"—from the original draft and have his readers cooperate in the production of meaning:[45]

> la intención fue—porque no le corté las páginas así, arbitrariamente, no, no fui arrancándolas y tirándolas—fue quitarle las explicaciones. Era un libro un poco didáctico, casi pedagógico: daba clases de moral y yo no sé cuántas cosas y todo eso tuve que eliminarlo porque no soy muy moralista y además... sí, fui dejando algunos hilos colgando para que el lector me... pues, cooperara con el autor en la lectura. Entonces, es un libro de cooperación. Si el lector no coopera, no lo entiende; él tiene que añadir lo que le falta. (P. 11)

Rulfo's formulation is a less contentious version of Julio Cortázar's call for a *lector cómplice*. Leaving aside the (later deeply regretted) recourse to an ancient phallogocentric association between femininity and passivity in the gendering of the companion term (*lector hembra*), Cortázar was attempting to name a new type of reader for a new type of writing. *Cómplice* is from the Latin *complex*, from *complicare*, meaning complexity. The new reader was to be an accomplice in complexity, in a writing that was fluid and ambiguous, open-ended and open-minded, a writing that owed more to the perspectival elasticity of twentieth-century art and thought than to the iron laws of causality and objectivism that came to dominate nineteenth-century realism. Meaning would now be produced rather than revealed. The reader would be an accomplice in a crime against the law that holds meaning to be the exclusive property of an Author, to be revealed solely by those in Authority. The new writing, in contrast, would be an "essentially anti-theological activity" opposed to tradition and authority, "God and his hypostases," and aligned instead with the values of critical openness and democracy.[46]

El llano en llamas is moved by this democratic spirit. But if the stories eschew the fantastic elements of the novel, they also quietly depart from the traditional discourse of realism. Stylistically they cultivate the demotic, limited-perspective first-person narrative, whereas their subject matter is often formed by events that fall below the threshold of History. The reason for these choices is both aesthetic and ethical. Aesthetically speaking, the limited-perspective narrative opens up innovative, oblique angles, and the use of a demotic idiom makes for a new, laconic poetics. Ethically speaking, the use of the vernacular and the refusal of History ensure that events are told in a would-be democratic manner consistent with the characters' own language and limited perspective. In "Nos han dado la tierra," it is "they," not the PRI or Cárdenas, who have given "us" the land. The avoidance of History, and of the traditional moralizing omniscient voice of realism, is the narrative corollary of the general modern rejection of the Mexican Roman trinity of authority, religion, and tradition. If there is to be criticism and dissent, these are to be worked out between characters and readers rather than pass by way of the priest's voice.

The novel, in contrast, presents and demands a more complex form of complicity, above all for reasons having to do with the question of time, which is not the time of tradition. If at the level of content the novel seems to depict a dead or timeless town, this is because it portrays not a traditional society, but a society from which the traditional life-blood has been drained. Even less does the novel conform to the time of tradition at the level of form. It demands not just a dynamic process of reading (reading is dynamic in its essence), but a heightened reading performance that hopes to align itself with the democratic values of participation and openness. Narrative time in the novel produces *différance* rather than repetition of the same; it performs the tentative construction of meaning rather than confirms a meaning given at the outset. Rulfo participates less in myth, whose form is much more bound by tradition, than in the ambiguous, fragmentary discourse of modernism. At every juncture, but most acutely up to its midpoint, *Pedro Páramo* frustrates the traditional expectations produced by the ancien regime of realism. Thus, to say that the novel's narrator or characters are "dead" represents a judgment formulated *post factum*, which ignores the fabric of the text. Narrator and characters are deliberately not presented to us as "dead" from the outset. Death is not a *factum* given as *fatum*, something decided in advance, known and accepted. Narrator and characters are introduced before being systematically annulled. This is the fate first of Abundio, then Eduviges, then Damiana, then Juan. And because we cannot erase the experience of seeing them first as "alive," the characters have a spectral existence. This spectral quality is reinforced by the text's fragmented structure. Our first encounter with Abundio suggests he is "alive," then we learn he is "dead," then we wait the entire duration of the novel until we see him alive before he first met Juan Preciado. The novel's complex web of repetitions and foreshadowings performs spectrality, rendering uncertain the flickering border between life and death in the crisscross weave of memory and narration.

Narrative fragmentation is a response to societal fracture but also to epistemological disjuncture. One of the guiding principles of modern art, fragmentation challenges traditional single-point perspective. Fragmentation is supposed to be the sign of a modern world whose sheer complexity renders its narrativization in traditional form impossible. The art of the fragment, it is said, is coterminous with pluralism and modern democracy, with participation in the making of meaning. But Rulfo's fragments must be read without seeing fragmentation, or complicity in the production of fragmented meaning, as an absolute good (or indeed invention) of modern democratic times, and without believing that reading is not in its very origin a mental processing of a highly sophisticated order. The nature of the fragment is not so clear-cut. On the one hand, the incomplete fragment leaves room for intervention and for a future that, although not altogether eluding the shadows and echoes of tradition, need not merely repeat tradition.[47] On the other hand, the discourse of fragmentation is still tied to a traditional notion of the text's depth, aura, and sanctity. The fragment always promises, and withholds at the same time, the secret totality of which it is by definition a mere part; it always suggests the existence of a whole to whose revelation we will never be an accomplice. What is more, the fragment can always end in the most terminal, authoritative laconicism to match anything from the pulpit. *Pedro Páramo* cultivates them. But we forgive them. Because their content, even when they contain cruel words, is not cruel. Rama rightly said that Rulfo's art is a return to poetry, to the exercise of epos, where cadence and sound can count for as much as, if not more than, logical meaning.

Conclusion

Three conclusions impose themselves. First, to hear in Rulfo a meaningful voice of pre-Colombian Mexico is, I think, to credit him with something that he did not and probably could not do. Native American culture only really came into his viewfinder in his photographic and administrative work. Second, the profound and very real differences between modern and traditional cultures in Mexico cannot be construed in strictly oppositional terms, with all the values of movement, development and futurity being ascribed to modernity, and those of stasis, repetition, and preteriteness assigned to tradition. Better to think of mixed rhythms or intersecting networks. Look, for instance, at Rulfo's photograph of the traditional *lavanderas* (Fuentes et al., *Juan Rulfo's Mexico*, p. 98). Not only has the position of the sinks made it difficult for him to take a head-on shot of the women's faces—one of his favored modes of stylizing eternity. There is also a child on the loose in the bottom of the frame. The child will not be able to escape the death-dealing drive of photography. Nevertheless, oblivious to the camera, he does not present the face of immobile oblivion. Furthermore, and shifting our own focus just a little, there is the electric light in the background. A solitary light, it forms part of the network connecting modern and traditional Mexico, tying the nation together in the name of illumination and progress. Where once divinities alone brought light, now they must compete with the Comisión Federal de Electricidad. "Luvina" colludes in the traditional view of tradition as stasis through a narrator who actively re-produces it, on account of what he frames and what he chooses to omit. Ultimately, though, the story cannot maintain the notion that tradition is where time stands still, where the present is a mere unquestioning repetition of the past. It is precisely in the clash between the traditional and the modern that the short stories' social interest lies. The novel, in contrast, hyperbolizes the "deadness" of Mexican society, but ascribes this morbidity to the virtual annihilation of tradition (a destruction in which premodern attitudes collude) rather than to its dominance. The third and final conclusion, then, is that the critical gesture begins with technique.

CHAPTER 8

This Is Not a Revolution: Carpentier on the Age of Enlightenment

The modern world has changed the meaning of the word *revolution*. The original meaning—the turning of the worlds and the stars—has another, now the more usual, placed beside it: a violent breaking with the old order and the establishment of a new, more just, or more rational order. The turning of the stars was a visible manifestation of circular time; in its new meaning, *revolution* became the most perfect expression of sequential, linear, and irreversible time. One implied the eternal return of the past; the other the destruction of the past and the building of a new society.

—Octavio Paz[1]

Para mí, no existe la modernidad en el sentido que se le otorga.

—Alejo Carpentier[2]

Although the modern world has changed the meaning of the word *revolution*, when Alejo Carpentier writes about the revolution most closely identified with modernity, he applies the ancient meaning of the word to it. Because he does not believe in the modernity of the French Revolution. Because he does not believe in the modernity of modernity. From the very first line of *El siglo de las luces*, the guillotine (*la Máquina*), the machine of a violent breaking, is juxtaposed with the constellations of the night sky, with the turning of the worlds and the stars.[3] The ephemeral product of instrumental reason is dwarfed by the vast permanent-seeming cosmos. Carpentier does not, however, "analyze" the relationship between the Machine and the stars.[4] Although *El siglo de las luces* is not devoid of analysis, by virtue of its association with Western rationalism, analysis is one of the things against which the novel sets its face (as it looks up to the stars).

Carpentier's novel is essentially a work of demystification in the tradition of Left counter-Enlightenment thought. The "century of lights" is depicted as irrational, arbitrary, and dark.[5] Carpentier's parti-pris is clear from the decision to call a novel the *siècle des lumières* but proceed to write about the French Revolution as though the latter were a simple substitute for the former.[6] The novel is not, however, just a work of denunciation. It utters a great "yes" to what more rigid forms of the Enlightenment sought to demote (popular belief, superstition, nonrational knowledge). The cue for this affirmative note comes from romanticism and a later antiethnocentrism. The latter makes itself felt most obviously in the positive role played by Ogé, but also in the Caribbeanization of religion and nature, both of which offer Grand Narratives able to shed light on the failings of revolution.[7] The more important of the two is nature. The novel's meditations on nature, which derive from the eighteenth and twentieth centuries, suggest that nature puts things into perspective. Above all what nature puts into perspective, what it puts in its (smaller than imagined) place, is the Revolution.

But if Antillean nature is the archetype of the baroque, that is, a joyous principle of endless creativity, nature also conforms to a teleotheological narrative in its prefiguration of human history and individual destiny. Critics have maintained that Carpentier ends the novel with Sofía and Esteban's romantic rebellion in the Madrid uprising against Napoleon because it was the overthrow of the Bourbon monarch that led to Spanish American independence.[8] But such an analysis must explain why the voluntaristic romantic existentialism that underpins the characters' actions in Spain is accompanied by a much more traditional deterministic thematics. This determinism is inscribed at the novel's propositional level in the discourse of revelationism that attaches to its treatment of religion and nature. But it is not confined there. In its very form, *El siglo de las luces* works essentially according to an old deterministic logic—what Borges calls "la primitiva claridad de la magia." Just before the world of Carpentier's three young protagonists is turned upside-down by events in revolutionary France, they are buffeted by a violent tropical storm that sweeps across the island. It is as though nature herself, in accordance with a universe ruled by omens and presages, destiny and fate, had announced the Great Upheaval. It is as though "magic," not rationality, governed the order of things. Beyond the text's express anti-Enlightenment content, the novel's narrative art harbors a premodern logic that distances it from analysis as from the autonomous subject of Enlightenment modernity.

Of Ripe Immaturity: Enlightenment and Popular Culture

The opening chapter of *El siglo de las luces* careers brilliantly through the adolescents' politico-sentimental education in Havana, an education that is clearly in line with Enlightenment values. The inadequation between tradition and the adolescents' aspirations is expressed primarily as a leave-taking of the Church and an embrace of travel (engine of the novel's action). Sofía resolves to break with the convent while Carlos and Esteban, dreaming of the promises of a new, secular world, fiddle with the celestial globe ("símbolo del Comercio y la Navegación") as the Mother Superior extols the joys of monastic life. From this point on, prayers cede to secular life; new books and scientific instruments arrive; the forbidden flute is brought out; the normal day is inverted. And then Víctor Hugues arrives. In truth, it seems that the novel's target at this point is not the Enlightenment, but the spirit of inner-worldly asceticism.[9] What the adolescents seem above all to reject are the combined values of austerity and material acquisitiveness characteristic of the dead merchant father.[10]

Everything that has happened thus far in the novel predates the arrival of Hugues.[11] Consequently, if the adolescents' enlightenment does not conform to the Kantian model of enlightenment as a self-willed leaving behind of immaturity ("Enlightenment is man's release from his self-incurred tutelage. Tutelage is man's inability to make use of his understanding without direction from another. Self-incurred is this tutelage when its cause lies not in lack of reason but in lack of resolution and courage to use it without direction from another. *Sapere aude!* 'Have courage to use your own reason!'—that is the motto of Enlightenment"), this is not due to the fact that their transition is willed by another.[12] Rather, it is due to the essential difficulty involved in conforming to Kant's prescription, which is premised on a fully grown individual who seems either to have been born mature or to have made himself mature without the office of any other human being.[13] In this novel, on the contrary, immaturity is of the essence. Immaturity appears in the text, which never ceases to stress the adolescents' youthfulness, as a condition of preparedness for enlightenment. Their youthfulness and immaturity are what make them ripe. And the freemason, freethinker,

Enlightenment Man who will make them feel truly young ("«Es la primera vez que me siento realmente joven»dijo Esteban"), who will for the first time lead them out into the Cuban night "después de la hora del rosario," is not just another father, another "paternalistic authority."[14]

The first chapter is a roll call of Enlightenment topoi: the embracing of modern mores in preference to traditional customs; the importance of science and new learning; the greater incorporation of women into public life and intellectual debate; the triumvirate of secularism, rationalism, and antimonarchism. And yet the chapter takes significant steps beyond the Enlightenment, adding in the more Romantic emphases of youth, travel and personal liberation, together with those things (such as popular culture, superstition, the magical content of religious belief, and nonrational knowledge) regarded as anathema by the proponents of reason and progress. The lessons imparted by the first chapter correspond to the spirit of the Kantian injuncture to judge for oneself, but not necessarily to the contents of Enlightenment thought. In addition to the classes on Enlightenment contents, the most extended of which concerns politics, and the burden of which is borne by freemasonry, there is a lesson on the body. In accordance with an old prejudice, this lesson is best learnt among the popular classes, or, better still, among the black popular classes. It is a lesson in corporeal rhythms (*baile, músicas, risas, desaforo, caderas, muslos*, "ritmo de una guaracha que siempre volvía al intencionado estribillo de ¿*Cuándo, mi vida, cuándo?*"), which ends with Sofía being seduced by Víctor. Then there is a lesson on black culture and the limitations of Western knowledge, when Ogé successfully overcomes Esteban's asthma and Sofía's prejudice with the aid of traditional, non-Western medicine. Indeed, it is the figure of Ogé, with his eclectic faith and no less eclectic medicine, who will emerge as the key teacher of the novel's central value: ethical pluralism.

The novel then proceeds, first in France and later in the colonies, to treat of the French Revolution's shortcomings and betrayals of its own political and philosophical ideals. And there are plenty of betrayals. The Revolutionaries turn against foreign supporters; Cayenne is made into a prison "mucho peor que cualquiera Bastilla" (p. 107); Víctor Hugues rescinds the Decree that had freed the slaves; Robespierre is executed. It often happens that the logic of the Revolution, and of the text, is that of the *volte-face*. No need for analysis; it suffices to highlight a rapid change of mind for the denunciation to be complete. At other times, an analysis of sorts is brought to bear on events, though not always successfully. When the character Sieger observes that the blacks in the

Americas did not need the French Revolutionaries to tell them they were free ("Los negros no los esperaron a ustedes para proclamarse libres un número incalculable de veces"), he makes a telling antiethnocentric point. The French Revolution did not invent, much less have a monopoly over, the instinct for freedom. However, his preceding phrase ("Todo lo que hizo la Revolución Francesa en América fue legalizar una Gran Cimarronada que no cesa desde el siglo XVI" [p. 270]) is more problematic. Confusing two different realms, it dismisses the juridical sphere on the grounds that it is secondary in relation to historical fact. By that logic, one could dismiss any and every law. If it is true that moral right is on the side of the slaves, it is no less true that, *in the world of the law-makers*, extending legal recognition to the slaves' freedom stands as a radical politico-juridical achievement.

The Two Functions of Religion: Birthright and Grand Narrative

One of the Revolution's more jarring *voltes-face* is its reauthorization of religion. Having outlawed religion for its part in the oppressive ancien regime, religious belief is suddenly reinstated. We must be careful with religion and belief. For the protagonists of the European Enlightenment, the Church was the principal obstacle to philosophical, scientific, and political progress. For the best part of one and a half millennia, right down to the 1650s, ecclesiastical authority had exerted a stranglehold on the parameters of knowledge in a Europe governed by monarchy, aristocracy, and the Church itself.[15] At least in Kant, the argument for the use of critical reason is a petition for a form of thought against tradition and history, above all for a self-validating thought freed from religious authority.[16] Typically for a counter-Enlightenment text, which does not run altogether against the spirit of Enlightenment, *El siglo de las luces* accords religion a more positive role. Although one could argue, certainly taking Ogé's philosophy as a benchmark, that "the Christian church survives, despite rationalist persecutions and prohibitions, as if it were a testimony to a spiritual and mythological impulse in human beings" (Dulog Matibag, p. 232), it would appear, rather, that the novel deploys religion in two, less conventional ways. First, religion is part of a cultural tradition that provides anchorage in a specific place (synchronic function). Religion is a tying back (*religare*) to tradition, a bond to community and to a certain way of life. This is the message of Esteban's stay in the Basque country. Second, religion is a link to tradition understood as lineage (diachronic function). The novel opposes to the would-be uniqueness of the Revolution a religious grand narrative, which knows how to put the French uprising in its place. In both cases, it is the conceptual violence condensed into the figures of rupture, cut, erasure, and *tabula rasa* that draws the novel's fire.

The first understanding of religion emerges from a key epiphanic passage, in the Hospital of Saint-Paul-de-Chartres in Cayenne, where Esteban declares the Revolution's principal failing to be a religious one. Why does the atheist Esteban consider the absence of true religion to be the Revolution's Achilles Heel? And why does he say this just after the Revolution has restored religion? It is a matter of historical record that the restoration of religion was an act of *realpolitik*. The earlier outlawing of religion merely deprived the leaders of the Revolution of "the only political element in traditional religion."[17] The restoration allows the Revolution to use for its own ends the population's fear of an avenging God and belief in a future state. However, insofar as it restores one of the fundamental pillars of the "Roman trinity," the Revolution shares the essentially paradoxical relationship with modernity that is the lot of all modern revolutions. Ironically, for phenomena commonly imagined as ruptures with the past *par excellence*, and to that extent the very symbol of a modernity understood as a decisive break with the past, modern revolutions are perhaps the sole type of event that recovers in decisive fashion the old Roman notion of founding.[18] The key point is that in this founding, Robespierre and Machiavelli were unroman in their belief that all means—chief among them violence—were justified to achieve the desired end. In other words, if revolution is to be thought of as a founding, it is more properly a founding as forging, a founding as making. It is this founding as forging, this "initiating a new order of things," in Machiavelli's phrase, the production of rapid change by means of conceptual no less than physical violence, which provokes Esteban's wrath.

Let us follow the novel's logic. It is no ordinary, we might say traditional, conception of religion. One even has a right to this religion, the text says unusually, without it being necessary to have faith. Esteban has witnessed what for him is the last straw. With the arbitrariness of the best of tyrants, the Revolution suddenly restores religion. Everything appears to be as it was. *And yet the religion it restores is not the same religion.* The "restoration" does not amount to putting things back the way they were.[19] The leaders of the Revolution create their own, amended pantheon to appropriate the authority that formerly belonged to the Church and thereby overcome the problem of legitimacy, which, by definition, since they constitute a break with the past and thus a severance of the bonds of tradition, is the problem faced by every revolutionary regime. The "restoration" seeks to tie people back to a past and a tradition that are not theirs. The Revolution lacks foundations, lacks solid godly foundations. Robespierre's God has been made too rapidly. He has never come among humankind nor does he belong to a great tradition; he is a god without history, an invalid god:

> la debilidad de la Revolución, que tanto atronaba el mundo con las voces de un nuevo *Dies Irae*, estaba en su ausencia de dioses válidos. El Ser Supremo era un dios sin historia. No le había surgido un Moisés con estatura suficiente para escuchar las palabras de la Zarza Ardiente, concertando una alianza entre el Eterno y las tribus de su predilección. No se había hecho carne ni había habitado entre nosotros. A las ceremonias celebradas en su honor faltaba la Sacralidad; faltaba la continuidad de propósitos, la inquebrantabilidad ante lo contingente y inmediato que inscribía, en una trayectoria de siglos, al Lapidado de Jerusalem con los cuarenta Legionarios de Sebastés; al Arquero Sebastián, al Pastor Ireneo, los doctores Agustín, Anselmo y Tomás, con el moderno Felipe de Jesús, mártir de Filipinas, por quien varios santuarios mexicanos se adornaban de Cristos chinos, hechas de fibra de caña de azúcar, con tales texturas de carne que la mano, al tocarlos, retrocedía ante una ilusión de pálpito aún viviente en la herida de Lanza—única Lanza de tal suerte enrojecida—que se les abría en el costado. (Pp. 261–262)

Esteban's meditation does not end there, however. For religion is not only a canonical tradition or lineage of saints and theologians; it is a way of life, a way of relating to people and place. Esteban's sentiments are those of a popular counterreformation. Religion is a *patrimonio*, which is one's birthright without it being necessary to have faith:

> Sin necesidad de orar, puesto que no tenía fe, Esteban se complacía en la compañía del crucificado, sintiéndose devuelto a un clima familiar. Aquel Dios le pertenecía por herencia y derecho; podía rechazarlo, pero formaba parte del patrimonio de los de su raza. (p. 262)

"Aquel Dios le pertenecía por herencia y derecho," "podía rechazarlo": according to an intractable logic, the rejection of Enlightenment anticlericalism is couched in the discourse of Enlightenment (the Rights of Man, freedom of choice or religious expression). It is a rejection that only becomes possible after Spinoza.

The second function of religion is further reaching. Religion is not only thematized in the novel as a way of being in the world and of relating to others. Religion, or, more properly, a religious narrative, offers a running commentary on the Revolution, an unashamedly Grand Narrative that furnishes a framework for the interpretation of events. And the interpretation it offers is that we have been here before. Carpentier situates the discourse of modernity in the context of a long tradition, such that the heralding of the new appears very old. The Revolution, and not just the Revolution, is understood as apocalypse, as a wiping away of the old order and the advent of a new beginning.[20] It is an idea that accords well with the "apocalyptic" historiography of the Enlightenment and with modernity's own image of itself as a radical break with the past.[21] But the idea is evidently very old and it is this antiquity, specifically its rootedness in Christian tradition, which the novel constantly signals by using the linguistic and figurative materials of the Old Testament narrative, above all whenever it is a question of violence. It suffices for there to be a bombardment or for foreign troops to invade a city, for the sound of the Old Testament, at times quite literally "algún versículo del Apocalipsis," to ring out. On the one hand, this may be attributed to the fact that the worldview and figures of speech embedded in the Christian narrative belong to the era being portrayed. On the other hand, there is a simple message here: viz., the discourse of apocalypse has been heard repeatedly throughout human history and will be heard again. This is why Carpentier can say: "Para mí, no existe la modernidad en el sentido que se le otorga, el hombre es a veces el mismo en diferentes edades y situarlo en su pasado puede ser también situarlo en su presente." In Paris, Esteban steeps himself in the messianic, apocalyptic thought of millennarism because he wants to establish a genealogy for the Revolution in order to grasp the full sense of its and his destiny. For this time, he is sure, it will come to pass. But in actual fact what Esteban views, teleologically, as the culmination of history, the novel sees as one more repetition of an age-old desire for a new and better world.

In the great subchapter on Esteban's sea journey through the Bocas del Dragón, the text recounts the incorporation of the Caribbean into the Grand Christian Narrative, into the "Auto Sacramental del Gran

Teatro del Mundo." A world-weary Esteban, gazing upon a landscape unchanged since Columbus set eyes upon it, dwells on the persistence of the myth of the Promised Land: "Según el color de los siglos, cambiaba el mito de carácter, respondiendo a siempre renovadas apetencias, pero era siempre el mismo: había, debía haber, era necesario que hubiese en el tiempo presente—cualquier tiempo presente—un Mundo Mejor" (p. 289). The myth belongs to Christian tradition (the Portuguese, the Spanish, the Pilgrim Fathers) but, in a sense that is no less part of the history of Christianity, it belongs also to those opposed to the Christian Narrative (the Carib, the *encyclopédistes*, the French Revolutionaries). The Revolution thus appears, to a jaundiced Esteban, as the latest fateful manifestation foretold of a long tradition of apocalypse. Therein, too, the main reason for the "prolonged century":

> A medida que transcurrían los días de la navegación, pintábasele lo vivido como una larga pesadilla—pesadilla de incendios, persecuciones y castigos, anunciada por el Cazotte de los camellos vomitando lebreles; por los muchos augures del Fin de los Tiempos que tanto habían proliferado en este siglo, tan prolongado que totalizaba la acción de varios siglos. (P. 290)

It is not just that so many things have happened in it; it is because the present century seems to contain many of the preceeding ones. The Grand Narrative of religion allows Carpentier to diminish the importance of the Revolution. The century of light looks curiously like the many others that have gone before. Like Esteban, the novel does not necessarily have faith; it does, however, have a sense of history.

The Grand Narrative of Nature

And yet, the novel is not content with the dimensions furnished by the religious narrative. It seizes upon a narrative that is greater even than religion—above all Christian religion, which is clearly a latecomer.[22] This narrative stretches to incorporate something that has been missing from the text's litany of counter-Enlightenment topoi, which otherwise includes popular and Afro-Caribbean culture, non-Western knowledge, tradition and religion. According to its detractors, in its attempted rationalization of the world the Enlightenment submits nature to calculation as a prelude to its scientific and industrio-technological manipulation.[23] This rationalization Weber called the "de-magification" or "disenchantment of the world." Carpentier's text attempts to revivify the magic of a world that, in latitudes remote from the centers of instrumental reason, has never lost its marvelous quality. Just as, earlier in Paris, Esteban finds his line of sight leading naturally from the *camino de Santiago* up to the sky, Sofía's later meditation on the constellations of the night sky will take her beyond Christianity to a pagan, and ultimately cosmic, dimension. The novel embraces nature as a cosmic force whose dimensions cannot be confined to the narrative of Christianity. Above all, nature reveals itself as a source of understanding.

A number of different traditions of thought on nature converge in the novel. Apart from Carpentier's well-known recourse to Jungianism, two eighteenth-century elements furnish the novel with its basic philosophy. They are natural history and a largely Rousseauesque Romanticism. Both elements are present in the three important scenes involving the adolescents and nature: (1) Sofía's sea journey to Haiti; (2) Esteban's tree-climbing episode in the Basse-Terre; (3) the hymn to America that is the *caracol* episode. *El siglo de las luces* will consistently frame nature as an epistemological laboratory, and the contemplation of nature as the trigger to a heightened understanding of things other than the strictly natural.[24] However, contemplation of nature's harmony will not get the characters onto the streets of Madrid. Carpentier reminds us that the Romantics were men of action.[25] (To that extent, the cousins must exceed Rousseau, who did not intend man's capacity for free will to be exercised in the name of social revolution.[26]) The novel's dramatic thrust demands a self ultimately hewn out of a Romantic existentialism, in which the self uses the relationship with nature as a means of arming itself for a return to political action.

At the beginning of the sea journey to Haiti (it is hard not to hear Rousseau in this journey compared by Sofía to an excursion on a Swiss lake, "de románticas orillas empeñascadas; *promenade en bateau*" [p. 88]), Sofía's proximity to nature brings understanding of nature together with understanding of the self. Her exposure to the sea, and observation of the life-cycle, leads to a giving over of the self to a corporeal sensuousness far removed from Rousseau's Calvinism. It is significant, however, that although the episode ends with Sofía's sexual initiation, much of the scene is given over to Ogé's philosophy. The sea episode is a lesson in philosophical pluralism as much as a sentimental education.

In the Romantic revolution in feeling, pure, spontaneous nature becomes the measure of truth. But this truth can only be apprehended when the individual immerses himself bodily in nature. To understand and commune with nature, one must walk. In the second important immersion in nature in the novel, Esteban outdoes the Rousseau of *Les Rêveries du promeneur solitaire* (1782). He not only walks, but climbs. The scene is organized and narrated according to a precise *dispositio*. Everything works to demonstrate the superior understanding that is achieved through the relationship to nature. There are four clear steps. First, the life-cycle in general; second, the specifically Antillean life-cycle ("en este mundo sin muertes invernales ni resurrecciones en Pascuas Floridas" [p. 159]); third, one aspect of the Antillean cycle (rain); finally, the conclusion (the transcendence gained from the relationship with nature serves, too, in man's relationship with society). Let us underscore the point: the meditation on nature ends with a meditation on the relationship between man and society. Although the text suggests that the encounter with American nature alienates Esteban from society ("se sentía ajeno a la época"), what it really says, by means of the classic Enlightenment topos of detachment-as-objectivity— which is also expressed in terms of height ("Trepando a su mirador, entendía Esteban la relación . . .")—is that this distance affords a better view. Nature gives perspective, understanding, cosmic vision, clarity to the place of the smallest detail in the order of things. Just before this episode, Esteban considers the minutiae of nature as a respite from the enormity of political events. By the end of it, even if he remains affectively distanced from revolutionary affairs, the minutiae of nature have given him a keen sense of the former's unpalatable contradictions:

> Cuando Esteban volvía de tales andanzas [. . .] se sentía ajeno a la época; forastero en un mundo sanguinario y remoto, donde todo resultaba absurdo. Las iglesias permanecían cerradas cuando, acaso, las habían vuelto a abrir en Francia. Los negros habían sido declarados ciudadanos libres, pero los que no eran soldados o marinos por la fuerza, doblaban el lomo de sol a sol, como antes, bajo la tralla de sus vigilantes, detrás de los cuales se pintaba, por añadidura, el implacable azimut de la guillotina. (P. 191)

The third encounter with nature, the great hymn to American nature, is the much-discussed *caracol* episode.[27] Roberto González Echevarría has interpreted the text's discourse on the spiral as Carpentier's critique of his own widespread recourse to the idea of cyclical time, which now becomes a less deterministic spiral time fusing the cyclical and the linear-progressive (*The Pilgrim at Home*, p. 247). This idea appears to be reinforced by the novel's Byronic ending, in which Sofía and Esteban actively drive history forward in the Madrid uprising against Napoleon. It also receives support from the fact that the passage is about evolutionism. Jo Labanyi argues that nature becomes the model for Carpentier's developmental understanding of History, an understanding perfectly incarnated in the figure of the spiral.[28] However, such analyses do not explain why the book's stress on will and becoming is matched at every step by a more traditional determinism. The shell episode is indeed about time but not in the way critics imagine. The key to its interpretation lies in something González Echevarría says about Carpentier's work in general, namely, that it consistently uses authentic historical sources at the same time as it deploys deliberate anachronisms. The authentic sources derive from eighteenth-century natural history and the anachronism from allusions to the twentieth-century idea of the double helix structure of DNA. What neither strain of evolutionism can suppress from Carpentier's text, however, is an older revelationism, which stands at the passage's beginning and end. The revelation at the beginning is an old form (mysticism) filtered through a modern one (*lo real maravilloso americano*); the end revelation is a modern idea (the double helix structure of DNA) filtered through an old one (the world as given).

The passage begins under the sign of mysticism. This mysticism is produced not by asceticism, as in the traditional conception, but by an exalted, almost giddy sense of physical well-being brought on by the radiancy of the setting, one of the small Antillean islands:

> A eso llamaba sus «borracheras de agua», ofreciendo el cuerpo desnudo al ascenso del sol, echado de bruces en la arena, o de boca arriba, abierto de piernas y de brazos, aspado, con tal expresión de deleite en el rostro que parecía un místico bienaventurado favorecido por alguna Inefable Visión. (p. 203)

These lines are written to prescription. They correspond point for point to Carpentier's theory of *lo real maravilloso*, and the passage will tirelessly deploy variations of the word *maravilla*.[29] The "Ineffable Vision" is Caribbean nature itself, whose magnificent "architecture" (the text abounds in architectural analogies) inspires the reverence due any cathedral. Though it recalls late-eighteenth-century deism, the hymn of thanksgiving (*Tedéum*, the text chants twice) is to Carpentier's religion, the American marvelous real.[30] Thus, what begins as Gothic ("caracoles [. . .] como creaciones góticas") slides inexorably toward the magnificent excess of the baroque (the coral "jungle" sustained "los primeros barroquismos de la Creación").

The experience in question bears more than a passing resemblance to the Rousseauesque sublime (though with a greater emphasis on corporeal sensuousness), in which nature is no longer a demonstration of order, as in the French Classical Age, but rather an invitation to reverence, which is better accepted in solitude and in the midst of a nature "untouched by man, if not actually hostile to him" (Hampson, p. 206). And so, like some Antillean Jean-Jacques, and in order to "olvidarse de la época," Esteban strikes out for a remote part of the islands, fighting his way through the harsh landscape. Alone, naked, and adamic, Esteban contemplates *un caracol*—just one ("abismábase en la contemplación de un caracol—de uno solo" [p. 209]). Although the entire passage is marked by mysticism, revelation will be a more programmatic affair. What Esteban sees first as he contemplates the shell is not the shell. He sees an abstraction: that is, the shell as Mediator between land and sea, structure and evanescence. The text's logic at this juncture is dualistic and Greek: the closer Esteban gets to the Antillean, the more it is framed by the ancient opposition between Apollo and Dionysus, order and disorder, form and formlessness, male and female:

> El caracol era el Mediador entre lo evanescente, lo escurrido, la fluidez sin ley ni medida y la tierra de las cristalizaciones, estructuras y alternancias, donde todo era asible y ponderable. De la Mar sometida a ciclos lunares, tornadiza, abierta o furiosa, ovillada o destejida, por siempre ajena al módulo, el teorema y la ecuación, surgían esos sorprendentes carapachos, símbolos en cifras y proporciones de lo que precisamente faltaba a la Madre. Fijación de desarrollos lineales, volutas legisladas, arquitecturas cónicas de una maravillosa precisión, equilibrios de volúmenes, arabescos tangibles que intuían todos los barroquismos por venir. (P. 209)

The shell as Mediator is supposed to undo the oppositional logic, since it partakes of the two things that it mediates. But the text reasserts the separateness of the sea, since the sea lacks what the shell symbolizes, even if the sea in reality produces that which symbolizes the lack. The dualism sustains itself by misconstruing the sea, which is posited as "fluidez sin ley ni medida," but which, by virtue of being "sometida a ciclos lunares," cannot but be subject to a certain regularity. Finally, we again have the baroque. The shell is the American, natural incarnation of the expansive, centrifugal energy Carpentier finds in Bernini's Saint Peter's in Rome. The shell is the cipher of nature's, especially American nature's, primordiality; a nature that prefigures the manmade world; nature as Ur-text or archetype in respect of which all future baroque forms will forever be derivative.

There then follows the meditation on the spiral, which I reproduce in full:

> Contemplando un caracol—uno solo—pensaba Esteban en la presencia de la Espiral durante milenios y milenios, ante la cotidiana mirada de pueblos pescadores, aún incapaces de entenderla ni de percibir siquiera la realidad de su presencia. Meditaba acerca de la poma del erizo, la hélice del muergo, las estrías de la venera jacobita, asombrándose ante aquella Ciencia de las Formas desplegada durante tantísimo tiempo frente a una humanidad aún sin ojos para pensarla. ¿Qué habrá en torno mío que esté ya definido, inscrito, presente, y que aún no pueda entender? ¿Qué signo, qué mensaje, qué advertencia, en los rizos de la achicoria, el alfabeto de los musgos, la geometría de la pomarrosa? Mirar un caracol. Uno solo. Tedéum. (P. 210)

As a spatial image of time, the spiral may well be more adequate than the circle, as critics have said. But this is not what the text is proposing. The discourse that surrounds the shell says something else. The spiral has always been there, the text says, it is just that people have been unable to see and to think it. What is it about the spiral that they have been unable to see and think? The answer that the text gives is that the spiral mediates between land and sea, uniting the two.

Now, on the one hand, the scene is straight out of late-eighteenth-century natural history. It was not until the eighteenth century—and principally in Buffon—that there was a gradual move away from a static conception of a divinely created and unchanging universe. The evidence of marine fossils (the passage speaks about fossilized fish) suggested the necessity of pushing back the origins of the earth way beyond the six thousand or so years that the Bible ascribed to the planet. When Esteban thus observes that the same forms are found on land as in the oceans, this is because there are distant kinships stretching back millennia and wholesale mutations that have taken place in a way thought impossible by traditional creationism. Buffon does not look for categorically differentiated species arranged according to a static order; instead he studies living creatures from the point of view of "their kinship, their transition from one type to another, their evolution and transformations" (Cassirer, p. 78).

Buffon's more flexible view of nature signals a departure not just from ancient attitudes toward the world, but from seventeenth-century rationalism. Cassirer maintains that eighteenth-century thought departs from the preceding century in the sense that it both has its point of origin there but also moves away from it. For the eighteenth century, order, law, and reason are not to be grasped as the a priori of phenomena; such regularity can be discovered in the phenomena themselves. This discovery does not take place within the confines of a closed system; reason should instead unfold gradually and with greater precision as knowledge of the facts progresses. "The mind must abandon itself to the abundance of phenomena and gauge itself constantly by them." Reason does not belong, as in the seventeenth-century conception, to the realm of the "eternal verities" shared by the human and the divine mind. The eighteenth-century conception of reason is that of an active principle, an intellectual force that guides the discovery and determination of truth:

> Reason is now looked upon rather as an acquisition than as a heritage. It is not the treasury of the mind in which the truth like a minted coin lies stored; it is rather the original intellectual force which guides the discovery and determination of truth. This determination is the seed and indispensable presupposition of all real certainty. The whole eighteenth century understands reason in this sense; not as a sound body of knowledge, principles, and truths, but as a kind of energy, a force which is fully comprehensible only in its agency and effects. What reason is, and what it can do, can never be known by its results but only by its function. And its most important function consists in its power to bind and to dissolve. It dissolves everything merely factual, all simple data of experience, and everything believed on the evidence of revelation, tradition and authority; and it does not rest content until it has analyzed all these things into their simplest component parts and into their last elements of belief and opinion. Following this work of dissolution begins the work of construction. Reason cannot stop with the dispersed parts; it has to build from them a new structure, a true whole. But since reason creates this whole and fits the parts together according to its own rule, it gains complete knowledge of the structure of its product. Reason understands this structure because it can reproduce it in its totality and in the ordered sequence of its individual elements. Only in this twofold intellectual movement can the concept of reason be fully

characterized, namely, as a concept of agency, not of being. (Cassirer, pp. 13–14)

Without altogether jettisoning the potential for man to erect himself into the new god that subordinates nature to his will, the eighteenth century has introduced a greater sense of the need to observe nature closely, rather than be guided by unquestioned doctrine. This is where natural history's openness toward the experience of nature comes into its own. For, in Buffon's eyes, as soon as we try to acclimatize ourselves to the sphere of the real, the purely analytical categories of mathematics are insufficient. Rather, "We must commit ourselves to the exclusive guidance of experience, for only experience can yield that kind of certainty of which the truth of physical objects is capable."[31] This openness to experience, and indeed the greater appreciation of the place of human affects—which predates Rousseau and develops independently of him (Cassirer, p. 108)—distinguishes eighteenth- from seventeenth-century thought and renders problematic the conventional image of the Enlightenment as a form of pure intellectualism given over to the merciless rationalization of the world.

On the other hand, and to return to our distributive logic begun some while back, although the eighteenth century seems to configure the *caracol* passage more, even, than does the baroque, it does not constitute the last word. Consider the text's insistence on spatial form. Everything in the passage, not just the *caracol*, is marked by the form of the spiral (*poma del erizo, hélice, estrías, rizos, achicoria, musgos, pomarrosa*). It is true that the spiral is as good a form as any other to represent late-eighteenth-century natural history's Great Chain of Being. But do we not see in the spiral, in a text written in the late 1950s and published in 1962, a reference to the double helix structure of DNA—the code, sign, message, or *advertencia* inscribed in spiral form at the heart of creation, for which humankind had to wait millennia to be able to see and think it?[32] All you have to do is look at a gene—just one. Though it identified the structure of the genetic material of all but a few living organisms, by virtue of the presence of random mutations the discovery of DNA did not amount to a "genetic blueprint." Notice, however, that in this passage the spiral is accompanied by a more traditional thematics. The spiral, sign, message, or *advertencia* is given, is always already there, inscribed, prescribed, like God's imprint in nature. Here is where the passage's Enlightenment faith in objectivity shines through. Despite mentioning "el Gran Alberto" (p. 32), the text remains firmly on the other side of twentieth-century relativity theory.

The world is given in advance; what remains is for humankind to develop a cognitive apparatus able to see and to think what is already there. "One has the impression that with Tournefort, with Linnaeus or Buffon, someone has at last taken on the task of stating something that had been visible from the beginning of time, but had remained mute before a sort of invincible distraction of men's eyes."[33] According to this teleological narrative, progress in human knowledge over millennia gradually gets closer to the thing itself, to a nature given, objective, set out once and for all, awaiting only (scientific) revelation. *Tedéum.*

Narrative Art and Magic

The Grand Narratives of religion and nature accomplish two major things. First, they reinscribe without embarrassment a certain popular antirationalism characteristic of the period; second, they cast doubt on the century's, and the Revolution's, singularity. The Greek word for violence, *bias*, means "against nature." *El siglo de las luces* uses nature against conceptual and political violence, where violence is an abrupt cutting off from a previous state of affairs. Nature in the novel is not singular novelty, but a principle of holistic continuity through change. Where, though, does this leave the characters' violent intervention in Madrid at the close of the novel?

Taking its lead in part from the eighteenth century, *El siglo de las luces* reserves a special place for characters' passionate will to intervene in human history. This place is not just for men of action in general; it is for a Caribbean, and, just as important, female, subjectivity. Four pages after the great natural history lesson of the shell episode, the text says that thought is not enough. There then follows a scene, packed with references to French existentialism and kindred postwar French movements, where Esteban berates himself for becoming the prisoner of Víctor Hugues's will.[34] Add to this the close of the novel, where the cousins take to the streets with Sofía's mantra "Hay que hacer algo" ringing in their ears, and it looks as though a romantic-existentialist voluntarism prevails. It is no surprise that doing, together with the link between knowing and doing, should correspond closely to a contemporary belief championed by the key figure of Ogé: "«Martínez de Pasqually [. . .] explicaba que la evolución de la Humanidad era un acto colectivo, y que, por lo tanto, la acción iniciada individual implicaba forzosamente la existencia de una acción social colectiva: quien más *sabe* más *hará* por sus semejantes»" (p. 82).

And yet critics have overlooked the fact that *El siglo de las luces* cannot but oppose this sense that everything can be overturned by dint of human will.[35] It would make no sense to condemn modernity's, and the Revolution's, apocalypticism only to allow the characters' youthful voluntarism to go unchallenged. Because it sets itself against the discourse of Enlightened modernity—against the narratives of apocalypse and revolution—it must also speak against youthfulness and immaturity, passion and will, action and force, that is, against all those things, which it elsewhere supports, that smack of radical voluntarism. The novel checks this voluntarism in two ways. First, by contriving to have the cousins take to the streets with the promise of violence *against Napoleon*. In other words, not with a revolutionary violence bent on founding "a new order of things," but with a violence aiming to *restore* the ties of an existing tradition (the Hispanic, not to say Bourbon). To that extent, Sofía and Esteban are more Roman than French Revolutionary Caribbean Creoles. Second, and more importantly, the novel counters voluntarism by means of an older logic over which the human subject has little control. This logic surfaces explicitly in the novel's treatment of nature and religion, and in its reinstatement of popular superstition as an antidote to Enlightenment reason (we are told that Esteban has become superstitious and that the first sea journey to Port-au-Prince assumed for Sofía "un significado providencial"). However, beyond the counter-Enlightenment antirationalism of the novel's express content, *El siglo de las luces* contains a form of superstition that distances it from *lo real maravilloso americano* as from modern rationality and analysis alike.

The superstition or "magic" that I have in mind is outlined by Borges in his essay "El arte narrativo y la magia."[36] We recall his argument. Novels and short fiction do not operate according to the dictates of modern (postscientific revolution) causality. Their logic is of the order of primitive magic, that is, more akin to the analogical reasoning of primitive peoples. The witchdoctor cuts his forearm so that the rain might flow from the sky in a way that mirrors the blood flowing from the wound. North American indians don bison skins and pound the ground in a thunderous dance so that the bison might come. The logic is that of sympathy, be it imitative or contagious. What is entailed is not the absence of causality, but a different order of the latter, "la primitiva claridad de la magia." This order of magic is, for Borges, the proper of narrative, which constitutes a precise game of "vigilancias, ecos y afinidades."

El siglo de las luces abounds in such magic. The adolescents' upheaval is preceded by a great tropical storm; what Víctor will become is anticipated by the game of charades, in which he always plays the ancient legislator or tribune. Then there are the repetitions: the parallel postmortem dinners; the two sea journeys on board the Arrow, which initiate new phases of Sofía's life; Sofía's visit to the graveyard visited many years before by Víctor, only to find that she is looking at the tomb of the last rightful owner of the Basílica de Santa Sofía. Borges's preference was for a narrative art of economy and allusion; Carpentier's art tends to the explicit. We are thus told that Sofía herself is struck by the coincidence of names, which she deems too extraordinary not to be "un anuncio, un aviso, una premonición" (p. 358).[37] None of the earlier things "causes" the later one in the modern sense of the word; they foreshadow, anticipate, presage, conjure according to a more mysterious, more premodern understanding of causality. This magic is, for Borges, nothing less than "narrative art." Narrative does not just thematize magic; it *is* magic, and to that extent entails an almost generic leave-taking of modern rationality and analysis.

This alternative, premodern logic is inscribed in the novel's central "magical" device, the painting *Explosión en una catedral*, which has hung abandoned in the adolescents's family home. Only on his return from France can Esteban see it properly, that is, recognize in it a prefiguration of everything that has happened to him and to the epoch:

> Había allí como una prefiguración de tantos acontecimientos conocidos, que se sentía aturdido por el cúmulo de interpretaciones a que se prestaba ese lienzo profético, antiplástico, ajeno a todas las temáticas pictóricas, que había llegado a esta casa por misterioso azar. Si la catedral, de acuerdo con doctrinas que en otros días le habían enseñado, era la representación—arca y tabernáculo—de su propio ser, una explosión se había producido en ella, ciertamente, aunque retardada y lenta, destruyendo altares, símbolos y objetos de veneración. Si la catedral era la Época, una formidable explosión, en efecto, había derribado sus muros principales, enterrando bajo un alud de escombros a los mismos que acaso construyeran la máquina infernal. Si la catedral era la Iglesia Cristiana, observaba Esteban que una hilera de fuertes columnas le quedaba intacta, frente a la que, rota a pedazos, se desplomaba en el apocalíptico cuadro, como un anuncio de resistencia, perdurabilidad y reconstrucciones, después de los tiempos de estragos y de estrellas anunciadoras de abismos. (P. 295)

Explosion within the self, within the epoch, and within the Church (why does the text reserve resistance and perdurability for the Church alone?). Everything is foretold, prefigured, prophesied, announced (*prefiguración, lienzo profético, anuncio*).

When the painting is next mentioned, Esteban, in a mixture of narcissism (there is no canvas that is not ultimately about me) and fatalism (the canvas as the always already spoken/painted), curses it for anticipating what will become of him. The reference is to the hard labor that awaits him in Ceuta: "«Hasta las piedras que iré a romper ahora estaban ya presentes en esta pintura»" (p. 346). If only I had had the eyes to see it . . . We have seen this logic before. We recall the shell episode: the fishermen who had not the eyes to see the spiral; Esteban who wonders what there is around him that he is incapable of understanding: "¿Qué habrá en torno mío que esté ya definido, inscrito, presente, y que aún no pueda entender?" It is the first time in the episode that the "I" speaks. Esteban pulls out of the abstract meditation on nature and turns to himself. Is there a sign around me, a warning (*advertencia*) that I have not yet apprehended? Is there something already inscribed in nature that will reveal my fate? In fact, signs are indeed present in nature, in the cathedralic forms of the American baroque ("la esbeltez catedralicia de ciertos caracoles"), which echo the cathedral of the portentous painting. There is a "magical" solidarity between nature and art, nature and religious text. When Esteban realizes his love for Sofía, the moment of epiphany ("una jubilosa revelación") is the maturation of that which was always already inside (if he had only had the eyes to see it): "Todo lo entiendes ahora. Sabes lo que maduraba en ti desde hace años" (p. 315). The novel harbors a teleological view of the process of maturation whereby the end-point was there in miniature from the beginning. Preformationism migrates from the natural to the human world. It is the traditional logic of destiny, of predestinationism, a teleotheology that, in a species of archipelagology, extends even to the landscape of the Caribbean.[38]

In conclusion, nature, the Bible, art, and assorted other emblems and motifs construct a web of repetitions, echoes, and presages in solidarity with the characters' fatalism.[39] It is not that human will is not important in the novel. However, for every reference to doing and becoming, the novel supplies a deterministic alternative. This extends to its final scene, where the painting's dark canvas simultaneously mirrors, after the event, the absence of one who has taken his destiny into his own hands (victory for romantic existentialism) and *prefigures* Esteban's annihilation (triumph of determinism). Even before it has uttered a single anti-Enlightenment statement, the magical narrative art of *El siglo de las luces* sets it against the central tenets of Enlightenment modernity, above all against the autonomous subject of reason in whom the violence of modernity's self-definition as a self-willed historical epoch finds its maximum expression.

Conclusion

At the beginning of the twentieth century, and in typical romantic fashion, the Spanish American *modernistas* set their face against the perceived philistinism of a modernizing society. Their opposition was not absolute. It was marked, rather, by the kind of messy entanglements that characterize daily life, compromises that seem on occasion to have been a cause for celebration rather than melancholy.[1] In contrast, the *modernistas* succumbed tamely to the contradictions of the philosophico-aesthetic discourse of modernity. That discourse does not value the chronologically new; it values the new that is simultaneously a negation of the past and an affirmation of something better. The word *modern* thus functions in two ways: on the one hand, it designates certain institutions, ideas, and objects that emanate from a period of history closely identified with the West, and that most mark out the historical phase of modernity from what preceded it; on the other hand, it means whatever negates and surpasses the past, on the understanding that that thing will one day in turn be exceeded by something more "modern." In their reflections on what it means to be modern, the *modernistas* make liberal use of the disjunctive conceptual habits and rhetorical figures of modern thought (cut, disinheritance, revolution), yet remain deeply wedded to the demands of a historical consciousness and to the most traditional of nineteenth-century axioms: historical progress.

Vallejo's case is different. Lucid about the political and economic realities of the 1920s, Vallejo advocates European- or North American–style industrialization as the most effective means to challenge the West. Appropriating the discourse of Enlightenment modernity, he turns it back on an imperialist Europe. It is not that Vallejo wishes to reproduce existing European politics, economics, styles, or ideas; he wants Latin America to copy the principle of creativity that underpins them, and then proceed to be more creative, more democratic, and more powerful than Europe. Vallejo subscribes firmly to the philosophico-aesthetic discourse of modernity, though not to an extant model of Europe: let us go beyond Europe, he says, by being more modern than Europe.

Borges and Carpentier take aim at the dominant tropology and temporality of the discourse of modernity. In Buenos Aires in the 1920s, Borges was an active participant in a youthful, iconoclastic cultural nationalism. By the late 1930s, he had witnessed the hardening of certain European and Argentine nationalisms into politically ugly and culturally narrow affirmations of difference. He saw, correctly, that these affirmations were underpinned by a nominalism that he identified as the philosophical "premisa general" of the modern age. In the case of Carpentier, a potentially constrictive rationality, which critics of rationalism have succeeded in rendering synonymous with the Enlightenment, shows its true political colors in the French revolutionaries' guillotine will to begin historical time anew. Where Vallejo thought that Enlightened reason could channel the forces of instrumental reason in a progressive direction, Carpentier infers that no such harnessing is possible and that, on the contrary, the point is to bring about the remagification of the world and the cosmos by expanding the very notion of reason. By Caribbeanizing reason.

El siglo de las luces suggests the need for another kind of expansion: that surrounding the concept of Spanish American modernity. The word *modernidad* has come to be reserved for a period in Spanish America coeval with the explosive technological changes of the Second Industrial Revolution. Combining a socioeconomic and a philosophico-aesthetic view of modernity, Beatriz Sarlo's "modernidad periférica" of Buenos Aires is at once a discursive and, perhaps above all, technological affair. Negation of past technology and proclamation of its own superiority, this is a modernity visible in the city's railways, telegraph wires, automobiles, trams, electricity lines, and cinemas, a modernity that has transformed the material fabric of everyday life. Carpentier, in contrast, has a different take on modernity in the subcontinent. By returning in quick succession to France, 1789, and to scenes of commercial activity and political debate in Havana in the same year, Carpentier not only makes the point that the Caribbean was a protagonist in the shaping of a modern republican West, but casts doubt on the tendency to equate *modernidad* with the twilight years of the nineteenth century, opting instead for the *longue durée*.

But that is not the only doubt Carpentier raises about modernity. *El siglo de las luces* works hard to persuade us that even a backdated modernity's attempts at apocalyptic self-periodization are inadequate.

Carpentier's initial doubt is not assuaged by simply bringing the start date of Latin American modernity forward a few years. What the work of Carpentier (and Borges) suggests is that modernity can only be considered a historical phase in the most general sense possible. Without discounting the palpable changes that have taken place in the region at precise moments in history, only by virtue of historiographical prejudice can one ascribe the origin and unfolding of all these changes to a rigidly delimitable historical epoch—above all to so tardy a period as the end of the nineteenth century. On the contrary, to respect the philosophico-aesthetic and socioeconomic dimensions of Spanish American modernity means taking seriously not only the fact that not everything in the modern age is modern, but also the reality that even the avowedly modern contents of modernity conceived of as a historical phase do not always have their origin in that same historical moment. The modern age and its contents are not absolutely modern, and thus never fully arrived in Spanish America at the end of the nineteenth or any other century. Because they do not possess a totalizable self-presence even at home, historical phases do not travel elsewhere; only elements of a historical phase travel elsewhere.

The task of the philosophical discourse of modernity was to produce a single practical definition of the modern. There have been constant attempts since to have done with this discourse, on account of its claim to be able to wrap the contents of the world's past into a universal history based on a single scale of development in which progress is defined "in terms of the projection of certain people's presents as other people's futures" (Osborne). Even though *modernismo* was an important affirmation of the new republics' cultural quasi-autonomy, universal history haunts it. The *modernistas*' present is projected as the positivists' future, but in progressing beyond the (positivist) past, the (*modernista*) present contains no traces of it. Complete with a new name, *modernismo* would be nothing but itself: an uncontaminated positivity folded back into itself without remainder. What I have repeatedly tried to show is that this (more or less modern) habit of thought, which consists in circumscribing the contents of a self-identical present, also animates certain avowedly antiethnocentric discourses of what is called postmodernity. It returns in William Rowe's concept of the field, and also in the will to periodize characteristic of much thinking on Spanish American modernity. In the desire to respect the latter's specificity without bringing it under the sway of universal history, one fails to see that it is always already a process. Rowe sees that the field is a process, but does not follow through the consequences of such a recognition and sets about instead attempting to totalize the field, to spatialize it so that, in conformity with the most traditional Western habit, it can be illuminated and, thus, known. One does not so easily get rid of Enlightenment (but they are also Ancient Greek) devices and desires. The razing of tradition and the past, which is a simplification of the present for the purpose of its mastery, does not just belong to Robespierre or, in an obviously less cataclysmic form, the *modernistas*; it inhabits the postmodern moment of cultural studies.

The postmodern, antiethnocentric moment of Latin American cultural studies is not always and everywhere the same. Alberto Moreiras's position on political progress differs from that of Beatriz Sarlo (who is unequivocal on the need for Enlightenment categories of thought), which differs from that of Néstor García Canclini (who gives greater consideration to non-Western cultures but cannot avoid awkward questions about the Enlightenment universality that secretes itself into his notion of the public sphere). Moreiras strives to respect the indigenous subaltern without recuperating it for a regulative Western order. But because he posits a subaltern figure that must irrupt in an unconditional instant (in order not to be anticipated by, and made to appear before, the court of Western reason), Moreiras's subaltern cannot appear in the name of "democracy," "tradition," or any other extant order known to the West. It must invent its own conditions of emergence without reference to the West, and those conditions must necessarily remain a secret to Moreiras.

The earlier generations of literary writers studied in this book are cognizant of and candid about the intractable relationship of Latin America to the Western tradition, and their own ethico-intellectual position within that relationship. Although they make overtures to non-Western cultures, or non-metropolitan cultures, such overtures are often accompanied by an honest awareness of their own limitations, which does not slide back into bad faith. Moved by one of the spirits of antiethnocentrism, Carpentier's work suggests that some of the major gains associated with modernity (*liberté, fraternité, égalité*) do not begin in Europe in 1789 and do not belong exclusively to the European tradition. By incorporating Afro-Caribbean culture into the narrative of the modern age, Carpentier underlines the fact that the modern age is composed of different historical temporalities, and that to sever oneself from tradition in the name of progress—which modernity desires but never quite manages to do—is to give up not only on popular culture but on the black (and mulatto) Caribbean.

Conclusion

The two writers who, by virtue of their rural upbringing, apparently have greater claim to non-Western culture, respond differently. In his explicit musings on indigenous Andean culture, the young Vallejo of *Los heraldos negros* experiments with a symbolist aesthetic of temporal disjuncture that mythologizes, and above all hypostatizes, indian culture. Influenced by Marxist–Leninist thought, but also by the debates kindled by APRA in Peru, the later Vallejo gives more room to Peru's indians as a living people. However, faithful to Marxism, he is also faithful to the European discourse of modernity, which puts economic and technological progress above all else. Vallejo was not embarrassed by this advocacy, which he saw as a simple matter of realpolitik, of the brute facts of semicolonialism.

Rulfo is a different, but not dissimilar, case. Rulfo did not write political essays militating for Western-style socioeconomic modernization. Mexico was in the middle of such a process, the shortcomings of which Rulfo was painfully aware. On the basis of comments he made about the marginalization of the indigenous, but also mestizo, rural poor, Rulfo has been constructed as a spokesperson for traditional-rural culture, without seeing the extent to which he also reserved an Enlightenment despair for the Jalisco peasantry. Overt moral condemnation may have disappeared, but in *Pedro Páramo* and "Luvina" the thematization of stagnation tips over into hyperbole, such that time seems to stand still and the characters take on the aspect of a people who are going nowhere. Religion and popular superstition do not step forward to provide local, communal means of negotiating a path through life's hardships; rather, they leave the characters as near-empty husks unable to counter the decimation of tradition with any action other than that of taking their own lives in a moment of jubilee.

All of the literature studied makes space for indigenous or non-metropolitan culture. Only Carpentier suggests that these cultures have an already existing ability to constitute themselves as viable alternatives to Western models of development, but even then, at least in *El siglo de las luces*, Carpentier is not about to advocate separatist development or an avant-garde subalternism that would owe nothing to the West. The reluctance on the part of all these writers to champion the radical subaltern as complete (though impossible) other of the West, and concomitant reluctance to turn themselves into (modern) figures of disinheritance from the West, doubtless constitutes one axis of the desire to see them relegated to pre-postmodern obsolescence.

And then there is literary form, the second axis. A certain demotic, antiethnocentric impulse, and critical distance, in their language and/or narrative structure might just suffice to absolve some of the literary figures dealt with in this book of their filiation with the European tradition. Something has happened, for instance, between *modernismo* and Vallejo. The overwhelmingly written character of *modernista* poetry cedes terrain to a modern, spoken written language in which local American experience—including the marginal, the vulgar, and the childish—finds its place. Likewise with Rulfo. Running counter to his Enlightenment despair at the popular classes, Rulfo's prose picks up on the rhythms and habits of vernacular speech, and can thus in some sense stand as an affirmation of the popular. Moreover, by excising the moralizing authorial voice from his text, Rulfo enacts in literary form the general excision of the Roman trinity of authority, religion, and tradition characteristic of modern societies. This demotic thrust is in sharp contrast to the grand style of Carpentier, who seems somehow less modern and, hence, less salvageable. Everything about Carpentier's style appears to confirm him as a grandee of letters who, like Borges, belongs to a different era or to a cultural sphere that cannot but distance him from the *res publica*.

Culturas híbridas, the landmark text of Latin American cultural studies, savages rather than salvages these last representatives of the literary Roman trinity. These contrary priests (García Canclini is writing specifically about Borges and Octavio Paz), "sacerdotes del mundo moderno del arte," urge artistic and philosophical modernity upon the region while clinging dearly to the traditional role of the Author as Authority. That book, which stands on the extreme wing of sociological, antiliterary cultural studies, does not believe, however, that the polyvocal vernacular represents by contrast an absolute good of modern democratic times. Seeing through the fact that the traditional-popular elements of Vallejo and Rulfo are the product of immense sophistication, *Culturas híbridas* goes further. It argues that *any* cultural production with a degree of sophistication that renders it inaccessible to the public sphere is bad. One hears in García Canclini's insistence on the public sphere, which resurfaces with renewed force in the wake of the Argentine collapse of 2001, a fear for the future of Latin American democracy.[2] This does not obviate the fact that *Culturas híbridas* reproduces a deeply simplistic understanding of the relationship between literary form and political value (the vox populi is democratic; the univocal, authoritarian). Such a reductive view of literature, the public sphere, and the relationship between the two, falls back on an instrumental model of communication, which shows no trace of the rethinking of communication theory carried out by postmodern theorists. Faithful to the paradigmatic move of cultural studies, which consists in establishing a connection (at worst, a homology) between symbolic production and the political and economic conditions of production and reception, it reduces the density—and temporality—of the literary text to a determinate ideology (input) and determinate power-effects (output). We have traveled the path from art as autonomous sphere to culture as homologous process. The neo-Leninist call for literature to be judged according to its function in social practice makes little attempt to address the problems of mediation and virtually none to allow the life-enhancing qualities of art to shine through. But cultural studies knows that. Better to track the life-affirming qualities of other forms of cultural production, those forms left on the margins of the public sphere—or stymied at birth—by the life-denying hegemony of cultural modernism.

García Canclini's iconic text from 1989 was an extreme antielitist statement of opposition to modern literature. It was, as they say, a book of its time, a time when the (literary) Wall was being torn down. A decade later, García Canclini is more conciliatory toward "slow" literature. It remains the case, however, that cultural studies is always close to a certain spirit of Leninism, a spirit that demands that cultural production—including academic production—be judged by the criterion of praxis, not objective value. Despite the obvious politicoteleology of its premise, that spirit does not seem to me such a bad thing. Concentrating on neglected cultural production, and on the social function of such production, it is an affirmative practice that expands the conception of culture and allows room for a different sensibility. Cultural studies is less good when it turns its attention toward so-called elite cultural production, and when this production is condemned by virtue of its dominant position or by virtue of its association with an entire historical epoch. This strain of cultural studies involves a violent wager that is nothing if not modern: in order to defeat Napoleon, one must revive the spirit of Robespierre. To defend the high-literary production of the first part of the twentieth century in Spanish America, a cultural modernism undeniably bound up with hegemonic forces of socioeconomic modernization, is not to restore Empire. It is to give credit to that writing's efforts to avoid moral simplifications, efforts to write about tradition and modernity positively and negatively at the same time. At the risk of turning its secrets into a program by publicizing them in the public sphere, we can say that much of the literary writing dealt with in this book anticipates Derrida's caveat from "Psyché, Invention de l'autre" (cited at the end of chapter 3): "Because the other is not the new." If writing inventively of and against modernity cannot involve taking refuge in tradition (i.e., following an order that will always be the same tomorrow), nor can it entail being a stranger to repetition, to memory, and to a certain traditionality. "La venue de l'invention ne peut se rendre étrangère à la répétition et à la mémoire. Car l'autre n'est pas le nouveau."

Notes

Introduction

1. See Néstor García Canclini, *La globalización imaginada* (Buenos Aires, Barcelona, México: Paidós, 1999), chapter 5 (pp. 129–139), where, calling himself "el antropólogo latinoamericano," he takes his distance from (North American literary) cultural studies.
2. See Alberto Moreiras for the most taut articulation of this position. "Introduction: Conditions of Latin Americanist Critique," *The Exhaustion of Difference: The Politics of Latin American Cultural Studies* (Durham and London: Duke University Press, 2001), pp. 1–25.
3. Stuart Hall, "Introduction," in *Formations of Modernity*, ed. Stuart Hall and Bram Gieben (Cambridge: Polity Press and the Open University, 1992; reprt. 1997).
4. See Hernán Vidal, "Restaurar lo político, imperativo de los estudios literarios y culturales latinoamericanistas," in *Nuevas perspectivas desde/sobre América Latina: el desafío de los estudios culturales*, ed. Mabel Moraña (Chile: Editorial Cuarto Propio/Instituto Internacional de Literatura Iberoamericana, 2000), p. 126. Vidal's proposal is that departments of Spanish cut themselves off not just from outmoded cultural forms and disciplinary habits, but from the Iberian Peninsula *tout court*.
5. See Moreiras, *The Exhaustion of Difference*, p. 3, for whom such literature is not sacrificed but simply read differently. My point is that that literature is not being read differently at all, but put through the machine of a presentist cultural studies.

Chapter 1   The Things that Travel

1. I use Latin America rather than Spanish America in this chapter because it more accurately reflects the compass of Latin American cultural studies. In subsequent chapters my focus narrows mainly on Spanish America.
2. An exception is Aníbal Quijano, "Modernity, Identity, and Utopia in Latin America," *boundary 2* 20:3 (Fall 1993), 140–155.

3. "Adoptamos con cierta flexibilidad la distinción hecha por varios autores, desde Jürgen Habermas hasta Marshall Berman, entre la *modernidad* como etapa histórica, la *modernización* como proceso socioeconómico que trata de ir construyendo la modernidad, y los *modernismos*, o sea los proyectos culturales que renuevan las prácticas simbólicas con un sentido experimental o crítico"; Néstor García Canclini, *Culturas híbridas. Estrategias para entrar y salir de la modernidad*, Nueva edición (Buenos Aires, Barcelona, México: Paidós, 2001), p. 40.
4. Michael Hardt and Antonio Negri, *Empire* (Cambridge, Massachusetts, and London: Harvard University Press, 2001), p. 70.
5. See, for instance, S.N. Eisenstadt, *Tradition, Change, and Modernity* (Florida: Robert E. Krieger Publishing Company, 1973; reprt. 1983), pp. 231–232.
6. Matei Calinescu, *Five Faces of Modernity: Modernism, Avant-Garde, Decadence, Kitsch, Postmodernism* (Durham: Duke University Press, 1987), p. 41. Also cited in Carlos J. Alonso, *The Burden of Modernity: The Rhetoric of Cultural Discourse in Spanish America* (New York and Oxford: OUP, 1998), p. 29.
7. Jonathan I. Israel, *Radical Enlightenment: Philosophy and the Making of Modernity 1650–1750* (Oxford: Oxford University Press, 2001), pp. 3–4.
8. Ernst Cassirer, *The Individual and the Cosmos in Renaissance Philosophy*, trans. Mario Domandi (Oxford: Basil Blackwell, 1963), p. 10.
9. See Calinescu, *Five Faces of Modernity*, pp. 13–14.
10. Jürgen Habermas, *The Philosophical Discourse of Modernity: Twelve Lectures*, trans. Frederick Lawrence (Cambridge: Polity Press, 1987; reprt. 1994), p. 5. I take Peter Osborne's point entirely that it should be Kant, not Hegel, who receives the credit for first dwelling on modernity. Peter Osborne, "Modernity Is a Qualitative, Not a Chronological, Category," *New Left Review* 192 (March–April 1992), 65–82.
11. Hall, "Introduction." See my Introduction for more discussion of Hall.
12. C.A. Bayly, *The Birth of the Modern World 1780–1914* (Malden, Oxford, and Victoria: Blackwell, 2004).
13. Enrique Dussel, "Beyond Eurocentrism: The World-System and the Limits of Modernity," in *The Cultures of Globalization*, ed. Fredric Jameson and Masao Miyoshi (Durham: Duke University Press, 1998), pp. 3–31.
14. Marshall Berman, *All That Is Solid Melts into Air: The Experience of Modernity* (London: Verso, 1983). See also Hannah Arendt, "Tradition and the Modern Age," *Between Past and Future: Eight Exercises in Political Thought* (Harmondsworth: Penguin Books, 1993), p. 27: "The modern age ris[es] with the natural sciences in the seventeenth century, reaching its political climax in the revolutions of the eighteenth, and unfolding its general implications after the Industrial revolution of the nineteenth."
15. See Hall and Gieben, *Formations of Modernity*, p. 6.
16. In the words of Hardt and Negri, "The constitution of modernity was not about theory in isolation but about theoretical acts indissolubly tied

to mutations of practice and reality. Bodies and brains were fundamentally transformed" (*Empire*, p. 74).
17. Octavio Paz, *Children of the Mire: Modern Poetry from Romanticism to the Avant-Garde*, trans. Rachel Phillips (Cambridge, Mass. and London: Harvard University Press, 1974; reprt. 1991), p. 5.
18. Following E.P. Thompson, David Harvey, *The Condition of Postmodernity: An Enquiry into the Origins of Cultural Change* (Cambridge, Mass. and Oxford: Blackwell, 1990; reprt. 2001), pp. 228 and 231, argues that the conception of modern time is intimately bound to industrial capitalism (with its timesheets and timekeepers). However, the obvious presence of clocks and chronometers in the factories, and of a certain disciplining of the workforce, should not blind us to the possibility that factory time introduces no great change in the understanding of time and may even be premodern, in the sense that clocks "go round" at a (more or less) uniform rate and know nothing of the great ruptures and changes supposedly characteristic of modernity. This is precisely why Bergson later rails at conventional clock time.
19. Paz, *Children of the Mire*, p. 3. Or again: "The modern age begins as a breaking away from Christian society. Faithful to its origins, it is a continual breaking away, a ceaseless splitting apart; each generation repeats the act by which we were founded, and in this repetition we deny and renew ourselves. Separation unites us with the original movement of our society, and severance throws us back on ourselves" (p. 27).
20. Western modernity's own time is "ahead" of the "backward" time of the colonies, producing the idea of the "*non-contemporaneousness of geographically diverse but chronologically simultaneous times*" (Osborne, "Modernity Is a Qualitative, Not a Chronological, Category," p. 75).
21. See Calinescu, *Five Faces of Modernity*, p. 49 on the impossibility of modernity as historical phase (at least according to Baudelaire).
22. "It is surely not difficult to see that our time is a birth and transition to a new period. The Spirit has broken with what was hitherto the world of its existence and imagination and is about to submerge all this in the past; it is at work giving itself a new form. . . . [F]rivolity as well as the boredom that open up in the establishment and the indeterminate apprehension of something unknown are harbingers of a forthcoming change. This gradual crumbling . . . is interrupted by the break of day, that like lightning, all at once reveals the edifice of the new world." Hegel (*Phenomenology of Mind*) cited in Habermas, *The Philosophical Discourse of Modernity*, p. 6.
23. In chapter 2 I deal with the question of why the intimate relationship between aesthetic and socioeconomic concepts of modernity does not prevent them from conflicting.
24. Beatriz Sarlo, *Una modernidad periférica: Buenos Aires 1920 y 1930* (Buenos Aires: Ediciones Nueva Visión, 1988).
25. For the European and North American angle, see Peter Conrad, *Modern Times, Modern Places: Life and Art in the Twentieth Century* (London: Thames and Hudson, 1998); Peter Watson, *A Terrible Beauty: The People*

and Ideas that Shaped the Modern Mind: A History (London: Phoenix Press, 2000); and Stephen Kern The Culture of Time and Space 1880–1918 (Cambridge, Mass.: Harvard University Press, 1983).

26. Cf. Brunner: "Incluso hoy [1992], la modernidad cultural de la región está recién en sus comienzos y no puede confundirse con las querellas entre los antiguos y los modernos en el seno de la cultura tradicional"; José Joaquín Brunner, "La ciudad de los signos," *América latina: cultura y modernidad* (Mexico: Grijalbo, 1992), p. 50.

27. Beatriz Sarlo, "The Modern City: Buenos Aires, The Peripheral Metropolis," in *Through the Kaleidoscope: The Experience of Modernity in Latin America*, ed. Vivian Schelling (London and New York: Verso, 2000), pp. 109–110.

28. Note that Sarlo also invokes the "large administrative buildings, schools and hospitals," that is, the institutions of modernity less assimilable to the ideal of speed and change. In chapter 6, I comment at greater length on Sarlo's understanding of modernity in relation to her work on Borges.

29. Jesús Martín-Barbero, *De los medios a las mediaciones. Comunicación, cultura y hegemonía* (Barcelona: Editorial Gustavo Gili, 1987; 5th ed. Mexico, 1998), pp. 150ff.; García Canclini, *Culturas híbridas*, p. 95; and Brunner, "La ciudad de los signos," p. 59.

30. Brunner, "La ciudad de los signos," pp. 50–51.

31. As Brunner puts it, only in the 1950s does schooling bring Enlightenment ("La escuela es el Kant de los pobres"), and television the critique of tradition ("Todo lo que es sólido se evapora en la televisión"); "La ciudad de los signos," p. 71.

32. Alonso, *The Burden of Modernity*, p. 32.

33. Paul Gilroy argues similarly with respect to modernity and the slave trade. Paul Gilroy, *The Black Atlantic: Modernity and Double Consciousness* (London and New York: Verso, 1993; reprt. 2002).

34. Strictly speaking, the developmentalist model imported into Latin America in the wake of the Second World War did not deny the possibility of integrating the indigenous population into a modernizing project, but the condition for including them was that they stopped being traditional, that is, "ceased to be indian" (Nelson Manrique, "Modernity and Alternative Development in the Andes," in Schelling, *Through the Kaleidoscope*, p. 241).

35. See Néstor García Canclini, "Los estudios culturales de los 80 a los 90: perspectivas antropológicas y sociológicas en América Latina," *Punto de vista* (Buenos Aires) 14:40 (July–Sept 1991), 41–48. According to Eisenstadt (*Tradition, Change, and Modernity*, p. xvii), the critique of sociology's affair with modernization theory dates back to the early and, especially, mid-1960s.

36. Perry Anderson, "Modernity and Revolution," *New Left Review* 144 (March–April 1984), 96–113.

37. Bruno Latour, *We Have Never Been Modern*, trans. Catherine Porter (New York: Harvester Wheatsheaf, 1993), p. 68.

38. Walter Benjamin, "Theses on the Philosophy of History," in *Illuminations*, ed. Hannah Arendt, trans. Harry Zohn (London: Fontana/Collins, 1977), pp. 259–260.

39. *Culturas híbridas*, p. 203. Juan Rulfo recognized this point long ago ("el hombre de allá [del campo] viene aquí, emigra a la ciudad, y aquí se produce un cambio. Pero él no deja hasta cierto punto de ser lo que fue"), but deals with it in contradictory fashion. Juan Rulfo, *Autobiografía armada* (Buenos Aires: Ediciones Corregidor, 1973), p. 73. I explore Rulfo's relationship to rural Mexico in chapter 7.
40. The epiphany is in fact overdetermined, not least by the 1980s paradigm-shift in Latin American cultural studies toward a Gramscian understanding of the negotiations at the heart of hegemony. I deal with this shift more fully in chapter 2.
41. Néstor García Canclini, *Las culturas populares en el capitalismo* (Mexico: Editorial Nueva Imagen, 1982; reprt. 1986), p. 104.
42. Equivocation is a hallmark of debates on the relationship among tradition, modernity, and postmodernity. At times, *Culturas híbridas* petitions loudly for the difference between Latin American modernity and postmodernity; at others, it suggests that the difference is a matter of an exacerbation in the latter of tendencies already at work in the former. Cf. Anthony Giddens, *The Consequences of Modernity* (Cambridge: Polity Press, 1990; reprt. 1994), p. 4: "The modes of life brought into being by modernity have swept us away from *all* traditional types of social order" versus "Obviously there are continuities between the traditional and the modern, and neither is cut of whole cloth"; and Fredric Jameson, *Postmodernism, or, the Logic of Late Capitalism* (London, New York: Verso, 1991; reprt. 1996), pp. xx, 1, and 2.
43. "The postmodern begins to make its appearance wherever the modernization process no longer has archaic features and obstacles to overcome and has triumphantly implanted its own autonomous logic (for which, of course, at that point the word *modernization* becomes a misnomer, since everything is already 'modern')." Jameson, *Postmodernism*, p. 366. Hardt and Negri's name for this logic is Empire.
44. The idea of the "*non-contemporaneousness* of *geographically diverse* but *chronologically simultaneous* times" becomes the basis for "universal history." "Such histories are 'modernizing' in the sense that the results of synchronic comparisons are ordered diachronically to produce a scale of development that defines 'progress' in terms of the projection of certain people's presents as other people's futures. [. . .] Some specific criterion must be introduced to set up a new differential, within the newly homogenized time, in order to provide a content for the concept of 'progress' [. . .], in order that there be some way to identify the historically, as opposed to the merely chronologically, 'new.' This is the role of so-called theories of modernity [. . .]: to provide a content to fill the form of the modern; to give it something more than an abstract temporal determinacy. It is at this point, historically, that the *geopolitical* dimension of the concept comes into its own, providing, via the discourse of colonialism, a series of criteria of 'progress' derived, first, from the history of European nation-states, and later, in modernization theory proper, from America" (Osborne, "Modernity Is a Qualitative, Not a Chronological, Category," p. 75).

45. At the root of this problem, as of so much else in contemporary theory, is Althusser. Osborne sees the crucial difficulty of Althusser's attempt to exit from Hegelianism as the problem of the idea of totality that one cannot do without but which has been negated in the first place. Althusser begins by thinking each instance of the whole as possessing its own peculiar time "relatively autonomous and hence relatively independent, even in its dependence, of the 'times' of the other levels." When Althusser comes to think of the type of articulation that would harmonize these autonomous times in the unity of the whole, he cannot do so, since there is no essential unity to his totality and therefore no common time within which to think the articulated coexistence of its various temporalities. Osborne (citing Althusser), "Modernity Is a Qualitative, Not a Chronological, Category," p. 81.
46. Cf. Renato Rosaldo in the Foreword to the English translation of *Culturas híbridas*: "When García Canclini argues that the processes of production and consumption imply that no realm of cultural production can remain independent of the marketplace (and vice versa), it should follow that entering and leaving modernity deconstructs—indeed, dissolves into hybridity—the very distinction between tradition and modernity that he resolutely maintains. Even if in certain cases commodities can enter and leave modernity with ease and perhaps remain relatively unchanged, human beings usually make such transitions with greater difficulty and emerge transformed to a greater or lesser degree by these late-twentieth-century rites of passage that permeate everyday life" (p. xv).
47. At stake, no surprise given the presence of the word throughout the book, is the understanding of "deconstruction." Cf. García Canclini, *La globalización imaginada*, p. 122, where the author comments on Stuart Hall's recourse to Derrida's (non-)concept *différance*. The object of Hall's observations is García Canclini's own concept of hybridization.
48. García Canclini, "Contradictory Modernities," in Schelling, *Through the Kaleidoscope*, p. 48.
49. "Fuimos colonizados por las naciones europeas más atrasadas, sometidos a la contrarreforma y otros movimientos antimodernos" (García Canclini, *Culturas híbridas*, p. 81).
50. Cf. Jameson, *Postmodernism*, p. 311: "The keen sense of the New in the modern period was only possible because of the mixed, uneven, transitional nature of that period, in which the old coexisted with what was then coming into being."
51. Anderson writes that at the end of the nineteenth century in continental Europe, cultural modernism was the result of the intersection of three different temporal orders: a semi-aristocratic ruling order, a semi-industrialized capitalist economy, and a semi-emergent labor movement. It is noticeable, however, that the term *temporality* falls from view in Anderson. Just as he is about to name the "different historical temporalities," he writes instead of "three decisive coordinates" ("Modernity and Revolution," p. 104) of what would appear to be just two historical temporalities.
52. Dussel's argument that the New World "contained the first 'barbarian' that modernity needed in its definition" ("Beyond Eurocentrism," p. 18)

NOTES

is a reminder that modernity's "first" is the West's (and not just the West's) umpteenth.
53. On this last point, see Gilroy, *The Black Atlantic*, p. 60.
54. Eisenstadt (*Tradition, Change, and Modernity* p. 258) writes of the "forces" of the "system" of modernity.
55. García Canclini writes in *La globalización imaginada* of "la modernidad de origen europeo" (p. 108).
56. The weakness of *Empire* lies in its simplistic radical libertarianism. Sporting the conceptual dress of poststructuralism, it seizes upon the continuous battle across time of order versus disorder, controlling structure versus irruptive event, the molar versus the molecular, yet distributes value in a trenchantly oppositional manner (order bad, disorder good). The book is crafted from a traditional continuist historicism, which sees the eternal conflict between the fires of liberty lit by a transhistorical multitude-victim and the fire-quenching forces of order. *Empire* cannot contemplate the possibility that all thinking and all politics are unavoidably complicitous in order and stability.
57. "If it has been the function of regional theories of modernity (economic, political, religious, aesthetic, sociological, and so forth) to totalize spatially across their respective domains, on the basis of specific, geopolitically determined but empirically derived criteria of the 'modern,' then the task of the philosophical discourse of modernity has been to unify and legitimate these enquiries within the scope of a single *practical* definition of the modern" (Osborne, "Modernity Is a Qualitative, Not a Chronological, Category," p. 78).
58. García Canclini, *Culturas híbridas*, p. 35: "También es posible pensar que perdió sentido ser moderno en este tiempo en que las filosofías de la posmodernidad descalifican a los movimientos culturales que prometen utopías y auspician el progreso." Contrast the above with Raymond Williams, "Culture Is Ordinary," in *Studying Culture: An Introductory Reader*, ed. Ann Gray and Jim McGuigan (London: Edward Arnold, 1993), p. 11: "Dirty water, an earth bucket, a four-mile walk each way to work, headaches, broken women, hunger and monotony of diet. The working people, in town and country alike, will not listen (and I support them) to any account of our society which supposes that these things are not progress: not just mechanical, external progress either, but a real service of life."
59. Eisenstadt's 1973 account of the new, "postmodern" movements of protest (*Tradition, Change, and Modernity*, p. 247) is already a prescient one.
60. "Hemos transitado de la modernidad ilustrada a la modernidad neoliberal" (García Canclini, *La globalización imaginada*, p. 81).

Chapter 2 Culture Is (Not) Ordinary

1. García Canclini, *Culturas híbridas*, p. 62.
2. García Canclini, *La globalización imaginada*.

3. This fact need not lead us to conclude that such goods therefore cease to be art. "If the commodity corrupts (art, philosophy, religion, morality, law, when their works become market values), it is because the becoming-commodity already attested to the value it put in danger. [. . .] If a work of art can become a commodity, and if this process seems fated to occur, it is also because the commodity began by putting to work, in one way or another, the principle of an art"; Jacques Derrida, *Specters of Marx: The State of the Debt, the Work of Mourning, and the New International*, trans. Peggy Kamuf (New York and London: Routledge, 1994), p. 162.
4. The least we can say about García Canclini and postmodernism is that he opts for it not because it represents the "tumultuous copresence of all styles" (the reason he gives), but because it is a way of thinking about culture that *recognizes and valorizes* the tumultuous copresence of all styles. One immediately comes up against the problem of trying to gather up all artistic and intellectual production under a single name and is left having to square the notion of postmodernism as an instrument of subalternism with Jameson's belief that postmodernism represents a "cultural dominant," that is, not just a style among others, but the cultural logic of late capitalism.
5. Cf. Jameson, *Postmodernism*, p. xv: " 'Culture,' in the sense of what cleaves almost too close to the skin of the economic to be stripped off and inspected in its own right, is itself a postmodern development"; and Harvey, *The Condition of Postmodernity*, p. 344: "Precisely because capitalism is expansionary and imperialistic, cultural life in more and more areas gets brought within the grasp of the cash nexus and the logic of capital circulation."
6. Cf. Jameson, *Postmodernism*, p. xxi: "To say that my two terms, the *cultural* and the *economic*, thereby collapse back into one another and say the same thing [. . .] is also to suggest that the base, in the third stage of capitalism, generates its superstructures with a new kind of dynamic."
7. Cf. Jameson, *Postmodernism*, p. 48: "What we must now ask ourselves is whether it is not precisely this semiautonomy of the cultural sphere which has been destroyed by the logic of late capitalism."
8. There are two concepts of autonomy in García Canclini. The absolute concept of autonomy (with which he disagrees) is used by the moderns to speak of the supposed independence of high-cultural production. The relative concept is used by García Canclini himself to highlight the difference between the autonomy achieved by the artistic and intellectual fields in Europe and the lack of such a thing in Latin America at the same time. Only from the 1930s does the subcontinent begin to develop "more" (the word is his) cultural autonomy. So then: No, not even Latin America from the 1930s on knows absolute cultural autonomy, since all cultural production is bound up with economic and other nonaesthetic concerns. Yes, Latin America does witness an expanding relative cultural autonomy (he says "more," not "complete"), in the sense that it becomes possible to make a living from cultural production by virtue of the new market opened up by the expansion of the middle classes.

NOTES   195

9. "The extinction of the 'great moderns' is not necessarily an occasion for pathos. Our social order is richer in information and more literate, and socially, at least, more 'democratic' in the sense of the universalization of wage labor (I have always felt that Brecht's term 'plebeianization' is politically more suitable and sociologically more exact in designating this levelling process, which people on the left can surely only welcome); this new order no longer needs prophets and seers of the high modernist and charismatic type, whether among its cultural producers or its politicians. Such figures no longer hold any charm or magic for the subjects of a corporate, collectivized, postindividualistic age; in that case, goodbye to them without regrets, as Brecht might have put it: woe to the country that needs geniuses, prophets, Great Writers, or demiurges!" (Jameson, *Postmodernism*, p. 306).

10. Raymond Williams, *Keywords: A Vocabulary of Culture and Society* (London: Fontana Press, 1976; reprt. 1988), p. 90.

11. Culture as "the outward and emphatically visible sign of a special kind of people, cultivated people," which, in reality, amounts to no more than "trivial differences of behaviour, [. . .] trivial variations of speech habit" (Williams, "Culture is Ordinary," p. 7). Unless otherwise indicated, all further references to Williams will be to this essay.

12. It is no surprise that the starkness of such an opposition is discursively difficult to maintain. One thinks of the way in which Sarmiento's headline distinction between *civilización* and *barbarie* is persistently undone in the fabric of his writing. For instance: "Había antes de 1810 en la República Argentina [. . .] dos civilizaciones diversas: la una española, europea, civilizada, y la otra bárbara, americana, casi indígena"; Domingo Faustino Sarmiento, *Facundo: Civilización y barbarie* (Santa Fe, Argentina: Editorial Castellví, 1966), p. 79.

13. Derrida plays on the French word *fait* ("fact" and "done") to make the point that even apparent givens require the responsibility of a constant making. Jacques Derrida, *Of Spirit: Heidegger and the Question*, trans. Geoffrey Bennington and Rachel Bowlby (Chicago and London: University of Chicago Press, 1987), p. 40.

14. For the differences between the Enlightenment and Marxist conceptions of popular culture, see Martín-Barbero, *De los medios a las mediaciones*, chapter 1. Raymond Williams sees the development of British cultural studies as, among other things, a leavetaking from certain aspects of Marxism, in particular the Marxist stress on the need for a directive culture and the belief that the working classes have no access to culture (Raymond Williams, "Culture is Ordinary," p. 10).

15. Cf. Jean Franco, "Afterword: The Twilight of the Vanguard and the Rise of Criticism," in *Critical Passions: Selected Essays*, ed. Mary Louise Pratt and Kathleen Newman (Durham and London: Duke University Press, 1999), p. 511: "The explanation for this difference lies, in part, in recent history. During the military regimes of the Southern Cone, the military took control of the universities. Research survived in independent institutions such as FLACSO and CENECA (Chile), CEBRAP (Brazil), and

CEDES (Argentina). Researchers in these institutions began to realize the importance of studying culture—particularly popular culture—for understanding the roots of authoritarianism."
16. Román de la Campa, "De la deconstrucción al nuevo texto social: pasos perdidos o por hacer en los estudios culturales latinoamericanos (hacia una economía política de la producción de capital simbólico sobre América Latina confeccionado en la academia norteamericana)," in Moraña, *Nuevas perspectivas*, p. 79.
17. Beatriz Sarlo's background is not strictly that of the social sciences, even if her literary criticism has always been profoundly marked by sociological concerns. See her observations in "Raymond Williams: una relectura," in Moraña, *Nuevas perspectivas*, p. 309.
18. Jesús Martín-Barbero, *Procesos de comunicación y matrices de cultura: itinerario para salir de la razón dualista* (México: Ediciones Gustavo Gili, 1987), p. 10.
19. See Sarlo, "Raymond Williams," p. 312.
20. Héctor Schmucler, "La investigación (1975): ideología, ciencia y política," in *Memoria de la comunicación* (Buenos Aires: Editorial Biblos, 1997), p. 133. This is a reprint of the article "La investigación sobre comunicación masiva," originally published in *Comunicación y cultura* (Buenos Aires) 4 (1975).
21. Dependency theory was never in any case a theory about culture; it remained strictly at the level of politics and economics. See Neil Larsen, "Los estudios culturales: aperturas disciplinarias y falacias teóricas," in Moraña, *Nuevas perspectivas*, p. 75, for a cynical view of this "reformist" decoupling from Marxism.
22. Martín-Barbero, *De los medios a las mediaciones*, pp. 221–222.
23. See Stuart Hall, who confesses himself "dumbfounded" by the rise of North American cultural studies, for some interesting remarks on the dangers of institutionalization. Stuart Hall, "Cultural Studies and Its Theoretical Legacies," in *Cultural Studies*, ed. Lawrence Grossberg, Cary Nelson, and Paula A. Treichler (New York and London: Routledge, 1992), p. 285. The least we can say of cultural studies in the United States and United Kingdom is that it is both symptom and cause. If, on the positive side, it both propels and responds to the emancipating and democratizing projects of modernity, on the negative side it both propels and responds to the expansive project of modernity as well as the populism latent in the democratizing project.
24. We may cite five changes that lay at the heart of the original cultural studies project. (1) The object: Expanding the notion of the field of culture, attention was to be directed toward cultural forms traditionally considered less worthy, such as the new media technologies. (2) The method: Moving away from the immanent approach characteristic of literary analysis, the more broadly conceived "cultural text" needed to be approached from a variety of methodological routes in order to explore its explicit ideological content or its conditions of production or, as in the case of the mass media, its channels of distribution and consumption. Interest is not in the narrowly aesthetic meanings of a "text" but rather in the social meanings it embodies. (3) The motive: It was not enough

to analyze the ideology of mass mediatic society; the point was to change it. Not only culture, but the study of culture, was political. (4) The site: Cultural studies in Britain was marked from the beginning by work carried out not just in nontraditional universities but also in altogether nonuniversity sites. Richard Hoggart, Raymond Williams, and Stuart Hall all worked as adult education tutors at one time or another, teaching people who had often struggled to break into what were then restricted university circles. (5) The ethos: Cultural studies was to be collaborative and cooperative rather than individualist.

25. This aspiration also lies at the heart of Alberto Moreiras's presentism. "If politico-intellectual activity must be understood as the development of a critical relationship with the present, then academic politics in the humanities are fundamentally conditioned by the latter" (*The Exhaustion of Difference*, p. 3). I return to Moreiras in chapter 3.

26. This is also the position of Moreiras, albeit for slightly different reasons. See *The Exhaustion of Difference*, p. 86.

27. Lenin's view of literary production was more open and flexible than it subsequently became in the hands of his followers: "There is no doubt," he wrote in *Concerning Art and Revolution*, "that it is literary activity that can least tolerate a mechanical egalitarianism, a domination of the minority by the majority"; Terry Eagleton, *Marxism and Literary Criticism* (London: Methuen, 1976), p. 41.

28. Cf. Moreiras, for whom all attempts at transformation, incorporation, and transculturation are just different ways of giving in to the existing hegemony. I pursue this argument in chapter 3.

29. See p. 47 for his assessment of literature and the other arts' exploration of the contradictions between the cultured and the popular.

30. García Canclini cites a Mexican interview with Susan Sontag, who is reminded by her interviewer that she had once written, in *Against Interpretation*, that, forced to choose between the Doors and Dostoevsky, she would side with Dostoevsky, but that she did not see why it was necessary to choose. In the late 1990s, the situation is different: "El problema ahora—agregó—es que la gente está tan fascinada con el entretenimiento de masas, que difícilmente puede pensar en otro nivel. La idea por la que tienes que pelear ahora tiene que ver con los conceptos de 'seriedad' y 'compromiso.' La pregunta ahora es ¿por qué va uno a querer otra cosa que el entretenimiento masivo?" (pp. 196–197).

31. Beatriz Sarlo, *Escenas de la vida posmoderna: Intelectuales, arte y videocultura en la Argentina* (Buenos Aires: Espasa Calpe/Ariel, 1994).

32. Jacques Derrida, *The Gift of Death*, trans. David Wills (Chicago and London: University of Chicago Press, 1995), p. 27.

Chapter 3   Fieldwork

1. William Rowe, *Hacia una poética radical: Ensayos de hermenéutica cultural* (Rosario: Beatriz Viterbo Editora and Lima: Mosca Azul Editores, 1996).

2. Or "paradigm," as he puts it in a recent paper: "siempre hay un paradigma—si entendemos por paradigma no sólo las teorías sino también los modos de trabajar los materiales, las reglas de la evidencialidad, que varían según las disciplinas" (William Rowe, "De la oclusión de la lectura en los estudios culturales: las continuidades del indigenismo en el Perú," in Moraña, *Nuevas perspectivas*, p. 453).
3. Gilles Deleuze and Félix Guattari, *What Is Philosophy?* trans. Graham Burchell and Hugh Tomlinson (London and New York: Verso, 1994), p. 108: "We do not lack communication. On the contrary, we have too much of it. We lack creation. *We lack resistance to the present.* The creation of concepts in itself calls for a future form, for a new earth and people that do not yet exist. Europeanization does not constitute a becoming but merely the history of capitalism, which prevents the becoming of subjected peoples. Art and philosophy converge at this point: the constitution of an earth and a people that are lacking as a correlate of creation."
4. Cf. Jacques Derrida, "Psyché, Invention de l'autre," in *Psyché, Inventions de l'autre* (Paris: Galilée, 1987), on literature (pp. 26–27) and on programmatic knowledge ("Partout le projet de savoir et de recherche est d'abord une programmatique des inventions") (p. 39).
5. See William Rowe, "Cultural Studies Questionnaire: William Rowe," *Journal of Latin American Cultural Studies* 6:2 (1997), 223.
6. I am reminded of the attendant madness of Foucault's remarks on the idea of "eventalization," which is the effort to construct around a singular event a " 'polyhedron' of intelligibility, the number of whose faces is not given in advance and can never properly be taken as finite"; Michel Foucault, "Questions of Method," trans. Colin Gordon, *Ideology and Consciousness* 8 (Spring 1981), p. 6.
7. See the key section on "Méthode" in Michel Foucault, *Histoire de la sexualité*, Vol. I: *La Volonté de savoir* (Paris: Editions Gallimard, 1976), pp. 121–135.
8. Jacques Derrida, "Force and Signification," in *Writing and Difference*, trans. Alan Bass (London, Melbourne, and Henley: Routledge and Kegan Paul, 1978; reprt. 1985): "simultaneity is the myth of a total reading or description, promoted to the status of a regulatory ideal. The search for the simultaneous explains the capacity to be fascinated by the spatial image [. . .]. But by saying 'simultaneity' instead of space, one attempts to *concentrate* time instead of *forgetting* it" (pp. 24–25). "Light is menaced from within by that which also metaphysically menaces every structuralism: the possibility of concealing meaning through the very act of uncovering it. *To comprehend* the structure of a becoming, the form of a force, is to lose meaning by finding it. The meaning of becoming and of force, by virtue of their pure, intrinsic characteristics, is the repose of the beginning and the end, the peacefulness of a spectacle, horizon or face. Within this peace and repose the character of becoming and of force is disturbed by meaning itself. The meaning of meaning is Apollonian by virtue of everything within it that can be seen" (p. 26).

9. Jacques Derrida, "Signature Event Context," in *Glyph*, Johns Hopkins Textual Studies 1 (Baltimore: Johns Hopkins University Press, 1977), pp. 185–186. It is important to recall the context of Derrida's own meditation on context. It forms part of a reply to John Searle's defence of Austin's, and his own, speech act theory. Searle argued that the intentional meaning of a speaker's utterance is determined by the context in which he speaks.
10. Derrida, "Limited Inc abc . . . ," in *Glyph*, Johns Hopkins Textual Studies 2 (Baltimore: Johns Hopkins University Press, 1977), p. 220.
11. "It is the *dream* of a purely *heterological* thought at its source. A *pure* thought of *pure* difference. Empiricism is its philosophical name, its metaphysical pretention or modesty. We say the *dream* because it must vanish *at daybreak*, as soon as language awakens" (Jacques Derrida, "Violence and Metaphysics: An Essay on the Thought of Emmanuel Levinas," in *Writing and Difference*, p. 151).
12. A dangerous word to use with respect to poststructuralism and especially Derrida, given the latter's insistence on the displacement of terms involved in a rigorous deconstructive practice. This displacement certainly does not amount, in Derrida's work, to opposing tradition to something like modernity. If there appears to be something like a return to tradition in moments of Derrida's work, such moments will frequently be remarked as returns to a nontraditional tradition or to a traditionality that must be thought of beyond the strictures of tradition.
13. In this respect, it is worth noting the similarities with Adorno and Horkheimer, which, although surprising, are not fortuitous. See Theodor W. Adorno and Max Horkheimer, "The Culture Industry: Enlightenment as Mass Deception," in *Dialectic of Enlightenment*, trans. John Cumming (London and New York: Verso, 1997), p. 164.
14. Nor by a historicist approach. Derrida criticizes structuralism *and* its supposed opposite, historicism, on the grounds that both share a common desire for a self-identical presence, be it in the form of a synchronic relationality wherein all the elements might be known simultaneously (structuralism) or in the shape of a past neatly gathered up in the latest avatar of a continuous process (historicism).
15. Martín-Barbero, *De los medios a las mediaciones*, p. 57.
16. See William Rowe and Vivian Schelling, *Memory and Modernity: Popular Culture in Latin America* (New York: Verso, 1991).
17. "Ese pluralismo asegura una equivalencia universal: 'todos los estilos parecen más o menos equivalentes e igualmente (poco) importantes.' Nadie podrá ser condenado por sus ideas estéticas, pero nadie tendrá los instrumentos que permiten comparar, discutir y validar las diferentes estéticas. El mercado, experto en equivalentes abstractos, recibe a este pluralismo estético como la ideología más afin a sus necesidades" (Sarlo, *Escenas de la vida posmoderna*, p. 158).
18. Cited in Moreiras, *The Exhaustion of Difference*, p. 249. The de Man text is *Aesthetic Ideology*.
19. The monsters/pets idea is cited by Moreiras from an essay by Derrida, "Some Statements and Truisms about Neologisms, Newisms, Postisms,

Parasitisms, and Other Small Seismisms," in *The States of "Theory": History, Art, and Critical Discourse,* ed. David Carroll (Stanford: Stanford University Press, 1990; reprt. 1994), pp. 63–94. It is worth noting that in that essay Derrida has some harsh words to say about cultural studies' willingness to sacrifice the study of the canonical texts of the high tradition.

20. Derrida writes of the duty to assume "the European, and *uniquely* European, heritage of an idea of democracy, while also recognizing that this idea, like that of international law, is never simply given, that its status is not even that of a regulative idea in the Kantian sense, but rather something that remains to be thought and *to come* [*à venir*]: not something that is certain to happen tomorrow, not the democracy (national or international, state or trans-state) of the *future*, but a democracy that must have the structure of a promise—*and thus the memory of that which carries the future, the to come, here and now*"; Jacques Derrida, *Aporias: Dying–Awaiting (One Another at) the "Limits of Truth,"* trans. Thomas Dutoit (Stanford: Stanford University Press, 1993), p. 19.

21. Fredric Jameson, "On 'Cultural Studies,' " *Social Text* 34 (1993), 32.

22. Jameson, *Postmodernism,* p. 188.

23. It is revealing that both Néstor García Canclini and Beatriz Sarlo err on the side of caution where multidisciplinarity is concerned, advocating the pedagogical necessity of an initial solid grounding in one discipline rather than what we might call an originary multidisciplinarity. Néstor García Canclini, "Cultural Studies Questionnaire: Néstor García Canclini," *Journal of Latin American Cultural Studies* 5:1 (1996), 83–87; Beatriz Sarlo, "Cultural Studies Questionnaire: Beatriz Sarlo," *Journal of Latin American Cultural Studies* 6:1 (1997), 85–92.

24. Cf. Derrida, "Psyché, Invention de l'autre," p. 61: "laisser venir l'aventure ou l'événement du tout autre. D'un tout autre qui ne peut plus se confondre avec le Dieu ou l'Homme de l'ontothéologie ni avec aucune des figures de cette configuration (le sujet, la conscience, l'inconscient, le moi, l'homme ou la femme, etc.). Dire que c'est là le seul avenir, ce n'est pas appeler à l'amnésie. La venue de l'invention ne peut se rendre étrangère à la répétition et à la mémoire. Car l'autre n'est pas le nouveau."

Chapter 4   *Modernismo*, Positivism, and (Dis)inheritance

1. Paul de Man, "Literary History and Literary Modernity," *Blindness and Insight: Essays in the Rhetoric of Contemporary Criticism* (London and New York: Oxford University Press, 1971), pp. 147–148.

2. This chapter is an amended version of "Modernismo, positivismo y (des)herencia en el discurso de la historia literaria," in *¿Qué es el modernismo? Nueva encuesta, nuevas lecturas,* ed. Richard A. Cardwell and Bernard J. McGuirk (Boulder: Society of Spanish and Spanish-American Studies, 1993), pp. 311–330.

NOTES

3. "At least one strand of artistic modernism is anti-modern and comes into being in violent or muffled protest against modernization, now grasped as technological progress in the largest sense. These anti-modern modernisms sometimes involve pastoral visions or Luddite gestures but are mostly symbolic, and, especially at the turn of the century, involve what is sometimes referred to as a new wave of anti-positivist, spiritualistic, irrational reactions against triumphant enlightenment progress or reason" (Jameson, *Postmodernism*, p. 304).
4. See Lily Litvak, *El Modernismo* (Madrid: Taurus, 1975), p. 12.
5. See Georg Simmel, "Las grandes ciudades y la vida anímica" (1903), cited in Rafael Gutiérrez Girardot, *Modernismo* (Barcelona: Montesinos, 1983), p. 126.
6. Rubén Darío, excerpt from "Ricardo Palma," in José Olivio Jiménez and Carlos Javier Morales, *La prosa modernista hispanoamericana: Introducción crítica y antología* (Madrid: Alianza Editorial, 1998), p. 69.
7. Angel Rama, *Rubén Darío y el modernismo (circunstancia socioeconómica de un arte americano)* (Venezuela: Universidad Central de Venezuela, 1970), p. 5.
8. Cited in Rama, *Rubén Darío y el modernismo*, p. 11. Leopoldo Lugones, for his part, remarked that *modernismo* was "la conquista de la independencia intelectual."
9. Julio Ramos, *Desencuentros de la modernidad en América Latina: literatura y política en el siglo XIX* (Mexico: Fondo de cultura económica, 1989).
10. Ivan Schulman, "Reflexiones en torno a la definición del modernismo," in Litvak, *El Modernismo*, p. 72.
11. See, for instance, the oft-quoted definition by Federico de Onís: "El modernismo es la forma hispánica de la crisis universal de las letras y del espíritu que inicia hacia 1885 la disolución del siglo XIX y que se había de manifestar en el arte, en la ciencia, la religión, la política, y gradualmente en los demás aspectos de la vida entera, con todos los carácteres, por lo tanto, de un hondo cambio histórico cuyo proceso continúa hoy" (cited in Rama, *Rubén Darío y el modernismo*, p. 26).
12. Guillermo Díaz Plaja speaks of the *modernistas*' "filosofía antitainiana," *Modernismo frente a noventa y ocho: una introducción a la literatura española del siglo XX*, 2nd edn. (Madrid: Espasa-Calpe, 1966), p. 140; Cf. Ricardo Gullón, *El modernismo visto por los modernistas* (Barcelona: Guadarrama, 1980), p. 12, on the "protesta [. . .] contra el positivismo y el materialismo"; Luis Alberto Sánchez, cited in Ned J. Davison, *The Concept of Modernism in Hispanic Criticism* (Colorado: University of New Mexico, 1966), p. 72, n.23, on the reaction against "prosaísmo realista y positivista"; and Litvak, *El Modernismo*, p. 12.
13. Auguste Comte, cited in D.G. Charlton, *Positivist Thought in France during the Second Empire 1852–1870* (Oxford: Clarendon Press, 1959), p. 6. All references to Comte are taken from Charlton.
14. Octavio Paz, "Traducción y metáfora," in Litvak, *El Modernismo*.
15. Pedro Salinas, cited in Davison, *The Concept of Modernism in Hispanic Criticism*, p. 37.

16. The slogan comes from José Deleito y Piñuela, in *Gente vieja* (Madrid), 30 April 1902 (cited in Litvak, *El Modernismo*, p. 389).
17. The difference between the positivist and the more canonical Enlightenment idea of progress is that where Kant saw the idea of progress as an advance both of and toward rationality (i.e., as exclusively a matter of human history), positivism held that "all time-processes were, as such, progressive in character, and that history is a progress merely because it is a sequence of events in time." Thus, against the eighteenth-century conception of progress, in the positivist view, nature, too, was fundamentally progressive. R.G. Collingwood, *The Idea of History*, ed. Jan Van der Dussen, revised ed. with Lectures 1926–1928 (Oxford and New York: Oxford University Press, 1994), p. 99.
18. Maurice Mandelbaum, *History, Man, and Reason: A Study in Nineteenth-Century Thought* (Baltimore: Johns Hopkins Press, 1971), p. 43.
19. Again, such a view of progress differs from the classical Enlightenment or Kantian understanding, and is attributable to a more encompassing view of history introduced by Schiller. "Whereas Kant restricts the task of history to the study of political evolution, Schiller includes in it the history of art, of religion, of economics and so forth, and here again he improves on his predecessor" (Collingwood, *The Idea of History*, p. 105).
20. The archive of *modernismo* could supply more. Cf. Julio Herrera y Reissig and Horacio Quiroga, in Jiménez and Morales, *La prosa modernista hispanoamericana*, pp. 84–85 and p. 86 respectively.
21. Rodó and Valle-Inclán cited in Max Henríquez Ureña, *Breve historia del modernismo* (Mexico: Fondo de Cultura Económica, 1954), p. 166 and 168. Italics are mine.
22. Cited in Allen W. Phillips, "Rubén Darío y sus juicios sobre el modernismo," in *Estudios críticos sobre el modernismo*, ed. Homero Castillo (Madrid: Editorial Gredos, 1968), p. 137.
23. The quotations from Hyppolite Taine are from his *Introduction à l'histoire de la littérature anglaise (L'Histoire, son présent et son avenir)*, ed. H.B. Charlton (Manchester: Manchester University Press, 1936).
24. "L'apparition d'une nouvelle structure, d'un système original, se fait toujours—et c'est la condition même de sa spécificité structurale—par une rupture avec son passé, son origine et sa cause. On ne peut donc décrire la propriété de l'organisation qu'en ne tenant pas compte, dans le mouvement même de cette description, de ses conditions passées: en omettant de poser le problème du passage d'une structure à une autre, en mettant l'histoire entre parenthèses"; Jacques Derrida, "La Structure, le signe et le jeu dans le discours des sciences humaines," *L'Ecriture et la différence* (Paris: Editions du Seuil, 1967), p. 426.
25. Taine's own discourse bears witness to a repressed difference whose traces (*empreintes*) nevertheless rear their head in the irruption of *le moment*, the historicity of the interior: "Quand le caractère national et les circonstances environnantes opèrent, ils n'opèrent point sur une table rase, mais sur une table où des empreintes sont déjà marquées. Selon qu'on prend la table à un moment ou à un autre, l'empreinte est dif-

férente; et cela suffit pour que l'effet total soit différent" (*Introduction*, p. 43).
26. "The advent of modernity increasingly tears space away from place by fostering relations between 'absent' others, locationally distant from any given situation of face-to-face interaction. In conditions of modernity, place becomes increasingly *phantasmagoric*: that is, locales are thoroughly penetrated by and shaped in terms of social influences quite distant from them. What structures the locale is not simply that which is present at the scene; the 'visible form' of the locale conceals the distanciated relations that determine its nature" (Giddens, *The Consequences of Modernity*, pp. 18–19).
27. Michel Foucault, *L'Ordre du discours: leçon inaugurale au Collège de France prononcée le 2 décembre 1970* (Paris: Editions Gallimard, 1971), p. 41.
28. It may not be overstated in the case of Leopoldo Lugones. Cf. Carlos Altamirano's excellent "La fundación de la literatura argentina," in *Ensayos argentinos: De Sarmiento a la vanguardia*, ed. Carlos Altamirano and Beatriz Sarlo (Buenos Aires: Centro Editor de América Latina, 1983), pp. 107–115.
29. In truth, be it in the form of the episteme or the *énoncé*, content occupied the entirety of Foucault's thinking in the two "archaeological" tracts, *Les Mots et les choses: une archéologie des sciences humaines* (Paris: Editions Gallimard, 1966) and *L'Archéologie du savoir* (Paris: Editions Gallimard, 1969).
30. See César Vallejo, *El romanticismo en la poesía castellana* (Lima: Mejía Baca & Villanueva, 1954).

Chapter 5   Vallejo, Semicolonialism, and Poetemporality

1. "En sa syntaxe et son lexique, dans son espacement, par sa ponctuation, ses lacunes, ses marges, l'appartenance historique d'un texte n'est jamais droite ligne. Ni causalité de contagion. Ni simple accumulation de couches. Ni pure juxtaposition de pièces empruntées"; Jacques Derrida, *De la grammatologie* (Paris: Éditions de Minuit, 1967), pp. 149–150.
2. See Gayatri Chakravorty Spivak, *A Critique of Postcolonial Reason: Toward a History of the Vanishing Present* (Cambridge, Mass.: Harvard University Press, 1999), p. 359. The first part of this chapter appeared as "Semicolonial Times: Vallejo and the Discourse of Modernity," *Romance Quarterly* 49:3 (Heldref Publications, Summer 2002), 192–205.
3. Frantz Fanon, *The Wretched of the Earth*, trans. Constance Farrington (Harmondsworth: Penguin Books, 1967; reprt. 1985), p. 27.
4. Stephen Henighan, "Caribbean Masks: Frantz Fanon and Alejo Carpentier," in *Postcolonial Perspectives on the Cultures of Latin America and Lusophone Africa*, ed. Robin Fiddian (Liverpool: Liverpool University Press, 2000), pp. 169–190.

5. Gayatri Chakravorty Spivak, "Can the Subaltern Speak?" *Marxism and the Interpretation of Culture*, ed. Cary Nelson and Lawrence Greenberg (Urbana and Chicago: University of Illinois Press, 1988), pp. 271, 280, and 281.
6. Jorge Klor de Alva, "The Postcolonization of the (Latin) American Experience: A Reconsideration of 'Colonialism,' 'Postcolonialism,' and 'Mestizaje,' " in *After Colonialism: Imperial Histories and Postcolonial Displacements*, ed. Gyan Prakash (Princeton: Princeton University Press, 1995), p. 244.
7. Cited in Manrique, "Modernity and Alternative Development in the Andes," p. 222.
8. Manrique, "Modernity and Alternative Development in the Andes," p. 221. Emphasis in the original.
9. César Vallejo, "¿Qué pasa en el Perú?" *La cultura peruana (crónicas)* (Lima: Mosca Azul Editores, 1987), p. 182.
10. Vallejo goes on to suggest that, owing to the absence of checks and balances imposed by a distant metropolis, Latin America's plight is even worse than that of recognized colonies.
11. See Manrique, "Modernity and Alternative Development," p. 227. The phrase "traditionalist modernization" comes from Barrington Moore via Fernando de Trazegnies.
12. In fact, *tercer cineastas* Solanas and Getino use a form of the same word as Vallejo (*semicolony*) to describe Latin America's condition. Fernando Solanas and Octavio Getino, "Towards a Third Cinema: Notes and Experiences for the Development of a Cinema of Liberation in the Third World," in *Twenty-five Years of the New Latin American Cinema*, ed. Michael Chanan (London: BFI and Channel Four TV, 1983), p. 18.
13. Iris M. Zavala, *Colonialism and Culture: Hispanic Modernisms and the Social Imaginary* (Bloomington and Indianapolis: Indiana University Press, 1992), p. 28.
14. García Canclini, *Culturas híbridas*, p. 86. García Canclini reserves the word *postmodern* for his approach.
15. José María Arguedas, "El complejo cultural en el Perú," *Formación de una cultura nacional indoamericana* (Mexico: Siglo veintiuno editores, 1975), pp. 1–8 (p. 3).
16. See "¿Qué pasa en el Perú?" (p. 179) for Vallejo's assessment of the country's hybridity.
17. Mirko Lauer, cited in Martín-Barbero, *De los medios a las mediaciones*, p. 206.
18. César Vallejo, *Obra poética*, ed. Américo Ferrari (Nanterre: Colección Archivos, 1988), p. 54. All poetry quotations are from this edition.
19. Raymond Williams, "Language and the Avant-Garde," in *The Politics of Modernism: Against the New Conformists*, ed. Tony Pinkney (London and New York: Verso, 1989), p. 71.
20. César Vallejo, "Oriente y occidente," *Desde Europa. Crónicas y artículos (1923–1938)*, ed. Jorge Puccinelli (Lima: Fuente de Cultura Peruana, 1987), p. 210.

21. Cf. José Martí, "Nuestra América": "Los jóvenes de América [...] [e]ntienden que se imita demasiado, y que la salvación está en crear. Crear es la palabra de pase de esta generación" (in Jiménez and Morales, *La prosa modernista hispanoamericana*, p. 70).
22. César Vallejo, "El espíritu universitario," in *La cultura peruana*, pp. 112–115 (p. 113).
23. César Vallejo, "La juventud de América en Europa," in *Desde Europa*, pp. 324–325 (p. 324).
24. César Vallejo, "La megalomanía de un continente," in *Desde Europa*, pp. 327–328 (p. 327).
25. César Vallejo, "Sociedades coloniales," in *La cultura peruana*, pp. 124–126 (p. 124).
26. Foucault, *Les Mots et les choses*, p. 274.
27. William Rowe, "Trauma and Memory: César Vallejo and the Poetics of Time in the Peruvian Twentieth Century," unpublished lecture, Kings College, University of London, 26 November 1996, p. 4. This address, together with the essay in note 34, has been published in Spanish in William Rowe, Ensayos Vallejianos (Berkeley and Lima: Latinoamericana Editores, 2006).
28. "However peoples theorized time, the idea that the theory reflected a naturalized mindset may be a modernist mistake. As much as it is for us, for them too, a theory of time may have been a site of conflict with the 'vulgar' experience of time" (Spivak, *A Critique of Postcolonial Reason*, p. 370, n. 80).
29. Paz, *Children of the Mire*, p. 110.
30. Federico Bravo, "Transtextuality in the Writing of César Vallejo: 'En mis falsillas encañona ...': From Verbal to Textual Etymon," in *The Poetry and Poetics of César Vallejo: The Fourth Angle of the Circle*, ed. Adam Sharman (Lewiston: Edwin Mellen Press, 1997), pp. 17–25 (p. 21).
31. Latour, *We Have Never Been Modern*, p. 74: "Every contemporary assembly is polytemporal."
32. Paz, *Children of the Mire*, pp. 85–86.
33. See Anderson for the same point made in the context of European modernism ("Modernity and Revolution," p. 105).
34. Rowe, "Williams and Vallejo: Modernism in the Americas," unpublished paper, p. 1. See note 27.

Chapter 6   Borges and a Differently Colored History

1. In the Prologue to *El otro, el mismo* (1965), Borges includes "la contradicción del tiempo que pasa y de la identidad que perdura" among his "hábitos"; Jorge Luis Borges, *Obras completas, Vol II, 1952–1972* (Barcelona: Emecé Editores, 1996), p. 235.
2. Whence the "horror sagrado" that accompanies Heraclitus's proverbial insight into linear time ("*Nadie baja dos veces a las aguas / Del mismo río*"). "Heráclito," from *La moneda de hierro* (1976), in Jorge Luis Borges, *Obras*

completas, Vol III, 1975–1985 (Barcelona: Emecé Editores, 1989), p. 156. It was another Ancient Greek, Herodotus, who pioneered the study of history, viz. the attempt to come to terms with a world of change and catastrophic disturbance of which the Greeks, unlike later medieval Europeans, were keenly aware. The Herodotean enterprise was only subsequently stifled by a hardening of the antihistorical tendency in Greek thought. See Collingwood, *The Idea of History*, pp. 20, 22–24, and 29.
3. Beatriz Sarlo, *Jorge Luis Borges: A Writer on the Edge* (London: Verso, 1993).
4. In a retrospective prologue to *Historia de la eternidad*, Borges writes of eternity as a "splendid artifice" that momentarily frees us from the intolerable oppression of "lo sucesivo"; in *Obras completas, Vol. I, 1923–1949* (Barcelona: Emecé Editores, 1996), p. 351.
5. Borges is critical of this museum metaphor in the Prologue added later, where immobility, "ocupación de un mismo lugar en distintos puntos del tiempo," is no longer held to rule out linear time and dynamism (*Obras completas, Vol. I*, p. 351).
6. I have borrowed the above from Cassirer, *The Individual and the Cosmos*.
7. Cf. Jameson, *Postmodernism*, p. 402 for a similar diagnosis.
8. Montevideo does not even need mythologizing: "Eres el Buenos Aires que tuvimos, el que en los años se alejó quietamente. [. . .] Puerta falsa en el tiempo, tus calles miran al pasado más leve" ("Montevideo," *Luna de enfrente*, in *Obras completas, Vol. I*, p. 63).
9. Sarlo cites Borges's tribute to Paul Valéry: "To propose lucidity to men in a lowly romantic era, in the melancholy era of Nazism and dialectical materialism, of the augurs of Freudianism and the merchants of *surréalisme*, such is the noble mission Valéry fulfilled (and continues to fulfill)" (p. 53).
10. "The city and modernity presuppose one another because the city was the stage for the changes wrought by modernity: it exhibited them in an ostensible and sometimes brutal fashion, disseminating and generalizing them" (p. 9).
11. Cf. Jameson, *Postmodernism*, pp. 304–305 on this issue.
12. "El inmortal," *El Aleph*, in *Obras completas, Vol. I*, p. 533. It is telling that Borges should preface the story with an expression of tradition taken from one who rejected the authority of tradition. See Norman Hampson, *The Enlightenment* (Harmondsworth: Penguin Books, 1968; reprt. 1982), p. 36.
13. "Mi vida entera," *Luna de enfrente*, in *Obras completas, Vol. I*, p. 70.
14. "Página para recordar al coronel Suárez, vencedor en Junín," *El otro, el mismo*, in *Obras completas, Vol. II*, pp. 250–251.
15. Cf. "La luna," *El hacedor*, in *Obras completas, Vol. II*, p. 196: "No sé dónde la vi [i.e., la luna] por vez primera, / si en el cielo anterior de la doctrina / del griego o en la tarde que declina / sobre el patio del pozo y de la higuera."
16. Oscar Masotta's conclusion is slightly different. When the protagonist of "El Aleph" laments the appearance of a new advertisement in Plaza

NOTES 207

Constitución, it is because the advertised new cigarettes remind him that time passes and that, as a consequence, his memory of the dead Beatriz will gradually go up in smoke. For Masotta, the work of mourning is an operation in which the identity of the other is *necessarily* negated. Only by accepting the negation of the other's essentiality, only by coming to terms with the other's banality (the new cigarettes will in turn be replaced), can the libido be recovered. Desire can only be the form of eternity if it is pathological desire. Oscar Masotta, *Lecturas de psicoanálisis. Freud, Lacan* (Buenos Aires: Paidós, 1992), p. 145. I am grateful to Alejandro Riberi for drawing my attention to this book.

17. As Borges puts it in "Nota sobre la paz": "hablar es resignarse a ser Góngora"; Jorge Luis Borges, *Borges en Sur (1931–1980)* (Barcelona: Emecé Editores, 1999), p. 33. Originally published in *Sur* 129 (July 1945). For the importance of expressionism (and *ultraísmo*) to Borges, see Edwin Williamson, *Borges: A Life* (New York, London: Viking, 2004), p. 60ff.

18. Cf. "La noche cíclica" (1940), *El otro, el mismo*, in *Obras completas, Vol. II*, p. 241 for a similar yoking together of nightfall, Greek philosophy, periodic fractions, and "Una esquina remota / [. . .] / que tiene siempre una tapia celeste."

19. In the poem "Caminata," *Fervor de Buenos Aires*, in *Obras completas, Vol. I*, p. 43, night makes room for memory and another time by "losing" "mediocre" reality. "Grandiosa y viva / como el plumaje oscuro de un ángel / cuyas alas tapan el día, / la noche pierde las mediocres calles."

20. Eternity "occurs" as an irruption as early as *Fervor de Buenos Aires*. See the poem "Rosas."

21. See "Elogio de la sombra," *Elogio de la sombra*, in *Obras completas, Vol. II*, p. 395 for the constellation of blindness/abstraction/thought/eternity. I touch on this poem in Adam Sharman, "Borges y el tiempo de la ceguera," in *Jorge Luis Borges. Intervenciones sobre pensamiento y literatura*, ed. William Rowe, Claudio Canaparo, and Annick Louis (Buenos Aires, Barcelona, Mexico: Paidós, 2000), pp. 249–262.

22. "La doctrina de los ciclos," *Historia de la eternidad*, in *Obras completas, Vol. I*, p. 385.

23. The image is repeated in "Los teólogos," *El Aleph*, in *Obras completas, Vol. I*, p. 551.

24. Poetry proceeds in the same way. "Sin prefijadas leyes, [la poesía] obra de un modo vacilante y osado, como si caminara en la oscuridad" ("Prólogo," *El otro, el mismo*, in *Obras completas, Vol. II*, p. 236). On blindness, see *Siete noches*, in *Obras completas, Vol. III*, pp. 276–286.

25. The impossibility of speaking of a "return" without readmitting the language and conceptuality of conventional chronology is restated in "El tiempo circular" (1943), *Historia de la eternidad*, in *Obras completas, Vol. I*, p. 394.

26. The same circumspection toward the doctrine of eternity, in the shape of a preference for similarity over identity, was already at work in *Fervor de*

Buenos Aires. In the poem "El truco," *Obras completas, Vol, I*, p. 22, the card game's limited permutations allow the players to *copy* the *antiguas bazas* (old tricks, trump cards, achievements) of Rosas's generation, that is, allow them momentarily, and figuratively, to "resuscitate" their elders ("un poco, muy poco") without *becoming* them.

27. A similar strategy informs the poem "Arte poética," *El hacedor*, in *Obras completas*, Vol. II, p. 221, except that here the refutation of the refutation allows back in what it looked to have refuted (the eternal nature of art).
28. Cf. Borges's famous remark on the kabbalah that his interest lies in its hermeneutic or cryptographic methods rather than in its doctrine ("Una vindicación de la Cábala," *Discusión*, in *Obras completas, Vol. I*, p. 209).
29. "Funes el memorioso," *Ficciones*, in *Obras completas, Vol. I*, pp. 485–490.
30. Elsewhere Borges calls Funes a "monster"; "A Fragment on Joyce," *The Total Library*, p. 220; originally published in *Sur* 77 (Feb 1941).
31. The origins of a textual character are always complex. It is worth noting that Borges's maternal grandfather died of the same illness as Funes. See the poem "Isidoro Acevedo," *Cuaderno San Martín* (1929), in *Obras completas, Vol. I*, p. 86. For the Locke dimension, see Evelyn Fishburn and Psique Hughes, *A Dictionary of Borges* (London: Duckworth, 1990), p. 143.
32. Borges uses the same idea, again with the word *abarrotado*, in a poem from 1936, "Insomnio," *El otro, el mismo*, in *Obras completas, Vol. II*, p. 237: "De fierro, / de encorvados tirantes de enorme fierro, tiene que ser la noche, / para que no la revienten y la desfonden / las muchas cosas que mis abarrotados ojos han visto, / las duras cosas que insoportablemente la pueblan."
33. Divergence from his beloved Berkeley, whose "Hay verdades tan claras que para verlas nos basta abrir los ojos" Borges cites in "Nueva refutación del tiempo," *Otras inquisiciones*, in *Obras completas, Vol. II*, pp. 137–138. And confirmation? Derrida reproduces the following words from Diderot, for whom idealism is a philosophy for the blind: "Those philosophers, madam, are termed idealists who, conscious only of their own existence and of a succession of external sensations, do not admit anything else; an extravagant system which should to my thinking have been the offspring of blind parents"; Jacques Derrida, *Memoirs of the Blind: The Self-Portrait and Other Ruins*, trans. de Pascale-Anne Brault and Michael Naas (Chicago: University of Chicago Press, 1993), p. 102.
34. *Discusión*, in *Obras completas, Vol. I*, pp. 267–274.
35. In *Obras completas, Vol. I*, pp. 617–627.
36. As if to confirm this, those stories and poems whose setting is more or less contemporary and that feature an instant of revelation, usually contrive to have the arrival of the fantastic or the advent of eternity—if the latter can advene—preceded by a verisimilitudinous detail. Tiredness in "Sentirse en muerte," loss of consciousness in "El Sur" and "Funes," a closing of the eyes in "El Aleph": all conform to the "reality effect" proper to realism.

It is as though the idea of an Ancient (Greek) time could not exist without the say-so of a modern aesthetic in which it must find expression.
37. Despite pronounced political differences, Borges is close to Walter Benjamin in this respect. It is not a matter of simply embracing tradition, and certainly not of doing away with it; it is a matter of wresting tradition from conformism. Benjamin, *Illuminations*, p. 257.
38. "The word Kabbalah means, if the texts I have read don't mislead me, something like 'received' or 'received tradition,' and this etymology sends us to a fact far distant from us. Today, we enjoy knowing that an idea is new. The notion of novelty is not an unpleasant one, but during the Middle Ages, let us say during the eleventh or twelfth century, and even during the Renaissance, the idea of novelty was a displeasing one. It was thought of as something arbitrary because essential things were already discovered"; Jorge Luis Borges, "The Kabbalah," in Jaime Alazraki, *Borges and the Kabbalah and Other Essays on His Fiction and Poetry*, (Cambridge: CUP, 1988), p. 57.
39. "The biblical scholar perceives revelation not as a unique and clearly delineated occurrence, but rather as a phenomenon of eternal fruitfulness to be unearthed and examined: 'Turn it and turn it again, for everything is in it' "; Gershom Scholem, *The Messianic Idea in Judaism: and Other Essays on Jewish Spirituality* (London: Allen and Unwin, 1971), p. 287. I am grateful to Sheldon Penn for drawing my attention to this quotation.
40. All three essays are to be found in *Otras inquisiciones*, in *Obras completas*, *Vol. II*, pp. 28–30, 48–63, 101–104.
41. Cf. Theodor W. Adorno and Max Horkheimer, *Dialectic of Enlightenment*, trans. John Cumming (London and New York: Verso, 1997), p. 27: "In its figures mythology had the essence of the *status quo*: cycle, fate, and domination of the world reflected as the truth and deprived of hope."
42. Jacques Derrida, "Otobiographies: The Teaching of Nietzsche and the Politics of the Proper Name," in *The Ear of the Other: Otobiography, Transference, Translation*, ed. Christie V. McDonald, trans. Avital Ronell (New York: Schocken Books, 1985), pp. 34–35.
43. "*Deutsches Requiem*," *El Aleph*, paradoxically, makes the same point. Paradoxically, because the narrator Otto Dietrich zur Linde both propounds the idea of novelty ("El nazismo, intrínsecamente, es un hecho moral, un despojarse del viejo hombre, que está viciado, para vestir el nuevo") and recognizes that history registers a "continuidad secreta" ("Arminio, cuando degolló en una ciénaga las legiones de Varo, no se sabía precursor de un Imperio Alemán"), a continuity that is nothing other than (a Nazi version of) Nietzschean will. It is not fortuitous that the paragraph which contains the latter begins thus: "Se ha dicho que todos los hombres nacen aristotélicos o platónicos. Ello equivale a declarar que no hay debate de carácter abstracto que no sea un momento de la polémica de Aristóteles y Platón; a través de los siglos y latitudes, cambian los nombres, los dialectos, las caras, pero no los eternos antagonistas. También la historia de los pueblos registra una continuidad secreta" (*Obras completas, Vol. I*, p. 580).

Chapter 7   Rulfo and the Mexican Roman Trinity

1. Ángel Rama, *Transculturación narrativa en América Latina* (Mexico: Siglo veintiuno editores, 1982).
2. References are to the English translation. Ángel Rama, "Processes of Transculturation in Latin American Narrative," *Journal of Latin American Cultural Studies* 6:2 (1997), 155–171.
3. The transculturators were at one, he writes in 1974, in regarding foreign techniques as "mere instruments with which to discover their internal equivalents" (p. 157).
4. See Carlos Blanco Aguinaga, "Realidad y estilo de Juan Rulfo," in *Nueva novela latinoamericana*, Vol. I, ed. Jorge Lafforgue (Buenos Aires: Paidós, 1972), pp. 85–113; Augusto Roa Bastos, "Los trasterrados de Comala," *Unomásuno* (22 Aug. 1981), pp. 2–3; Martin Lienhard, *La voz y su huella. Escritura y conflicto étnico-cultural en América Latina 1492–1988*, 3rd edn. (Lima: Editorial Horizonte, 1992), pp. 180–189; William Rowe, *Rulfo: El llano en llamas (Critical Guide)* (London: Grant and Cutler, 1987).
5. "Pero el hecho de haber exterminado a la población indígena les trajo una característica muy especial, esa actitud criolla que hasta cierto punto es reaccionaria, conservadora de sus intereses creados" (Rulfo, cited in Rama, *Transculturación narrativa*, p. 104).
6. There was and is a substantial Huichol population in northern Jalisco; many Huicholes and people from other ethnic groups (including Purhepechas) migrated to the state capital Guadalajara; there were and are various other groups, such as the Nahuatl speakers of Tuxpan, in southern Jalisco. It is significant, by contrast, that Rulfo's parents were from the region of Los Altos, one of the enclaves of emphatically non-indian people in Jalisco (more like *criollos* than *mestizos*) frequently held up by the Jaliscan elite as emblems of the state. I am indebted to Trevor Stack for the above.
7. Cited in Rama, *Transculturación narrativa*, p. 114.
8. Some 150 photographs have been collected in Carlos Fuentes et al., *Juan Rulfo's Mexico*, trans. Margaret Sayers Peden (Washington and London: Smithsonian Institution Press, 2002).
9. On at least one occasion, Rulfo explicitly takes issue with attempts to designate him as a "regional" or "rural" writer: "Dicen que soy un escritor rural. Pero eso no me interesa que lo digan; eso de que soy un escritor regional. Porque yo no sé lo que quieren decir con eso. En primer lugar, todos los escritores son regionales. Cada uno expresa su región. Tampoco cuadra eso de rural porque yo utilice personajes del pueblo o campesinos. Eso no implica exactamente que vivan en el campo. Pueden vivir en una población grande pero estar en contacto con el campo"; Juan Rulfo, *Autobiografía armada* (Buenos Aires: Ediciones Corregidor, 1973), p. 70.
10. See Rulfo, *Autobiografía armada*, pp. 61–62.

NOTES   211

11. Jacques Derrida, *Given Time: I. Counterfeit Money*, trans. Peggy Kamuf (Chicago and London: University of Chicago Press, 1992), p. 152. The phrase originally refers to a story by Baudelaire.
12. Both fifteenth-century European and Aztec cultures knew the custom of offering food to the dead. See Pamela Voekel, *Alone before God: The Religious Origins of Modernity in Mexico* (Durham and London: Duke University Press, 2002), p. 213 on Europe; and Elizabeth Carmichael and Chloë Sayer, *The Skeleton at the Feast: The Day of the Dead in Mexico* (London: British Museum Press, 1991), p. 31, on the Aztecs.
13. Octavio Paz, *El laberinto de la soledad*, 2nd edn. (Mexico: Fondo de cultura económica, reprt. 1988), pp. 50–51.
14. On the *phantasma* as the living dead in Plato, see Jacques Derrida, *Specters of Marx*, p. 147.
15. Rulfo in Luis Harss, *Los nuestros*, 2nd edn. (Buenos Aires: Editorial Sudamericana, 1968), p. 325.
16. "Their [i.e., Toltec and Aztec] underlying philosophy of life (union of opposites, death as transformation and seed of new life, etc.) lasted well into the Spanish conquest and helped to give Mexico its overall 'toltequistic' characteristics"; Juan Schobinger, "The Amerindian Religions," in *The Church in Latin America 1492–1992*, ed. Enrique Dussel (Kent: Burns and Oates, 1992), p. 35.
17. See G.C. Vaillant, *Aztecs of Mexico: Origin, Rise, and Fall of the Aztec Nation* (Harmondsworth: Penguin Books, 1972), p. 178. Cf. Augusto Roa Bastos objecting to mythical readings of *Pedro Páramo* that alight solely on Western myths: "Por qué no también el lugar expiatorio de Mictlan en tierra azteca: el inframundo de la cosmogonía náhuatl donde cruje el viento negro de los cuchillos de obsidiana del que hablan los códices? El lugar adonde iban a purgar su culpa los que morían de enfermedad así el señor como el esclavo [. . .]. No está acaso Comala más cerca, raigalmente, de Mictlan que del trasmundo de [Luciano de] Samosata?" (p. 3). It is true that if one wants to "go mythical," Mictlan might prove as valid an intertext as the Greek underworld. The point, I think, is that the novel is much closer to Catholic than to either Greek or Aztec myth, and that Roa Bastos effectively christianizes the latter—filling it with moral significance (purgative guilt)—in order to bring it closer to the novel. Martin Lienhard's attempt to draw a parallel between Juan Preciado and Quetzalcóatl is similarly strained, relying on the fact that an archetypal story such as Juan's journey can touch off echoes with the most diverse cultural myths, if one tries hard enough. Lienhard's Aztec reading reaches its limits when he insists on the "re-creative" dimension of the novel in a deliberate attempt to pre-Colombianize it (see Lienhard, *La voz y su huella*, pp. 183–184).
18. Juan Rulfo, *Pedro Páramo*, 7th edn., ed. José Carlos González Boixo (Madrid: Ediciones Cátedra, 1990), p. 120. All references to the novel are to this edition.
19. Hannah Arendt, "What Is Authority?" in *Between Past and Future: Eight Exercises in Political Thought* (Harmondsworth: Penguin Books, 1993), p. 120.

20. Insofar as the Church's repetition is a significant appropriation, it is clear that the authority in question is not a once-and-for-all established authority, but a continuously reinvented principle. For this same point, see Thomas Paine, *The Rights of Man*, ed. Christopher Bigsby (London: J.M. Dent, 1993), p. 31.
21. Enrique Dussel, "The Church and Emergent Nation States (1830–80)," in Dussel, *The Church in Latin America 1492–1992*, p. 107.
22. Rulfo observes in the interview with Harss that the conquistadores were often criminals from Spain who changed their name by adopting a "nombre geográfico" (Harss, *Los nuestros*, p. 307).
23. Giddens, *The Consequences of Modernity*, p. 102.
24. The other function of this scene, strange as it might seem for Rulfo, is that of psychological realism. The scene paves the way for the transformation of Pedro—seemingly overnight—into a plausibly ruthless figure.
25. The "populist" view is advanced by Carlos Monsiváis, "Sí, tampoco los muertos retoñan. Desgraciadamente," in *Juan Rulfo: Homenaje nacional* (México: Instituto Nacional de Bellas Artes, 1980). It should be said that Marx's view is not opposed to the "populist" one. Precisely in that famous quotation about religion as opiate, Marx recognizes that religious distress is a protest against real distress ("it is the sigh of the oppressed creature"). Marx's point was that it was necessary to abolish religious illusion so that people could see the truth of their worldly oppression and do something about it. See Bowker, *The Meanings of Death* (Cambridge: Cambridge University Press, 1991; reprt. 1996), p. 11.
26. Rulfo, apropos the Cristeros war: "son pueblos muy reaccionarios, pueblos con ideas muy conservadoras, fanáticos" (in Harss, *Los nuestros*, p. 308).
27. Arendt ("What Is Authority?" p. 128) argues that the doctrine of the Final Judgement originally comes from Plato, and that the introduction of the Platonic myth into Christian doctrine strengthened religious authority to the point where it became a more forbidding prospect than secular power.
28. The women's preference for death has close affinities with the practice of slave suicide as a release from terror and servitude. See Gilroy, *The Black Atlantic*, p. 63.
29. Rama maintained that of the two processes of transculturation ("the first operating between the external metropoli and the Latin American urban centers, and the second, between the latter and their internal regions"), the second was "the most original, or the specifically Latin American" ("Processes," p. 159).
30. In accordance with a traditional understanding of place—and the same could be said of "La Cuesta de las comadres," "Anacleto Morones," or "La herencia de Matilde Arcángel"—the characters of "Luvina" do not themselves inhabit "traditional rural Mexico"; they live in San Juan Luvina.
31. The geography of the two places also receives a similar symbolization. Each is associated with death and purgatory, that is, with a certain end of time.

32. In "Es que somos muy pobres" the mother uses the religious language of exemplarity only to make prostitution into a pathologically exemplary, genetic condition (like sister like sister).
33. William Rowe, *Rulfo: El llano en llamas* (*Critical Guide*) (London: Grant and Cutler, 1987), p. 51.
34. Juan Rulfo, "Luvina," *El llano en llamas*, ed. Carlos Blanco Aguinaga (Madrid: Ediciones de Cátedra, 1988), p. 126. All references to the stories are to this edition.
35. "Mi obra no es de periodista ni de etnógrafo, ni de sociólogo. *Lo que hago es una transposición literaria de los hechos de mi conciencia*. La transposición no es una deformación sino el descubrimiento de formas especiales de sensibilidad" (*Autobiografía*, p. 72).
36. This rather supports Rulfo's confession to a journalist that "Yo, de mujeres no entiendo" (Jesús Torbado, "Entrevista. Con Juan Rulfo, de contrabando, en California," *El País*, 19 September 1982, p. 11).
37. Cf. Rama: "El conflicto modernizador instaura el movimiento sobre la permanencia, [. . .] pone en movimiento a la cultura estática y tradicionalista de la región enquistada" (1982, p. 96).
38. Blanco Aguinaga, "Realidad y estilo," pp. 101 and 103.
39. Joseph Sommers, *After the Storm: Landmarks of the Modern Mexican Novel* (University of New Mexico Press, 1968), pp. 74 and 88. Cf. Rulfo: "Y claro, los muertos no viven en el espacio ni en el tiempo" (in Harss, *Los nuestros*, p. 330).
40. The point is made by Ángel Rama, "Una primera lectura de 'No oyes ladrar los perros' de Juan Rulfo," *Revista de la Universidad de México* 29:12 (August 1975), 7.
41. Jean Franco, "Journey to the Land of the Dead: Rulfo's *Pedro Páramo*," in Franco *Critical Passions: Selected Essays*, p. 439. At the very close of the novel, Rulfo restates the connection between time and air: "De pronto su corazón se detenía y parecía como si se detuviera el tiempo y el aire de la vida" (p. 194). Again, the *parecía como si* is revealing.
42. Blanco Aguinaga, cited in Rowe, *Rulfo: El llano en llamas*, p. 55.
43. Rama is even more forthright in the early essay, giving the impression that the form of *Pedro Páramo* is generated solely by a "retreat back into tradition" (p. 161).
44. The parallels with Welles's film are particularly striking: the study of a very modern form of power in which a seemingly all-powerful man dies with the still-open wound of a childhood cut short.
45. Some 300 pages were reduced to 150 (Juan Rulfo, "Pedro Páramo treinta años después," *El Espectador Magazin dominical*, 147, 19 January 1986, p. 3; originally published in *Libros de México*, December 1985). There are possible contradictions in what Rulfo says, since he also suggests that what was reduced was the role of Susana San Juan. No contradiction, of course, if the didacticism was largely attached to the parts of the novel dealing with her.
46. Roland Barthes, "The Death of the Author," in *Image Music Text*, ed. Stephen Heath (London: Fontana, 1977), p. 147. Cf. Rulfo's

formulation: "Lo más difficil que tuve que salvar para escribir el *Pedro Páramo*, fue eliminarme a mí mismo, matar al autor, quien es, por cierto, el primer muerto del libro" (interview with Waldemar Verdugo Fuentes, "Juan Rulfo," http://magosdeamerica.galeon.com/album756854.html [originally published in *Vogue*]).

47. "If something is given to be read that is totally intelligible, that can be totally saturated by sense, it is not given to the other to be read. Giving to the other to be read is also a *leaving to be desired*, or a leaving the other room for an intervention by which she will be able to write her own interpretation"; Jacques Derrida in Jacques Derrida and Maurizio Ferraris, *A Taste for the Secret*, trans. Giacomo Donis (Cambridge: Polity Press, 2001), p. 31.

Chapter 8 Carpentier on the Age of Enlightenment

1. *Children of the Mire: Modern Poetry from Romanticism to the Avant-garde*, trans. Rachel Phillips (Cambridge, Mass.: Harvard University Press, 1991), p. 29.
2. Cited in Michael Moody, "Georg Lukàcs, the Historical Novel, and *El siglo de las luces*," *Revista de estudios hispánicos* 13 (1979), 45–63 (56).
3. Alejo Carpentier, *El siglo de las luces* (Barcelona: Seix Barral, 2001). All references to the novel are to this edition.
4. "Ya *El siglo de las luces* había analizado detalladamente el advenimiento de la modernidad en Hispanoamérica"; Roberto González Echevarría "Modernidad, modernismo y nueva narrativa: *El recurso del método*," *Inter-American Review of Bibliography* 30 (1980), 157–163 (161).
5. "El libro se llama así porque el Siglo de las Luces, que se ha dado como el ejemplo de la cordura, del pensamiento filosófico de la paz y de la calma y todo lo que usted quiera, es uno de los siglos más sangrientos— economía basada en la esclavitud, represiones, castigos, hechicerías, matanzas de protestantes, etcétera, que se ha visto en la historia. Por lo tanto, hay juego de palabras en el título" (Carpentier cited in Eugenio Dulog Matibag, *The Sleep of Reason: Alejo Carpentier and the Crisis of Latin American Modernity*, unpublished dissertation, May 1987, 47:11, p. 8).
6. It is not the only awkward blurring perpetrated by the novel. When the action spills over into the nineteenth century, offering up a "siglo prolongado" that allows Carpentier to recruit Goya's *Los desastres de la guerra* for the denunciation of Enlightenment reason and French imperialism, everything seems to take place under the aegis of the Same. Either the French Revolution and Napoleon's invasion of Madrid are avatars of the same undifferentiated historical force (the violent overcoming of others) or, worse, the second is made the essential consequence of the first (the Revolution as hidden God, First Cause). The discourse of inheritance offers a variation on this theme: "l'héritier de la Révolution n'est-il pas

Napoléon qui entreprendra l'annexion de l'Espagne, et les mêmes hommes qui ont renversé Capet le tyran ne sont-ils pas les bourreaux du *Dos* et du *Tres de Mayo* [. . .]?" Jean M. Goulemot, "Romans de langue espagnole et révolution française (*Las memorias de un hombre de acción, El siglo de las luces*)," *Revue de littérature comparée* 4 (1989), 513–524 (516).

7. Ogé, who is called only Doctor Ogé, is probably based on Jacques Ogé, a mulatto whose brother Vincent was killed, as in the novel, for leading a mulatto uprising against the Santo Domingo authorities. See Ralph Korngold, *Citizen Toussaint* (London: Victor Gollancz, 1945), p. 47.

8. See, for instance, Jo Labanyi (who follows Julio Ortega), "Nature and the Historical Process in Carpentier's *El siglo de las luces*," *Bulletin of Hispanic Studies* 57 (1980), 55–66 (58–59).

9. " 'Inner-worldly ascetic' religion produced a culture whose central values were: 1) seeking mastery over the natural world; 2) seeking mastery over other people who are seen as being prone to sinfulness, wickedness, sensuality and laziness; 3) seeking mastery over the self—by controlling impulses to the sensual enjoyment of bodily experiences arising from wearing fine clothes, make-up, or perfumes, consuming good food and wine, or other alcoholic drinks, and above all sexual pleasure, both inside and outside marriage. Weber claimed that this set of cultural values had emerged *uniquely* from the later forms of Calvinism in the late 1500s and early 1600s, especially among Puritan groups in Britain, Holland and New England where early capitalism took firm root. The religious culture of inner-worldly asceticism had provided the seedbed for the formation of the 'rational spirit' of modern capitalism" (Robert Bocock, "The Cultural Formations of Modern Society," in Hall and Gieben, *Formations of Modernity*, pp. 254–255). In Weberian terms, the adolescents' Catholic father could accommodate himself to the ostensibly *Protestant* spirit of capitalism, first, through "elective affinity" (the "fit" between a socioeconomic group and a set of cultural beliefs and values), but, second, by virtue of ongoing processes of rationalization and secularization that together exceeded Protestantism.

10. A short while later, both Carlos and, more ambivalently, Sofía return to the father's mercantile ways.

11. To read the novel as a historically accurate portrayal of the Cuba of 1789 is to reach the same conclusion: namely that Hugues does not introduce modernity into the household. By virtue of the English invasion of Havana (1762–1763), the island had clearly already come into contact with certain aspects of modernity. See Roberto González Echevarría, *Alejo Carpentier: The Pilgrim at Home* (Austin: University of Texas Press, 1990), p. 227: "New industrial and commercial ideas and practices revolutionized the socioeconomic fabric of the island and forced the Spanish colonial regime to liberalize its rule after regaining Havana. These changes began to erode the colonial system that had been in force since the sixteenth century and had kept the island outside the mainstream of intellectual, social, and historical currents."

12. Dulog Matibag, *The Sleep of Reason*, p. 198. The quotation is from Immanuel Kant, "What Is Enlightenment?" in *Foundations of the*

Metaphysics of Morals and What Is Enlightenment? trans. Lewis White Beck (Indianapolis: The Liberal Arts Press, 1959), p. 85.
13. In point of fact, Kant's idea of enlightenment is more complex, and certainly does not dispense with tutelage. Kant does not say that the right to criticize should be exercised everywhere and at all times. There are times when the use of reason should be curbed and one should submit to the guidance of others. Kant calls this the private use of reason and refers to its use in a civil post or office entrusted to an individual. In contrast, that same member of the community has the right to make public use of reason in an unfettered way and without tutelage. This public use of reason in Kant is reserved exclusively for the function of the scholar. Thus the clergyman must make his sermon conform to the symbol of the Church that he serves (he must censor his use of private reason and simply obey), but he can and should exercise his public use of reason when, as a scholar, he publicly expresses his carefully considered thoughts on the errors of the symbol or on ways to improve the Church.
14. Dulog Matibag, *The Sleep of Reason*, p. 198. For a similar reading, see Beatriz Pastor, "Carpentier's Enlightened Revolution, Goya's Sleep of Reason," in *Representing the French Revolution: Literature, Historiography, and Art*, ed. James A.W. Heffernan (Hanover: University Press of New England, 1992), p. 264. The novel encourages the comparison between Víctor and the dead father but also draws a clear distinction: "(Sofía nunca había pensado en eso. Cuando el padre vivía, tan austero como era, jamás hubiera tolerado que alguien saliese de la casa después de la hora del rosario.)" (p. 46)
15. Israel, *Radical Enlightenment*, p. 3.
16. There is some debate as to just how anti-religious the Enlightenment was. Strictly speaking, with the exception of Spinoza and Bayle, the early Enlightenment sought to accommodate the new thinking to Christian belief and the authority of scripture (Israel, *Radical Enlightenment*, p. 15). Although Cassirer is prepared to say that by the time of the French *encyclopédistes*, war has been declared on religion, and above all on the concept of original sin, he goes on to say that the Enlightenment thinkers were against dogma, not ignorance, and consequently against superstition rather than faith as such. "Not atheism, but superstition, is the major evil to be attacked"; "ignorance is not so far from the truth as prejudice" (p. 162). He concludes that the Enlightenment principle of tolerance towers above all else and becomes the expression of a new and positive religious ethos, of an expanded concept of God. Cassirer's key point is that this new ethos is not a matter of receptivity but activity. "It is not supernatural power nor divine grace which produces religious conviction in man; he himself must rise to it and maintain it" (p. 164). In other words, Cassirer finds active humanity—and humanism—at the heart of both the period's religious belief *and* its thought in general. This activity in religion is not a matter of pure intellectualism, as conventional accounts of the Enlightenment have maintained, since it cannot be a question of reducing belief to the acceptance of certain theoretical

propositions. Such a move would merely put religion back in the hands of doctrinaire theologians and thus negate the principle of enlightened reason. Both religion and philosophy, in other words, share a common ethical orientation: tolerant of difference, but intolerant of intolerance. Cassirer provides sufficient evidence from thinkers of the Enlightenment themselves to suggest that Esteban's reflections on religion do not altogether run counter to the spirit of Enlightenment. Ernst Cassirer, *The Philosophy of the Enlightenment*, trans. Fritz C.A. Koelln and James P. Pettegrove (Boston: Beacon Press, 1951; reprt. 1960), pp. 134, 161, 162, and 164–169.
17. Arendt, "What Is Authority?" p. 133.
18. Arendt, "What Is Authority?" p. 136.
19. Despite recognizing the unroman violence of the revolutionary act of founding, Arendt appears in places to sanction an overly continuist view of history: "the revolutions of the modern age appear like gigantic attempts to repair these foundations, to renew the broken thread of tradition, and to restore, through founding new political bodies, what for so many centuries had endowed the affairs of men with some measure of dignity and greatness" ("What Is Authority?" p. 140). In fact, the French Revolution would not be an attempt to repair specifically Roman foundations (which suggests a continuity of the contents of the Roman trinity). The Revolution recognizes the need for foundations (and to that extent is Roman) but those foundations are not the same.
20. The same page that announces news of the Revolution also announces the apocalypse: "Los términos de *libertad, felicidad, igualdad, dignidad humana*, regresaban continuamente en aquella atropellada exposición, justificando la inminencia de un Gran Incendio que Esteban, esta noche, aceptaba como una purificación necesaria; como un Apocalipsis que estaba anhelante de presenciar cuanto antes, para inciar su vida de hombre en un mundo nuevo" (p. 81).
21. On the Enlightenment's "apocalyptic" historiography, see Collingwood, *The Idea of History*, p. 80.
22. "Por el nombre de las constelaciones remontábase el hombre al lenguaje de sus primeros mitos, permaneciéndole tan fiel que cuando aparecieron las gentes de Cristo, no hallaron cabida en un cielo totalmente habitado por gentes paganas. Las estrellas habían sido dadas a Andrómeda y Perseo, a Hércules y Casiopea. Había títulos de propiedad, suscritos a tenor de abolengo, que eran intransferibles a simples pescadores del Lago Tiberiades—pescadores que no necesitaban de astros, además, para llevar sus barcos a donde Alguien, próximo a verter su sangre, forjaría una religión ignorante de los astros . . ."(p. 350).
23. Theodor W. Adorno and Max Horkheimer, *Dialectic of Enlightenment*, trans. John Cumming (London and New York: Verso, 1997), p. 9. In Marx's famous passage from the *Grundisse*, it is capital, not the Enlightenment, that drives beyond nature worship to subjugate nature to human needs. See Harvey, *The Condition of Postmodernity*, pp. 110–111.

24. Understanding, *entendimiento*, lies at the heart of Carpentier's famous essay "De lo real maravilloso americano," in *Tientos y diferencias* (Cuba: Ediciones Unión, 1966), p. 90.
25. "The Romantic man was action and vigor and movement and will and declaration and violence"; Alejo Carpentier, "The Baroque and the Marvelous Real," in *Magical Realism: Theory, History, Community*, ed. Lois Parkinson Zamora and Wendy B. Faris (Durham, N.C.: Duke University Press, 1995), p. 97.
26. Hampson, *The Enlightenment*, pp. 211 and 215. Although by the end of the novel Esteban has become a keen reader of Chateaubriand (an ardent critic of the Revolution), and notwithstanding the fact that it is Esteban himself who draws the parallel between his own plight and that of Chateaubriand's René (Carpentier changes the relationship from brother/sister in *René* to cousins in *El siglo*, thereby circumventing the problem of incest and paving the way for a good romantic ending), both Sofía and Esteban are pointedly unchateaubriandesque, preferring the "Ancient" route of a *grande existence politique* ruled out by the French author. See Chateaubriand, Préface d'*Atala* (1805), *Atala-René* (Paris: Garnier-Flammarion, 1964), p. 63.
27. Carpentier's Caribbean is not an undifferentiated whole, not always the subject of homage. Whereas Guadeloupe is the object of celebration, the natural habitat of Cayenne is viewed by Esteban in an entirely negative light (see subchapter 29).
28. Labanyi equates Nature to History and History to the Revolutionary Process, and on the basis of the spiral image of development reads the novel's depiction of revolution in a positive light: though a revolution may decay, it will release the seeds which will germinate a new idealism. My view is that the novel is much more pessimistic, we might even say fatalistic, about revolution; that harmony with nature allows Esteban to see the revolution's contradictions; and that Carpentier's organicism is put to a more traditional use—in a discourse of preformationism that finds its way into Labanyi's own text (p. 60): "Carpentier exploits the organic image of the seed to develop his notion of the dynamic continuity of History. Just as the seed contains within it the whole development of the plant, so the germs of the future are contained within the past."
29. "Lo maravilloso comienza a serlo de manera inequívoca cuando surge de una inesperada alteración de la realidad (el milagro), de una revelación privilegiada de la realidad, de una iluminación inhabitual o singularmente favorecedora de las inadvertidas riquezas de la realidad, de una ampliación de las escalas y categorías de la realidad, percibidas con particular intensidad en virtud de una exaltación del espíritu que lo conduce a un modo de «estado límite»" (Alejo Carpentier, "De lo real maravilloso americano," pp. 96–97).
30. Deism, also known as "natural religion," held that God created the universe but does not subsequently intervene in it (no providence); the world operates instead according to rational natural rules.
31. Cassirer, *The Philosophy of the Enlightenment*, p. 78. Cassirer is in part paraphrasing Buffon's introduction to his *Histoire naturelle* (1749).

32. Crick, Watson, and Wilkins made the discovery in 1953 and were awarded the Nobel Prize in 1962.
33. Michel Foucault, *The Order of Things: An Archaeology of the Human Sciences* (London: Tavistock, 1970; reprt. 1985), p. 132. Cf. Cassirer: "The whole eighteenth century is permeated by this conviction, namely, that in the history of humanity the time had now arrived to deprive nature of its carefully guarded secret, to leave it no longer in the dark to be marveled at as an incomprehensible mystery but to bring it under the bright light of reason and analyze it with all its fundamental forces" (*The Philosophy of the Enlightenment* p. 47).
34. Esteban's life has become a "Teatro del Absurdo"; "había dejado de pertenecerse a sí mismo: su existir, su devenir, estaban regidos por la Voluntad ajena . . ."(p. 214).
35. See Jo Labanyi's otherwise excellent analysis of the role played by instinct, which is "a source of action (change) based on the fulfilment—rather than repression—of natural energies" (p. 63).
36. Jorge Luis Borges, "El arte narrativo y la magia," *Discusión* (1932), in *Obras completas, Vol. 1*, pp. 226–232. Cf. Adorno and Horkheimer, *Dialectic of Enlightenment*, p. 19 for a similar discussion.
37. Another example: The parallel between the two meals that follows the respective deaths of the father and Jorge is drawn by one of the characters and, when she can no longer do so, by the narrator: "«¡Qué casualidad!—dijo Sofía—. Me parece recordar que comimos casi lo mismo después de que murió . . .» (y dejó la voz en suspenso, pues del padre nunca se hablaba en la casa)" (p. 328).
38. The Golfo Prodigioso is viewed as a "prior state" of the Antilles—"un anteproyecto que reuniera, en miniatura, todo lo que, en escala mayor, pudiera verse en el Archipiélago" (p. 227). It is true for Sofía that her time with Víctor will prove to be but an "anteproyecto [. . .] en miniatura" of her larger destiny, which she fulfills, "en escala mayor," on the streets of Madrid.
39. "Se sintió orgullosa, predestinada, al pensar que la Muerte [. . .] le otorgaba un tratamiento de favor" (p. 325).

Conclusion

1. See Rubén Darío, "El Retorno," *La Nación*, 4,800, Buenos Aires, 21 August 1912, p. 8, cited in Rama, *Rubén Darío y el Modernismo*, p. 26, on the coexistence of *modernista* activity with the daily business of Argentine merchants and bankers.
2. Néstor García Canclini, "Ocho acercamientos al latinoamericanismo en antropología," conference paper, University of Manchester, 21–22 June 2002.

Bibliography

Adorno, Theodor W. and Max Horkheimer, *Dialectic of Enlightenment*, trans. John Cumming (London and New York: Verso, 1997).
Alonso, Carlos J., *The Burden of Modernity: The Rhetoric of Cultural Discourse in Spanish America* (New York and Oxford:OUP, 1998).
Altamirano, Carlos, "La fundación de la literatura argentina," in *Ensayos argentinos: De Sarmiento a la vanguardia*, ed. Carlos Altamirano and Beatriz Sarlo (Buenos Aires: Centro Editor de América Latina, 1983), pp. 107–115.
Anderson, Perry, "Modernity and Revolution," *New Left Review* 144 (March–April 1984), 96–113.
Arendt, Hannah, *Between Past and Future: Eight Exercises in Political Thought* (Harmondsworth: Penguin Books, 1993).
Arguedas, José María, "El complejo cultural en el Perú," in *Formación de una cultura nacional indoamericana* (Mexico: Siglo veintiuno editores, 1975), pp. 1–8.
Barthes, Roland, "The Death of the Author," in *Image Music Text*, ed. Stephen Heath (London: Fontana, 1977), pp. 142–148.
Bastos, Augusto Roa, "Los trasterrados de Comala," *Unomásuno* (22 August 1981), 2–3.
Bayly, C.A., *The Birth of the Modern World 1780–1914: Global Connections and Comparisons* (Malden, Oxford and Victoria: Blackwell, 2004).
Benjamin, Walter, *Illuminations*, ed. Hannah Arendt, trans. Harry Zohn (London: Fontana/Collins, 1977).
Berman, Marshall, *All That Is Solid Melts into Air: The Experience of Modernity* (London: Verso, 1983).
Blanco Aguinaga, Carlos, "Realidad y estilo de Juan Rulfo," in *Nueva novela latinoamericana, Vol. I*, ed. Jorge Lafforgue (Buenos Aires: Paidós, 1972), pp. 85–113.
Bocock, Robert, "The Cultural Formations of Modern Society," in *Formations of Modernity*, ed. Stuart Hall and Bram Gieben (Cambridge: Polity Press and the OU, 1992), pp. 229–274.
Borges, Jorge Luis, "The Kabbalah," in Jaime Alazraki, *Borges and the Kabbalah and Other Essays on His Fiction and Poetry*, (Cambridge: CUP, 1988), pp. 54–61.
———, *Obras completas, Vol. III, 1975–1985* (Barcelona: Emecé Editores, 1989).
———, *Obras completas, Vol. 1, 1923–1949* (Barcelona: Emecé Editores, 1996).
———, *Obras completas, Vol. II, 1952–1972* (Barcelona: Emecé Editores, 1996).
———, *Borges en Sur (1931–1980)* (Barcelona: Emecé Editores, 1999).

Bowker, John, *The Meanings of Death* (Cambridge: Cambridge University Press, 1991; reprt. 1996).
Bravo, Federico, "Transtextuality in the Writing of César Vallejo: 'En mis falsillas encañona . . .': From Verbal to Textual Etymon," in *The Poetry and Poetics of César Vallejo: The Fourth Angle of the Circle*, ed. Adam Sharman (Lewiston: Edwin Mellen Press, 1997), pp. 17–25.
Brunner, José Joaquín, *América Latina: cultura y modernidad* (Mexico: Grijalbo, 1992).
———, *Cartografías de la modernidad* (Santiago: Dolmien, 1994).
Calinescu, Matei, *Five Faces of Modernity: Modernism, Avant-Garde, Decadence, Kitsch, Postmodernism* (Durham: Duke University Press, 1987).
Carmichael, Elizabeth and Chloë Sayer, *The Skeleton at the Feast: The Day of the Dead in Mexico* (London: British Museum Press, 1991).
Carpentier, Alejo, "De lo real maravilloso americano," in *Tientos y diferencias* (Cuba: Ediciones Unión, 1966), pp. 85–99.
———, "The Baroque and the Marvelous Real," in *Magical Realism: Theory, History, Community*, ed. Lois Parkinson Zamora and Wendy B. Faris (Durham, N.C.: Duke University Press, 1995), pp. 89–108.
———, *El siglo de las luces* (Barcelona: Seix Barral, 2001).
Cassirer, Ernst, *The Individual and the Cosmos in Renaissance Philosophy*, trans. Mario Domandi (Oxford: Basil Blackwell, 1927; reprt. 1963).
———, *The Philosophy of the Enlightenment*, trans. Fritz C.A. Koelln and James P. Pettegrove (Boston: Beacon Press, 1951; reprt. 1960).
Charlton, D.G., *Positivist Thought in France During the Second Empire 1852–1870* (Oxford: Clarendon Press, 1959).
Chateaubriand, "Préface d'Atala (1805)," *Atala-René* (Paris: Garnier-Flammarion, 1964).
Collingwood, R.G., *The Idea of History*, rev. ed. Jan van der Dussen (Oxford and New York: Oxford University Press, 1994).
Conrad, Peter, *Modern Times, Modern Places: Life and Art in the Twentieth Century* (London: Thames and Hudson, 1998).
Darío, Rubén, "Ricardo Palma" (excerpt), in *La prosa modernista hispanoamericana: Introducción crítica y antología*, ed. José Olivio Jiménez and Carlos Javier Morales (Madrid: Alianza Editorial, 1998), pp. 68–69.
Davison, Ned J., *The Concept of Modernism in Hispanic Criticism* (Colorado: University of New Mexico, 1966).
De la Campa, Romain. "De la deconstrucción al nuevo texto social: pasos perdidos o por hacer en los estudios culturales latinoamericanos (hacia una economía política de la producción de capital simbólico sobre América Latina confeccionado en la academia norteamericana)," in Mabel Moraña, *Nuevas perspectivas desde/sobre América Latina*, pp. 77–95.
de Man, Paul, "Literary History and Literary Modernity," in *Blindness and Insight: Essays in the Rhetoric of Contemporary Criticism* (London and New York: Oxford University Press, 1971), pp. 142–165.
Deleuze, Gilles and Félix Guattari, *What Is Philosophy?* trans. Graham Burchell and Hugh Tomlinson (London and New York: Verso, 1994).
Derrida, Jacques, "La Structure, le signe et le jeu dans le discours des sciences humaines," in *L'Écriture et la différence* (Paris: Éditions du Seuil, 1967), pp. 409–428.

BIBLIOGRAPHY

———, *De la grammatologie* (Paris: Éditions de Minuit, 1967).
———, "Signature Event Context," in *Glyph*, Johns Hopkins Textual Studies 1 (Baltimore: Johns Hopkins University Press, 1977), pp. 172–197.
———, "Limited Inc abc . . . ," in *Glyph*, Johns Hopkins Textual Studies 2 (Baltimore: Johns Hopkins University Press, 1977), pp. 162–254.
———, "Force and Signification," in *Writing and Difference*, trans. Alan Bass (London, Melbourne, and Henley: Routledge and Kegan Paul, 1978; reprt. 1985), pp. 3–30.
———, "Violence and Metaphysics: An Essay on the Thought of Emmanuel Levinas," in *Writing and Difference*, pp. 79–153.
———, "Otobiographies: The Teaching of Nietzsche and the Politics of the Proper Name," in *The Ear of the Other: Otobiography, Transference, Translation*, trans. Avital Ronell, ed. Christie V. McDonald (New York: Schocken Books, 1985), pp. 3–38.
———, "Psyché, Invention de l'autre," in *Psyché, Inventions de l'autre* (Paris: Galilée, 1987), pp. 11–61.
———, *Of Spirit: Heidegger and the Question*, trans. Geoffrey Bennington and Rachel Bowlby (Chicago and London: University of Chicago Press, 1987).
———, "Some Statements and Truisms about Neologisms, Newisms, Postisms, Parasitisms, and Other Small Seismisms," in *The States of "Theory": History, Art, and Critical Discourse*, ed. David Carroll (Stanford: Stanford University Press, 1990; reprt. 1994), pp. 63–94.
———, *Given Time: I. Counterfeit Money*, trans. Peggy Kamuf (Chicago and London: University of Chicago Press, 1992).
———, *Aporias: Dying-Awaiting (One Another at) the "Limits of Truth,"* trans. Thomas Dutoit (Stanford: Stanford University Press, 1993).
———, *Memoirs of the Blind: The Self-Portrait and Other Ruins*, trans. Pascale-Anne Brault and Michael Naas (Chicago: University of Chicago Press, 1993).
———, *Specters of Marx: The State of the Debt, the Work of Mourning, and the New International*, trans. Peggy Kamuf (New York and London: Routledge, 1994).
———, *The Gift of Death*, trans. David Wills (Chicago and London: University of Chicago Press, 1995).
———, *Demeure: Fiction and Testimony*, trans. Elizabeth Rottenberg (Stanford: Stanford University Press, 2000).
Derrida, Jacques and Maurizio Ferraris, *A Taste for the Secret*, trans. Giacomo Donis (Cambridge: Polity Press, 2001).
Díaz Plaja, Guillermo, *Modernismo frente a noventa y ocho: una introducción a la literatura española del siglo XX*, 2nd edn. (Madrid: Espasa-Calpe, 1966).
Dulog Matibag, Eugenio, *The Sleep of Reason: Alejo Carpentier and the Crisis of Latin American Modernity*, unpublished dissertation, May 1987, 47:11.
Dussel, Enrique, "The Church and Emergent Nation States (1830–80)," in *The Church in Latin America 1492–1992*, ed. Enrique Dussel (Kent: Burns and Oates, 1992), pp. 105–116.
———, "Beyond Eurocentrism: The World-System and the Limits of Modernity," in *The Cultures of Globalization*, ed. Fredric Jameson and Masao Miyoshi (Durham: Duke University Press, 1998), pp. 3–31.
Eagleton, Terry, *Marxism and Literary Criticism* (London: Methuen, 1976; reprt. 1983).

Eisenstadt, S.N., *Tradition, Change, and Modernity* (Florida: Robert E. Krieger Publishing Company, 1973; reprt. 1983).
Fanon, Frantz, *The Wretched of the Earth*, trans. Constance Farrington (Harmondsworth: Penguin Books, 1967; reprt. 1985).
Fishburn, Evelyn and Psique Hughes, *A Dictionary of Borges* (London: Duckworth, 1990).
Foucault, Michel, *Les Mots et les choses: une archéologie des sciences humaines* (Paris: Éditions Gallimard, 1966).
———, *L'Archéologie du savoir* (Paris: Éditions Gallimard, 1969).
———, *L'Ordre du discours: leçon inaugurale au Collège de France prononcée le 2 décembre 1970* (Paris: Éditions Gallimard, 1971).
———, *Histoire de la sexualité Vol. I La Volonté de savoir* (Paris: Éditions Gallimard, 1976).
———, "Questions of Method," trans. Colin Gordon, *Ideology and Consciousness* 8 (Spring 1981), 3–14.
———, *The Order of Things: An Archaeology of the Human Sciences* (London: Tavistock, 1970; reprt. 1985).
Franco, Jean, "Afterword: The Twilight of the Vanguard and the Rise of Criticism," in *Critical Passions: Selected Essays*, ed. Mary Louise Pratt and Kathleen Newman (Durham and London: Duke University Press, 1999), pp. 503–516.
———, "Journey to the Land of the Dead: Rulfo's Pedro Páramo," in *Critical Passions*, pp. 429–446.
Fuentes, Carlos et al., *Juan Rulfo's Mexico*, trans. Margaret Sayers Peden (Washington and London: Smithsonian Institution Press, 2002).
García Canclini, Néstor, *Las culturas populares en el capitalismo* (Mexico: Editorial Nueva Imagen, 1982; reprt. 1986).
———, "Los estudios culturales de los 80 a los 90: perspectivas antropológicas y sociológicas en América Latina," *Punto de vista* (Buenos Aires) 14:40 (July–Sept 1991), 41–48.
———, "Cultural Studies Questionnaire: Néstor García Canclini," *Journal of Latin American Cultural Studies* 5:1 (1996), 83–87.
———, *La globalización imaginada* (Buenos Aires, Barcelona, México: Paidós, 1999).
———, *Culturas híbridas: Estrategias para entrar y salir de la modernidad* (Buenos Aires, Barcelona, México: Editorial Paidós, 2001; 1st ed. Editorial Grijalbo, 1990).
———, "Contradictory Modernities," in *Through the Kaleidoscope: The Experience of Modernity in Latin America*, ed. Vivian Schelling (London and New York: Verso, 2000), pp. 37–52.
———, "Ocho acercamientos al latinoamericanismo en antropología," unpublished conference paper, University of Manchester, 21–22 June 2002.
Giddens, Anthony, *The Consequences of Modernity* (Cambridge: Polity Press, 1990; reprt. 1994).
Gilroy, Paul, *The Black Atlantic: Modernity and Double Consciousness* (London and New York: Verso, 1993; reprt. 2002).
González Echevarría, Roberto, "Modernidad, modernismo y nueva narrativa: *El recurso del método*," *Inter-American Review of Bibliography* 30 (1980), 157–163.

——, *Alejo Carpentier: The Pilgrim at Home* (Austin: University of Texas Press, 1990).

Goulemot, Jean M., "Romans de langue espagnole et révolution française (*Las memorias de un hombre de acción, El siglo de las luces*)," *Revue de littérature comparée* 4 (1989), 513–524.

Gullón, Ricardo, *El modernismo visto por los modernistas* (Barcelona: Guadarrama, 1980).

Gutiérrez Girardot, Rafael, *Modernismo* (Barcelona: Montesinos, 1983).

Habermas, Jürgen, *The Philosophical Discourse of Modernity: Twelve Lectures*, trans. Frederick Lawrence (Cambridge: Polity Press, 1987; reprt. 1994).

Hall, Stuart, "Cultural Studies and its Theoretical Legacies," in *Cultural Studies*, ed. Lawrence Grossberg, Cary Nelson, and Paula A.Treichler (New York and London: Routledge, 1992), pp. 277–294.

——, "Introduction," in *Formations of Modernity*, ed. Stuart Hall and Bram Gieben (Cambridge: Polity Press and the Open University, 1992; reprt. 1997), pp. 1–16.

Hampson, Norman, *The Enlightenment* (Harmondsworth: Penguin Books, 1968; reprt. 1982).

Hardt, Michael and Antonio Negri, *Empire* (Cambridge, Mass. and London: Harvard University Press, 2001).

Harss, Luis, *Los nuestros*, 2nd ed. (Buenos Aires: Editorial Sudamericana, 1968).

Harvey, David, *The Condition of Postmodernity: An Enquiry into the Origins of Cultural Change* (Cambridge, Mass. and Oxford: Blackwell, 1990; reprt. 2001).

Henighan, Stephen, "Caribbean Masks: Frantz Fanon and Alejo Carpentier," in *Postcolonial Perspectives on the Cultures of Latin America and Lusophone Africa*, ed. Robin Fiddian (Liverpool: Liverpool University Press, 2000), pp. 169–190.

Henríquez Ureña, Max, *Breve historia del modernismo* (Mexico: Fondo de Cultura Económica, 1954).

Herrera y Reissig, Julio, "Conceptos de crítica" (excerpt), in *La prosa modernista hispanoamericana: Introducción crítica y antología*, ed. Jiménez and Morales (Madrid: Alianza Editorial, 1998), pp. 83–86.

Hobsbawm, Eric, "Introduction: Inventing Traditions," in *The Invention of Tradition*, ed. Eric Hobsbawm and Terence Ranger (Cambridge: Cambridge University Press, 1983; reprt. 1985), pp. 1–14.

Israel, Jonathan I., *Radical Enlightenment: Philosophy and the Making of Modernity 1650–1750* (Oxford: Oxford University Press, 2001).

Jameson, Fredric, *Postmodernism, or, the Logic of Late Capitalism* (London and New York: Verso, 1991; reprt. 1996).

——, "On 'Cultural Studies,' " *Social Text* 34 (1993), 17–52.

Kant, Immanuel, "What Is Enlightenment?" in *Foundations of the Metaphysics of Morals and What Is Enlightenment?* trans. Lewis White Beck (Indianapolis: The Liberal Arts Press, 1959).

Kern, Stephen, *The Culture of Time and Space 1880–1918* (Cambridge, Mass.: Harvard University Press, 1983).

Klor de Alva, Jorge, "The Postcolonization of the (Latin) American Experience: A Reconsideration of 'Colonialism,' 'Postcolonialism,' and 'Mestizaje,' " in *After Colonialism: Imperial Histories and Postcolonial Displacements*, ed. Gyan Prakash (Princeton: Princeton University Press, 1995), pp. 241–275.

Korngold, Ralph, *Citizen Toussaint* (London: Victor Gollancz, 1945).
Labanyi, Jo, "Nature and the Historical Process in Carpentier's *El siglo de las luces*," *Bulletin of Hispanic Studies* 57 (1980), 55–66.
Larsen, Neil, "Los estudios culturales: aperturas disciplinarias y falacias teóricas," in *Nuevas perspectivas desde/sobre América Latina: el desafío de los estudios culturales*, ed. Mabel Moraña (Chile: Editorial Cuarto Propio/Instituto Internacional de Literatura Iberoamericana, 2000), pp. 73–75.
Latour, Bruno, *We Have Never Been Modern*, trans. Catherine Porter (New York: Harvester Wheatsheaf, 1993).
Lienhard, Martin, *La voz y su huella. Escritura y conflicto étnico-cultural en América Latina 1492–1988*, 3rd edn. (Lima: Editorial Horizonte, 1992).
Litvak, Lily, *El Modernismo* (Madrid: Taurus, 1975).
Mandelbaum, Maurice, *History, Man, and Reason: A Study in Nineteenth-Century Thought* (Baltimore: Johns Hopkins Press, 1971).
Manrique, Nelson, "Modernity and Alternative Development in the Andes," in *Through the Kaleidoscope: The Experience of Modernity in Latin America*, ed. Vivian Schelling (London and New York: Verso, 2000), pp. 219–247.
Martí, José, "Nuestra América" (excerpt), in *La prosa modernista hispanoamericana: introducción crítica y antología*, ed. José Olivio Jiménez and Carlos Javier Morales (Madrid: Alianza Editorial, 1998), pp. 69–71.
Martín-Barbero, Jesús, *Procesos de comunicación y matrices de cultura: itinerario para salir de la razón dualista* (México: Ediciones Gustavo Gili, 1987).
———, *De los medios a las mediaciones. Comunicación, cultura y hegemonía* (Barcelona: Editorial Gustavo Gili, 1987; 5th edn. Mexico, 1998).
Martínez Carrizales, Leonardo (ed.), *Juan Rulfo: Los caminos de la fama pública. Juan Rulfo ante la crítica literario-periodística de México: una antología* (Mexico: Fondo de Cultura Económica, 1998).
Masotta, Oscar, *Lecturas de psicoanálisis. Freud, Lacan* (Buenos Aires: Paidós, 1992).
Monsiváis, Carlos, "Sí, tampoco los muertos retoñan. Desgraciadamente," in *Juan Rulfo: Homenaje nacional* (México: Instituto Nacional de Bellas Artes, 1980), pp. 35–44.
Moody, Michael, "Georg Lukàcs, the Historical Novel, and *El siglo de las luces*," *Revista de estudios hispánicos* 13 (1979), 45–63.
Moraña, Mabel (ed.), *Nuevas perspectivas desde/sobre América Latina: el desafío de los estudios culturales* (Chile: Editorial Cuarto Propio/Instituto Internacional de Literatura Iberoamericana, 2000).
Moreiras, Alberto, *The Exhaustion of Difference: The Politics of Latin American Cultural Studies* (Durham and London: Duke University Press, 2001).
Osborne, Peter, "Modernity Is a Qualitative, Not a Chronological, Category," *New Left Review* 192 (March–April 1992), 65–82.
Pastor, Beatriz, "Carpentier's Enlightened Revolution, Goya's Sleep of Reason," in *Representing the French Revolution: Literature, Historiography, and Art*, ed. James A.W. Heffernan (Hanover: University Press of New England, 1992), pp. 261–276.
Paz, Octavio, "Traducción y metáfora," in *El Modernismo*, ed. Lily Litvak. (Madrid: Taurus, 1975), pp. 91–117.

———, *Children of the Mire: Modern Poetry from Romanticism to the Avant-Garde*, trans. Rachel Phillips (Cambridge, Mass. and London: Harvard University Press, 1974; reprt. 1991).

———, *El laberinto de la soledad*, 2nd ed. (Mexico: Fondo de cultura económica, reprt. 1988).

Phillips, Allen W., "Rubén Darío y sus juicios sobre el modernismo," in *Estudios críticos sobre el modernismo*, ed. Homero Castillo (Madrid: Editorial Gredos, 1968), pp. 118–145.

Quijano, Aníbal, "Modernity, Identity, and Utopia in Latin America," *boundary 2* 20:3 (Fall 1993), 140–155.

Quiroga, Horacio, "Aspectos del modernismo," in *La prosa modernista hispanoamericana: introducción crítica y antología*, ed. José Olivio Jiménez and Carlos Javier Morales (Madrid: Alianza Editorial, 1998), pp. 86–87.

Rama, Angel, *Rubén Darío y el modernismo (circunstancia socioeconómica de un arte americano)* (Venezuela: Universidad Central de Venezuela, 1970).

———, "Una primera lectura de 'No oyes ladrar los perros' de Juan Rulfo," *Revista de la Universidad de México* 29:12 (August 1975), 1–8.

———, *Transculturación narrativa en América Latina* (Mexico: Siglo veintiuno editores, 1982).

———, "Processes of Transculturation in Latin American Narrative," *Journal of Latin American Cultural Studies* 6:2 (1997), 155–171.

Ramos, Julio, *Desencuentros de la modernidad en América Latina: literatura y política en el siglo XIX* (Mexico: Fondo de cultura económica, 1989).

Rosaldo, Renato, "Foreword" to Néstor García Canclini, *Hybrid Cultures: Strategies for Entering and Leaving Modernity*, trans. Christopher L. Chiappari and Silvia L. López (Minneapolis and London: University of Minnesota Press, 1995), pp. xi–xvii.

Rowe, William, *Rulfo: El llano en llamas* (Critical Guide) (London: Grant and Cutler, 1987).

———, *Hacia una poética radical: Ensayos de hermenéutica cultural* (Rosario: Beatriz Viterbo Editora and Lima: Mosca Azul Editores, 1996).

———, "Trauma and Memory: César Vallejo and the Poetics of Time in the Peruvian Twentieth Century," unpublished lecture, Kings College, University of London, 26 November 1996.

———, "Cultural Studies Questionnaire: William Rowe," *Journal of Latin American Cultural Studies* 6:2 (1997), 223–226.

———, "De la oclusión de la lectura en los estudios culturales: las continuidades del indigenismo en el Perú," in Mabel Moraña, *Nuevas perspectivas desde/sobre América Latina*, pp. 453–459.

———, "Williams and Vallejo: Modernism in the Americas," unpublished paper.

Rowe, William and Vivian Schelling, *Memory and Modernity: Popular Culture in Latin America* (New York: Verso, 1991).

Rulfo, Juan, *Autobiografía armada* (Buenos Aires: Ediciones Corregidor, 1973).

———, "Pedro Páramo treinta años después," *El Espectador Magazin dominical*, 147, 19 January 1986, pp. 3–4.

———, *El llano en llamas*, ed. Carlos Blanco Aguinaga (Madrid: Ediciones de Cátedra, 1988).

———, *Pedro Páramo*, ed. José Carlos González Boixo, 7th edn. (Madrid: Ediciones Cátedra, 1990).

———, Interview with Waldemar Verdugo Fuentes, "Juan Rulfo," http://magosdeamerica.galeon.com/album756854.html.

Sarlo, Beatriz, *Una modernidad periférica: Buenos Aires 1920 y 1930* (Buenos Aires: Ediciones Nueva Visión, 1988).

———, *Jorge Luis Borges: A Writer on the Edge* (London: Verso, 1993).

———, *Escenas de la vida posmoderna: Intelectuales, arte y videocultura en la Argentina*, 9th edn. (Buenos Aires: Espasa Calpe/Ariel, 1997).

———, "Cultural Studies Questionnaire: Beatriz Sarlo," *Journal of Latin American Cultural Studies* 6:1 (1997), 85–92.

———, "Raymond Williams: una relectura," in Mabel Moraña, *Nuevas perspectivas desde/sobre América Latina*, pp. 309–317.

———, "The Modern City: Buenos Aires, The Peripheral Metropolis," in *Through the Kaleidoscope: The Experience of Modernity in Latin America*, ed. Vivian Schelling (London and New York: Verso, 2000), pp. 108–123.

Sarmiento, Domingo Faustino, *Facundo: Civilización y barbarie* (Santa Fe, Argentina: Editorial Castellví, 1966).

Schelling, Vivian, "Introduction: Reflections on the Experience of Modernity in Latin America," in Vivian Schelling, *Through the Kaleidoscope: The Experience of Modernity in Latin America*, pp. 1–33.

Schmucler, Héctor, "La investigación (1975): ideología, ciencia y política," in *Memoria de la comunicación* (Buenos Aires: Editorial Biblos, 1997), pp. 131–143.

Schobinger, Juan, "The Amerindian Religions," in *The Church in Latin America 1492–1992*, ed. Enrique Dussel (Kent: Burns and Oates, 1992), pp. 23–42.

Scholem, Gershom, *The Messianic Idea in Judaism: and Other Essays on Jewish Spirituality* (London: Allen and Unwin, 1971).

Schulman, Ivan, "Reflexiones en torno a la definición del modernismo," in *El Modernismo*, ed. Lily Litvak (Madrid: Taurus, 1975), pp. 65–95.

Sharman, Adam, "Modernismo, positivismo y (des)herencia en el discurso de la historia literaria," in *¿Qué es el modernismo? Nueva encuesta, nuevas lecturas*, ed. Richard A. Cardwell and Bernard J. McGuirk (Boulder: Society of Spanish and Spanish-American Studies, 1993), pp. 311–330.

———, "Borges y el tiempo de la ceguera," in *Jorge Luis Borges. Intervenciones sobre pensamiento y literatura*, ed. William Rowe, Claudio Canaparo, and Annick Louis (Buenos Aires, Barcelona, Mexico: Paidós, 2000), pp. 249–262.

———, "Semicolonial Times: Vallejo and the Discourse of Modernity," *Romance Quarterly* 49:3 (Summer 2002), 192–205.

Solanas, Fernando and Octavio Getino, "Towards a Third Cinema: Notes and Experiences for the Development of a Cinema of Liberation in the Third World," in *Twenty-Five Years of the New Latin American Cinema*, ed. Michael Chanan, (London: BFI and Channel Four TV, 1983), pp. 17–27.

Sommers, Joseph, *After the Storm: Landmarks of the Modern Mexican Novel* (University of New Mexico Press, 1968).

BIBLIOGRAPHY

Spivak, Gayatri Chakravorty, "Can the Subaltern Speak?" *Marxism and the Interpretation of Culture*, ed. Cary Nelson and Lawrence Greenberg (Urbana and Chicago: University of Illinois Press, 1988).

———, *A Critique of Postcolonial Reason: Toward a History of the Vanishing Present* (Cambridge, Mass.: Harvard University Press, 1999).

Taine, Hyppolite, *Introduction à l'histoire de la littérature anglaise* (*L'Histoire, son présent et son avenir*), ed. H.B. Charlton (Manchester: Manchester University Press, 1936).

Torbado, Jesús, "Entrevista. Con Juan Rulfo, de contrabando, en California," *El País*, 19 September 1982, p. 11.

Vaillant, G.C., *Aztecs of Mexico: Origin, Rise, and Fall of the Aztec Nation* (Harmondsworth: Penguin Books, 1972).

Vallejo, César, *El romanticismo en la poesía castellana* (Lima: Mejía Baca & Villanueva, 1954).

———, *La cultura peruana (crónicas)* (Lima: Mosca Azul Editores, 1987).

———, *Desde Europa. Crónicas y artículos (1923–1938)*, ed. Jorge Puccinelli (Lima: Fuente de Cultura Peruana, 1987).

———, *Obra poética*, ed. Américo Ferrari (Nanterre: Colección Archivos, 1988).

Vidal, Hernán, "Restaurar lo político, imperativo de los estudios literarios y culturales latinoamericanistas," in Mabel Moraña, *Nuevas perspectivas desde/sobre América Latina*, pp. 121–126.

Voekel, Pamela, *Alone Before God: The Religious Origins of Modernity in Mexico* (Durham and London: Duke University Press, 2002).

Watson, Peter, *A Terrible Beauty: The People and Ideas that Shaped the Modern Mind: A History* (London: Phoenix Press, 2000).

Williams, Raymond, *Keywords: A Vocabulary of Culture and Society* (London: Fontana Press, 1976; reprt. 1988).

———, "Culture is Ordinary," in *Studying Culture: An Introductory Reader*, ed. Ann Gray and Jim McGuigan (London: Edward Arnold, 1993), pp. 5–14.

———, "Language and the Avant-garde," in *The Politics of Modernism: Against the New Conformists*, ed. Tony Pinkney (London and New York: Verso, 1989), pp. 65–80.

Williamson, Edwin, *Borges: A Life* (New York, London: Viking, 2004).

Zavala, Iris M., *Colonialism and Culture: Hispanic Modernisms and the Social Imaginary* (Bloomington and Indianapolis: Indiana University Press, 1992).

Index

abstraction, 1–2, 3, 121, 127, 171
  see also modernity; Nietzsche
Adorno, Theodor W. and Max
  Horkheimer, 14, 53, 61
aesthetics, 10, 30–1, 52, 73, 99, 102
  see also autonomy; Symbolism
Afro-Caribbean, 182
  see also black culture
Aleph, El, see Borges, Jorge Luis
Althusser, Louis, 192 n.45
analogical reasoning, *see* magic
Anderson, Perry, 15, 21, 192 n.51
Andean culture, 56, 86, 93–6, 100–1, 102, 183
ánimas en pena, 139, 145–7
antiethnocentrism, xi, 17, 163, 182, 184
Antilles, 169–70
antimodern modernism, *see* modernism
antirationalism, 175
apocalypse, 166–7
Arendt, Hannah, 140–1, 164, 188 n.14, 212 n.27, 217 n.19
Argentina
  and avant-garde urban *criollismo*, 117
  and modernity, 11, 113–14
  and modernization, xiv, 113–14, 115
  and nationalism, 111, 180
  and erosion of traditional ties, 116
  and nineteenth-century tradition, 114, 115
Arguedas, José María, 56, 92
Aristotelianism, 112, 209 n.43
  see also nominalism

art, 28, 29, 47
  and crafts, 29
  and culture industry, 30–2, 45
  high, 29–31
  (counter)public value of, 44–6
  see also autonomy
articulation, xii, 18–19, 63–5
  see also homology
authority, 73, 139–41
  see also Roman trinity
autonomy, of art/aesthetics, 28–32, 52, 59, 71–3, 194 n.8
avant-gardes, xii, 39–42, 53–4, 59, 60–1, 65–6, 97, 102, 116–17
avant-garde subalternism, *see under*
  Latin American cultural studies
Aztecs, 138, 139

Bacon, Francis, 118, 206 n.12
baroque, 170, 171–2, 178
Baudelaire, Charles, 7, 10
Bayly, Christopher Alan, 5
Benjamin, Walter, 15, 60–1, 209 n.37
Berman, Marshall, 6, 11, 12
Bhabha, Homi, 87
black culture, 162, 182
Blanco Aguinaga, Carlos, 150, 151
blindness as metaphor, 121, 122–3, 127, 129
Bocock, Robert, 215 n.9
body, 162, 170
Boedo, 116, 128, 129
Bolívar, Simón, 88–9

Borges, Jorge Luis, xiv, 109–33, 180
  El Aleph, xiv, 130–1
  "El Aleph", 129–31
  "El arte narrativo y la magia", 176–7
  "*Deutsches Requiem*", 209 n.43
  "La doctrina de los ciclos", 122, 126, 131
  "El escritor argentino y la tradición", 127–8, 129
  "Funes el memorioso", 126–9
  Historia de la eternidad, 110
  "Historia de la eternidad", 111, 119–21, 125, 133
  El idioma de los argentinos, 110, 120
  "El inmortal", 118
  "The Kabbalah", 129–30
  "Nueva refutación del tiempo", 124–5
  "Una oración", 126
  Otras inquisiciones, 110
  "Sentirse en muerte", 120–2, 125
  "El tiempo circular", 123–4, 132
Bourdieu, Pierre, 40
Bravo, Federico, 104
Brunner, José Joaquín, 1, 12, 190 n.26, 190 n.31
Buenos Aires, 11, 110, 113–16, 120, 180
Buffon, Georges Louis Leclerc, comte de, 172–4

caciquismo, 143
Calinescu, Matei, 3–4, 189 n.21
capitalism
  and colonialism, 90
  and modernity, 15, 16
  and narrative of modernization, 18
  and postmodernity, 17–18
Caribbean, xv, 160, 166, 170, 175, 178, 180, 218 n.27
Carpentier, Alejo, xv, 159–78, 180–1, 182, 184
  "Lo real maravilloso americano", 218 n.24, n.29
  El siglo de las luces, xv, 159–72, 174–8

Cassirer, Ernst, 4, 172–4, 216 n.16, 219 n.33
Catholicism, 138–9, 145–7
  see also Christianity; Church; religion
Chateaubriand, François René, vicomte de, 218 n.26
Christianity, 112, 144–7
  see also apocalypse; Catholicism; religion
Church, 141, 144–7, 177
  see also Enlightenment; French Revolution
circular time, *see* time, of eternity
Citizen Kane, see Welles, Orson
city, 113–16, 117, 206 n.10
classical Antiquity, 70, 139
Collingwood, R. G., 76, 202 n.17, 202 n.19, 206 n.2
colonial Hispanism, Catholic, 15
colonialism, xiii, 2, 5, 9, 18, 22, 23, 80, 85, 86–93, 106
community, and religion, 163–6
Comte, Auguste, 74, 76, 78
Comunicación y cultura (journal), 36–7
context, 55–60, 67, 83, 110–11, 113, 126, 127, 131, 132
creativity, 97–8, 179
Creoles, xiii, 88–9, 92, 115, 117, 136
  see also criollismo
criollismo, 116–17, 128
  see also Creoles
Cristeros War, 141, 144
Cuba, 161, 162, 215 n.11
cultura letrada, 61
culturas populares en el capitalismo, Las, see García Canclini, Néstor
cultural hermeneutics, 49, 56
cultural studies, 196 n.23, 196 n.24
  British, 33–4
  and high culture, xvi, 61, 185
  and immanence, 52–3
  institutionalization of, 58
  Latin American, *see* Latin American cultural studies
  and Leninism, 185

and Marxism, 35
presentism of, xvi
and relationality, 52
synchronicism of, 59–60
and shared idiom with Theory, xv
culture
　anthropological concept of, 33–4
　as the arts, 33
　black, *see* black culture
　indigenous, *see* indigenous culture
　mass, *see* mass popular culture
　modern, *see* modern culture
　popular, *see* mass popular culture or traditional popular culture
　and power, xii, 53
　traditional culture, *see* traditional popular culture
　see also art; transculturation
culture industry, 30–2, 43, 45

Darío, Rubén, 74, 77–8, 219 n.1
"Era un aire suave", 93–4
"Sinfonía en gris mayor", 93
death, 138, 156
decolonization, 86–7, 88
deconstruction, 50, 192 n.47
deism, 218 n.30
Deleuze, Gilles and Félix Guattari, 50, 52, 57, 198 n.3
de Man, Paul, 62, 67
democracy, 28, 45, 115, 133, 155, 184
dependency
　intellectual, 98–9
　theory, 36, 37, 91, 196 n.21
Derrida, Jacques, 50, 194 n.3, 195 n.13, 198 n.8, 199 n.9, n.11, n.12, n.14, n.19, 200 n.20, 202 n.24, 203 n.1, 208 n.33
　on democracy, 62
　on meaning and context, 55, 59–60
　on Nietzsche's politics, 131
　on the other, 186, 200 n.24
　on responsibility, xii, 28, 45–6,
　on simultaneity, 54

desarrollismo, 147
　see also development
determinism, 110–11, 130, 160, 170, 174, 178
　see also magic; predestinationism; prefiguration; preformationism
development
　and indians, 14, 190 n.34
　model of economics, 3, 35, 36
　and modernity, 191 n.44
　and postmodernity, 17
　social, 76–8
　see also desarrollismo; modernization
Díaz Plaja, Guillermo, 81
discourse of modernity, *see* modernity, philosophical discourse of
DNA, 170, 174
Dussel, Enrique, 5, 6, 22, 192 n.52

East
　and West, 96
Eisenstadt, S. N., 190 n.35, 193 n.54, n.59
elitism, xii, 28, 38
empiricism, *see* nominalism
Enlightenment, 97, 161–2
　autonomous human subject of, 178
　view of Church, 163
　Kantian model of, 161, 216 n.13
　concept of modernity, 70
　and popular culture, 35, 70, 107, 144, 195 n.14
　idea of progress, 202 n.17
　rationalization, 22, 167–8, 173–4
　and religion, 144, 216 n.16
Eternal Return, 121, 122–4, 131–2
eternity, *see under* time
ethics, 125–6
Europe
　as prime mover of early modernity, xi, 1, 2, 4–6, 7–8
　and geopolitical conceptual legacy, 3, 10–11, 21–4, 97–9
　see also colonialism; imperialism; semicolonialism

evolutionary metaphysics, 76
  see also progress
existentialism, 168, 175, 178

Fanon, Frantz, 86–7
fantastic, literature of the, 139, 150
fascism, 132
field, concept of, xii–xiii, 49–50, 59, 66
Final Judgement, 145–7
Foucault, Michel, 198 n.6, 203 n.29
  on power, 53
  on ritual, 80, 82
foundation, 140–1, 164
  see also Roman trinity
fragmentation, 156–7
French Revolution, xv, 159–60, 162–7
Franco, Jean, 150, 195 n.15

García Canclini, Néstor, xi, 1, 182, 187 n.1, 188 n.3, 192 n.47, 193 n.58, 194 n.4, n.8, 200 n.23
  culturas populares en el capitalismo, Las, 16
  Culturas híbridas, x–xi, 3, 12–14, 15–16, 17–19, 23, 27–32, 33, 34–5, 37–42, 44,47, 92, 184
  globalización imaginada, La, xii, 19, 27, 43, 44–5, 45–7
Generation of 1898, 81
Giddens, Anthony, 142–3, 191, n.42, 203 n.26
Gilroy, Paul, 190 n.33, 212 n.28
González Echevarría, Roberto, 169, 170, 215 n.11
Gramsci, Antonio, 37, 191 n.40

Habermas, Jürgen, 4, 9
Hall, Stuart, xi, 4–5, 63–4, 65, 196 n.23, 197 n.24
Hardt, Michael and Antonio Negri, 6, 22, 188 n.16, 191 n.43, 193 n.56
Harvey, David, 189 n.18, 194 n.5
Hegel, Georg Wilhelm Friedrich, 20, 189 n.22
hegemony, ix, 38, 41

heraldos negros, Los, see Vallejo, César
Heidegger, Martin, 50–1
Henighan, Stephen, 87
Henríquez Ureña, Max, 81
hermeneutics, 51, 54, 57
  see also cultural hermeneutics
Herodotus, 206 n.2
Historia de la eternidad, see Borges, Jorge Luis
historical temporalities, 15–16, 18, 21, 38, 86
historicism
  and modernity, 68, 69, 78–80
history, 138, 155–6
  cultural, 41–2
  and literature, 86, 104
  universal, 181, 191 n.44
Hitler, Adolf, 132
homology, 64, 82
  see also articulation
human will, 175–6, 178
  see also voluntarism
hybridity, 14–17, 103
hyperbole, 143, 148, 150

ideology critique, 30, 36–7
idioma de los argentinos, El, see Borges, Jorge Luis
illumination, metaphorics of, 54
imaginary, see social imaginary
immanence, plane of, xii, 52, 64
imperialism, xiii, 90–1
indians, see indigenous culture
indigenous culture, xiii, 14, 18, 87–90, 138–9, 183, 190 n.34
  mythification of, 93–6, 97
  see also Andean culture
inner-worldly asceticism, 161
instrumentalism, 46–7, 184–5
interdisciplinarity, 65
interpretation, ground of, 51
intertextuality, 104–5, 152
Israel, Jonathan I., 4, 7–8, 216 n.16
iterability, 55, 59
  see also context

Jalisco, 136, 210 n.6
Jameson, Fredric, 17–18, 32, 63, 64–5, 191 n.42, n.43, 194 n.5, n.6, n.7, 195 n.9, 201 n.3

Kabbalah, 130–1
Kant, Immanuel, 161, 163, 216 n.13
  see also Enlightenment
Klor de Alva, Jorge, 88

Labanyi, Jo, 170
language, *see* literature; orality
Larsen, Neil, 196 n.21
Latin American cultural studies
  and Anglo-Saxon cultural studies, 35, 38
  and avant-garde subalternism, 62–3
  differences within, ix, 182
  history of, 35–8
  and literature, ix, xii, xvi, 184–5
  and Marxist-Leninism, 35–8
  on modernity, x–xi, 1, 3, 11–14
  postmodern turn of, xi, 30, 35, 37, 185
  and tradition, 59–63, 182
  see also Brunner, José Joaquín; cultural studies; García Canclini, Néstor; Martín-Barbero, Jesús; Moreiras, Alberto; Sarlo, Beatriz
Latin American modernity, ix–xi, 12
  as altered abstraction from Western modernity, xi, 1–2, 3, 21
  as historical phase, x, 1–2, 179, 181
  disavowal of indigenous traditions, 14
  and tradition, 14, 137, 143
  as qualitative category, xi
  and Second Industrial Revolution, xi, 1, 11–14
Latour, Bruno, 15–16, 20–1
Lenguajes (journal), 36–7
Leninism, xiii, 37, 38, 40, 41–2, 91, 185, 197 n.27
Lienhard, Martín, 211 n.17

literary history, xiii, 69, 70, 76, 81–3
literature
  codification of, xiii, 65, 82–3
  and cultural studies, ix, 184–5, 187 n.5
  and form, xiv, 184, *see also* technique
  and function in Latin America, 71–2
  and history, 104, 137–8
  and demotic language, 39, 107, 135, 155, 184
  and literariness, 65–6
  as multitemporal heterogeneity, 105–6
  political effectiveness of, 40–1
  and Roman trinity, xv, 154–7
  value of, 62
  see also aesthetics; autonomy; technique; transculturation
llano en llamas, El, *see* Rulfo, Juan
Lugones, Leopoldo, 114, 128, 201 n.8, 203 n.28

Machiavelli, Niccolò, 164
magic, 176–8
Mandelbaum, Maurice, 76
Manrique, Nelson, 89, 190 n.34
market, 14, 31, 43–6, 61–2, 199 n.17
Marx, Karl, 212 n.25, 217 n.23
Marxism, 30, 35, 36, 37, 87, 98, 195 n.14
Martí, José, 205 n.21
Martín-Barbero, Jesús, xiii, 1, 12, 35, 36, 37, 60–1
Martín Fierro (journal), 116–17, 128
Masotta, Oscar, 206 n.16
Massignon, Louis, 96–7
mass popular culture, xiii, 30, 32, 35, 44, 61–2, 115
meaning, 55
mestizos, 92, 136, 147
Mexico
  and cult of the dead, 138–9
  and *desarrollismo*, 147, 183
  and father figure, 142
  and Roman trinity, xiv, 139, 141

Mexico—*continued*
  stagnation of, 150
  traditional and modern, 157–8
  see also Jalisco
Meyer, Jean, 136
modern culture
  as the arts, 33
  autonomy of, 28, 29–31
  bipolar habits of, 28, 29, 30, 33, 39, 137
  and culture industry, 32
  as distinction, 29, 33
  high, xvi, 27, 29–30, 42, 47, 54, 185
  and market, 30, 31, 32, 43
  and the new, 10, 40, 60, 116
  political potential of, 40
  power of, 28
  versus premodern culture, 143
  slow, 27, 44–6
  see also autonomy; avant-gardes; modernism, specialization
modernism, ix, xii, 28, 92, 137, 153–6, 185
  antimodern, 70, 118, 201 n.3
  and hegemony, 38–9
  and modernity and modernization, 14, 38–41
modernismo, xiii, 67–83, 93, 116–17, 179
  and colonialism, 80
  and European tradition, 70
  and positivism, 74–80, 181
modernity
  and colonialism, 2, 5, 6, 9, 18, 22, 23, 80, 191 n.44
  conventional definition of (as break with tradition), 1, 4, 8
  characteristics of, 5, 6–7
  early culture of, 7
  as differential, x, 2, 4–5, 20–1, 25, 95, 106, 181–2
  and Europe, xi, 1, 5–6
  experience of, 10, 60–1
  as general and specific, 24
  as historical phase, 4, 6, 21, 181
  and history, 69
  Latin American, *see* Latin American modernity
  geopolitical conceptual legacy of, xi, 3, 10–11, 21–4, 97–9
  two modes of, 22
  and cult of the new, 10, 40, 60, 61, 116, 166
  and nominalism, 117, 118
  philosophical discourse of, 3, 7, 8, 14, 23, 30, 32, 39, 96, 106, 166, 179, 180, 181, 191 n.44, 193 n.57
  philosophico-aesthetic concept of, 2, 7–11, 23, 68
  and postmodernity, 17, 191 n.42
  as proper name, 2, 20
  as qualitative category, x, 2, 9–10
  as generalizable model of social experience, 10, 21
  socioeconomic concept of, 2, 4–7, 23
  time of, 8–10, 15, 100
  and tradition, 109, 110, 118, 157, 186
  non-Western beginnings of, xi, 4, 21
  and USA, xi, 5, 22
  Western, 1, 5, 22, 153
  as world-system, 5
  see also Benjamin, Walter; de Man, Paul; Enlightenment; French Revolution
modernization, 11–12, 14, 16, 17, 70, 72–3, 90, 115–16, 191 n.43
  see also Buenos Aires, modernism; transculturation
modern traditionalism, 129–30
Monsiváis, Carlos, 150, 151
Moreiras, Alberto, 61–3, 182, 187 n.5, 197 n.25, 197 n.28
multidisciplinarity, *see* interdisciplinarity

Index

multitemporal heterogeneity, 15, 86, 92, 95, 99, 105–6
  see also literature; modernity; postmodernity
myth, 114, 116, 117, 150, 152, 154
  see also indigenous culture; transculturation

narrative art, 176–8
  see also technique
national identity, 128, 130–1
nationalism, xiv, 111, 126–33, 180
  see also nominalism
native American, *see* indigenous culture
natural history, 168, 170, 172–5
nature, 160, 167–72, 175
Nazism, 133, 209 n.43
neocolonialism, 91
  see also imperialism
Nietzsche, Friedrich, 67–9, 127
  see also Eternal Return
nominalism, xiv, 55, 112–13, 126, 127, 132, 180
  see also modernity; nationalism

Old Testament, 142, 145–6, 166
orality, 107, 151, 152–3, 155, 184
Osborne, Peter, 9–10, 18, 188 n.10, 191 n.44, 192 n.45, 193 n.57
Otras inquisiciones, see Borges, Jorge Luis

pagan cult of ancestors, 39
patriarchy, 144, 145
  see also Mexico, father figure
Paz, Octavio, 8–9, 39, 74–6, 102–3, 106, 138, 142, 159, 189 n.19
Pedro Páramo, see Rulfo, Juan
peninsulares, xiii, 89
Peru
  and appropriation of discourse of modernity, 97–9, 106
  continuity of colonial structures and social subject in, 89
  mestizaje in, 92
  semicolonial condition of, 90
  and traditionalist modernization, 90
  and the West, 104
philosophy
  difference between C17th and C18th, 173–4
philosophical discourse of modernity, *see* modernity, philosophical discourse of
plane of immanence, *see* immanence
Platonism, xiv, 111–12, 119–20, 132–3, 145, 209 n.43
poetry, 86, 93, 99, 102–4
polis, 72, 140
politics, xvi, 36–7, 40–1, 58–9, 66, 71–3
popular culture, *see* mass popular culture or traditional popular culture
Portugal, 78, 88, 92
positivism, xiii, 70, 74–6, 79, 82
postcolonialism, xiii, 87
postcolonial theory, 86, 87–8, 91–2
  see also colonialism
postmodernism
  aesthetic of, 32
  as death of aesthetic autonomy, 31
  as cultural response, 14–15, 16
  as valorization of all styles, 32
  as subaltern force or cultural dominant, 194 n.4
postmodernity
  and art, 31
  concept of, 17–18
  as historical phase, 14, 16
  as continuation of modernity, 18–19, 24, 181
  and modernization, 18
poststructuralism, 55
power, 37, 53, 81, 82, 140–1, 142
praxis, 37, 40, 42
pre-Colombian culture, 16, 93–5, 138, 139
  see also indigenous culture
predestinationism, xv, 178
  see also determinism

prefiguration, 177–8
preformationism, 178, 218 n.28
  see also determinism
premodern culture
  versus modern culture, 142–3
  logic of, xv,161, 176–8
  order of, 115–16, 118
presentism, xvi, 197 n.25
proper names, 2, 20, 78
progress, xiii, 10, 15, 69, 76, 80–1, 99, 191 n.44, 202 n.17
  see also development; evolutionary metaphysics; modernity, as qualitative category; positivism
public sphere, xii, 7, 8, 28, 44–7, 184

Rama, Ángel, 71, 79, 135–6, 137, 151–4, 157, 212 n.29
Ramos, Julio, 71–3
rationalism
  and realism,153
  philosophical, 22, 160, 173–4
rationalization, *see* Enlightenment; nature
reading, 49, 50, 58, 65–6, 155, 156, 214 n.47
realism, 153, 155, 156
reality effect, 208 n.36
lo real maravilloso americano, 170, 218 n.29
reason, 173–4
reductionism, 42, 104, 184
regionalism, 152–3
relationality, 52, 60
religion, 74, 112, 138–41, 142, 143, 144–7, 163–7
  see Church; Enlightenment; French Revolution
resignification, 95, 102, 114, 130, 147
responsibility, *see* Derrida, Jacques
revelation, 54, 129, 160, 170, 175, 178
  see determinism; structuralism
revolution, 159, 217 n.19
ritual, 39, 80, 82–3, 100–1, 102
Roa Bastos, Augusto, 211 n.17

Rodó, José Enrique, 77
Rome, 140–1
Romanticism, 162, 168–9, 178
Roman trinity, xiv, 7, 139–41, 142, 154, 164
  see also literature
Rosaldo, Renato, 192 n.46
Rousseau, Jean-Jacques, 168, 171
Rowe, William, xii, 49–61, 64, 65, 86, 99–103, 181, 198 n.2
Rulfo, Juan, xiv, 135–9, 141–158, 183, 184, 191 n.39, 210 n.9
  El llano en llamas, 147, 155–6
  "Luvina", xiv, 147–51, 158, 183
  Pedro Páramo, xiv, 138–9, 141–7, 150, 151, 154, 156, 157, 158, 183
  and photography, 137, 157–8
  "Talpa", 151
rural degree zero, 137

sacralizing desacralizations, 40
Santiago de Chuco, 100, 103
Sarlo, Beatriz, x, 1, 11, 35, 44, 61–2, 80, 110, 113–18, 182, 190 n.28, 196 n.17, 199 n.17, 200 n.23, 206 n.10
Sarmiento, Domingo Faustino, 14, 114, 195 n.12
Schmucler, Héctor, 37
Schobinger, Juan, 211 n.16
Scholem, Gershom, 209 n.39
Second Industrial Revolution, x, 1, 11–14, 25, 60, 180
Second World War, xiv, 3, 111, 132
secrecy, 46
semicolonialism, xiii, 90–1, 107
siglo de las luces, El, see Carpentier, Alejo
signs, 55
simultaneity, 5, 11, 111
slaves, 162–3, 169
Social Darwinism, 81
social imaginary, 56–7
socio-attributionist theory of art, 30

sociology of culture, 27, 61
Sommers, Joseph, 150
Sontag, Susan, 197 n.30
sound, 56–7
space, 54, 174
Spain, 71, 74, 77, 81, 88, 92
specialization, 29–30, 39
Spivak, Gayatri Chakravorty, 87–8, 205 n.28
Stein, Gertrude, 51
structuralism, xvi, 54, 63, 198 n.8
   see also articulation; homology
subaltern, 62, 183
   see also Latin American cultural studies, avant-garde subalternism
superstition, 176
symbolic action, 41–2
Symbolism, 94–5
synchronicism, 59–60

Taine, Hyppolite, 77–8, 202 n.25
technique, xiv, 137, 143, 149, 151–8, 184
teleological reasoning, 41–2, 122–3
temporality, *see* time
Theory, xv, 50
time
   Andean concept of, 100
   and concept of authority, 140
   of desire, 119–20
   and development, 149–50
   of eternity, xiv, 109–13, 119, 120–1
   and life and death, 138
   linear, 109, 121, 125
   of modernity, 8–10, 15, 100
   of modernity and colonialism, 189 n.20
   of modern literature, 102–3, 106
   of nostalgia, 119
   and the novel, 156
   and poetry, xiv, 99, 102–4
   of postcolonial moment, 87, 90, 91
   spiral as spatial image of, 172
   traditional concept of, 8, 148–51
   see also Eternal Return; modernity, qualitative understanding
tradition
   and Church, 141
   and Creoles, 89
   and democracy, 62–3
   European, ix, xi, 22–4, 62, 70
   and modernity, 14, 16, 20, 60, 109, 137, 143, 157, 186
   oral, 152
   and politics, 66
   in postmodernity, 15, 16–19
   and religion, 141, 163
   Roman concept of, 140–1
   and seniority, 140–1, 144, 147
   and social imaginary, 56–7
   time of, 8, 147–151
   as *traditio*, 1, 8, 109, 118
   traditional view of, xiv, 149, 158
   and women, 147, 149
   see also classical Antiquity; indigenous culture; Roman trinity
traditionalist modernization, 90
traditional popular culture, xiii, 16, 29, 30, 35, 60, 61, 109, 136, 141, 147, 151–3, 183
   see also indigenous culture; transculturation
transculturation, xiv, 135–9, 141, 147, 151–4

United States of America
   as center of late modernity, 5
   cultural studies in, 35
   and development model of modernization, 35–6
urbanization, 14, 16, 38
Uruguay, 126, 127, 128–9

Valle-Inclán, Ramón del, 77
Vallejo, César Abraham, xiii, 56, 83, 85–107, 179–80, 183, 184
   "Aldeana", 94

Vallejo, César Abraham—*continued*
  "A mi hermano Miguel", 103
  "Los arrieros", 94–5
  "Idilio muerto", 105
  Los heraldos negros, 85, 93–5
  "La megalomanía de un continente" (article), 98
  "Nostalgias imperials", 93, 95
  "Oriente y occidente" (article), 96–7
  "Terceto autóctono", 93–4
  Trilce, 85, 86
  Trilce VI, 86, 99, 102, 104–5
value, 61–3
vanguardismo, xii, 153
Verón, Eliseo, 36
violence, 27, 87, 164, 175, 178
voluntarism, xv, 175–6, 178
  see also human will

Weber, Max, xi, 29, 215 n.9
Welles, Orson, 154, 213 n.44
West
  and East, 96–7
  and Latin America, xiii, 3, 41, 90–2, 96, 180
  and transculturation, 136, 137, 152–4
Westernization of Latin America, 92, 98
Western tradition, 107, 139–41, 182
Western modernity, *see* modernity, Western
Williams, Raymond, 33–4, 95, 193 n.58, 195 n.11, n.14, 199 n.24
women, 100–2, 144–7, 149, 175

Zavala, Iris M., 92

CABRINI COLLEGE LIBRARY
610 KING OF PRUSSIA ROAD
RADNOR, PA 19087-3699

DEMCO